THE
GREAT
SECRET

Talks On The Songs Of Kabir

THE GREAT SECRET

Talks On The Songs Of Kabir

OSHO

JAICO PUBLISHING HOUSE
Ahmedabad Bangalore Bhopal Bhubaneswar Chennai
Delhi Hyderabad Kolkata Lucknow Mumbai

Published by Jaico Publishing House
A-2 Jash Chambers, 7-A Sir Phirozshah Mehta Road
Fort, Mumbai - 400 001
jaicopub@jaicobooks.com
www.jaicobooks.com

Copyright © 2012 OSHO International Foundation.
All rights reserved

First Publication Copyright © 1981, OSHO International Foundation.
Copyright ©-all revisions 1953-2012 OSHO International Foundation.
All rights reserved

OSHO is a registered trademark of
OSHO International Foundation, used under license.

www.osho.com

THE GREAT SECRET
ISBN 978-81-7992-785-4

First Jaico Impression: 2008
Sixth Jaico Impression: 2012

No part of this book may be reproduced or utilized in
any form or by any means, electronic or
mechanical including photocopying, recording or by any
information storage and retrieval system,
without permission in writing from the publishers.

Printed by
Snehesh Printers
320-A, Shah & Nahar Ind. Est. A-1
Lower Parel, Mumbai - 400 013.

CONTENTS

Introduction   vi

1   Tale Of Love, Untellable   1

2   Tell And Still It's Hidden   43

3   Drunk With Boundless Youth   80

4   A True Lover Never Dies   112

5   One Who Walks Alone   147

6   Why Wander Away?   183

7   Enter Your Temple   222

8   Why Go To Others?   259

9   Relax In Joy   298

10   Come What May, Allow   333

INTRODUCTION

For first-time readers of Osho this book itself will be introduction enough. Those familiar with Osho's recent books will need to remember that these discourses were delivered in 1975 to a predominantly Hindu gathering. By then only a few hundred Westerners had found him.

The discourses are commentaries on ten of Kabir's poems, in which Kabir sings of his love of God. Osho too talks of God: "You will only be able to love others when you become so overwhelmed by the love of God that it begins to overflow from your very being." And at the same time he reminds us that, "God is not a person to be communicated with." "God is not the way you describe him. He is something like this and something like that." "There is great difficulty in trying to describe him." "Anything I say about him will be incorrect."

Recent friends of Osho may find it strange to hear him using the name of God in this way. It was ten years after these Kabir discourses that he shocked his disciples, who thought of ourselves as iconoclastic, rebellious freethinkers who had finished with the idea of a personal God a long time ago, by showing us how subtly our conditioning still looked for something, someone out there who knew more than we did. And in 1989 another series, dedicated to Friedrich Nietzsche entitled *God is Dead, Now Zen is the Only Living Truth*, showed yet again that our minds may know that God is dead, but our blood and bones still haven't realized that he was never alive, that "he is a fiction," "an insult to man," "a

The Great Secret

puppeteer who has made you beggars and slaves," "a lie" that has dragged behind it the muck-cart of organized religion and the hypocrisy of our society.

In later discourses, by talking the truth, Osho has hit every vested interest of society so hard that it has provoked savage, fearful retaliation from the governments of the world. So to read these commentaries of 1975 is to be taken back to a calmer world, before society had felt Osho's power and reacted so violently, to a world filled by the great subjects of Kabir's songs — love, truth, death, enlightenment.

A story told by Osho in a recent discourse may be relevant to the change of language over those ten years. "I was watching a film about Jesus. And I love the man. Unless I love somebody I don't criticize him." He told the story of the rich young man going to Jesus who tells him to give all that he has to the poor. Osho says "You ask him too much, too early. A master should not be in a hurry." The young man "has just inherited an empire and you ask him to distribute it all!" "He had come and he was ready, but asking him too much when the time is not ripe shows too much hurry." "In fact before a person becomes alert and aware you should not ask such impossible things." He takes us at our own pace.

And once you are at ease again with the word 'God' these discourses will fill you to overflowing. With what will they fill you? That is the great secret — words like wisdom, understanding, truth, ecstasy, love, God, all fall far short. Osho has spoken on Kabir more than on any other mystic. "I love Kabir." Love is the subject.

— Swami Anand Robin, M.A. (Cantab.)

TALE OF LOVE, UNTELLABLE

Love's not grown in gardens;
Love's not sold at market.
He who wants it, king or commoner,
Gives his head and takes it.

Studying great books many have died.
None ever become learned.
Two letters and a half in love,
Who studies them is learning.

Narrow is the lane of love.
Two will never fit.
When I was, the Lord was not.
Now He is; I am not.

Kabir says: clouds of love
Came on me showering;
Soaked the heart,
Greening the inner jungle.

A heart dry of love;
God again untasted.
Thus is man
In this world:
His arising wasted.

Roused, ecstatic
With His name,
Love-drunk,
Overflowing,
Reveling in
His vision.
Why bother
With liberation?

Tale of love, untellable.
Not a bit's ever told.
The sweets of a dumb one —
He enjoys...and smiles.

I look at you and am convinced of one thing, that you once had something — some treasure, some symmetry, some secret, some key — but you have lost it. Every moment, asleep or awake, you are always busy looking for something. It is quite possible you do not know exactly what you are searching for and that you are unaware of what you have lost, but I see the hunger in your eyes. It is apparent in every beat of your heart.

This quest has been going on for countless lives. Sometimes you call it the search for truth. But you have never known truth, so how can you lose it? And sometimes you call it the search for God. But your meeting with Him has never taken place, so how can you be separated from Him?

You go in search to the temples, to the mosques, to Kashi and to Mecca...you knock on every door you come across in the hope you will find what you have lost. But as long as you do not know exactly what it is you have lost your search cannot be fulfilled. Your own experience will tell you the same thing — you have knocked on many doors, but you have always returned empty-handed. The doors are not to be blamed for this.

Before you set out in search you should know what it is you are looking for, what it is you have lost. If an illness is incorrectly diagnosed how can you know the right medicine to take? Even if a doctor is here what good will he do?

Nanak fell ill — the illness was the same as yours — and the people in his house sent for a physician. Whenever someone is ill we automatically send for a doctor; we don't understand there are some diseases that have nothing whatsoever to do with doctors. In any case the physician came, took hold of Nanak's wrist and started to take his pulse. Nanak began to laugh. "There is no illness there," he said. "You will discover nothing by taking my pulse. The illness is of the heart." The doctor had no idea what Nanak was talking about. Doctors have their own worlds and they diagnose illnesses by taking one's pulse. Nanak needed a master, a spiritual physician, and not a medical doctor.

The master is also a physician, not of the body but of the heart. And the master's first task is to make it clear to you what it is you are seeking. Then the search becomes very easy. When the diagnosis is correct it is not too difficult to find the proper medicine. Diagnosis is half the cure. But if the diagnosis is incorrect, then even vast quantities of medicine will be of no use to you.

What generally happens is that you become enamored of words. You begin to think, "Ah yes, this is what I have lost. It is God I have lost. It is freedom I have lost." Then you set out on your search. And it is wrong from the very beginning.

As I talk to you, I look into your hearts and I see that the throne within you is unoccupied. The throne is there, and someone must have sat on it at one time or another, but at present he is away, he is wandering somewhere else. Your heart is that throne; the king, love itself, has left it behind and has gone roaming in some far off place.

The search for love is possible; every child is born with love. Before you can search for something you have to lose it, and although every child is born with love it gets lost along the way, somewhere in the course of his upbringing. Education, society and culture play important roles in this process. And because of this lost love a sort of vacuum, a sort of vacancy, a sort of emptiness is created within you. You are in search of that love — not of God. You have never met God. But if you regain love then you are standing at His door. You have never known God. He is unknown to you; you cannot search for him. To search for someone, there must be some kind of relationship, some kind of acquaintance. And you have no such familiarity with God.

Truth surrounds you. How will you find it? Truth is there already; the basic problem is that you have no vision. The sun is always shining but you are blind. What should a blind man seek? The sun or sight? If you have no sight, even if the sun is sitting next to you what will you do? You will not be able to see it; you will remain in darkness. Sight is needed. That sight is love. God is ever-present. He is all around you. But you have lost your vision; you have lost the means of experiencing Him.

Love is the ability to experience. Love is sensitivity. Love is the experience in which all your impurities are washed away and you throw open all your doors, all your gates. Then whosoever stands at your door is no longer an enemy or a friend but a beloved, and you open your door to him. When you begin to feel the whole world is yours, when you begin to see the beloved in whosoever comes to your door, when you no longer see strangers or enemies, when you begin to see only friends everywhere — when this phenomenon takes place in you, know that you have found love. And for the man who has found love what else remains to be found? The man who has found love has found the key to the door of God.

Understand the significance of love carefully. Nothing is greater than love, not even God. God is achieved through love, but love is not achieved through God. The presence of God does not guarantee love, but the presence of love will surely bring Him to you. As Jesus has said, "Love is God."

The basic question, the fundamental problem, is seeking love. So let us clarify at the outset how love has been lost, because the way to regain it will only be clear when we know and understand how it has been lost in the first place.

The road you take to find love is the same road on which you lost it. But you have to reverse your direction. You will have to turn around and walk the opposite way. The same ladder leads to heaven or to hell. One end is in hell and the other is in heaven.

You begin to lose love as you become more and more attached to material things. This is hell; this is the end of the ladder that is grounded in material things. But as love grows, God becomes manifest. And this is the other end of the ladder. This is where the other end is fixed. Love is a ladder, a path. If you abandon love you begin a downward journey; as you embrace it you begin an upward path.

If you ask me, I will tell you to forget God, to forget truth. I will tell you to seek only love. All the rest will follow. Just as your shadow follows you, God follows love. But no matter how hard you seek, you will achieve nothing without love. This is because the seeker is dull and insensitive. He has neither the capacity nor the fitness for the search. He is asleep, unconscious. He is full of hatred, anger and hostility; he is submerged in the poison of malice. And only the nectar of love brings forth joy.

Every child is beautiful, lovely. And this is because he is born with love. But then, by and by, a disorder somehow occurs within him. Every child is so lovely; every child is so beautiful. Have you ever seen an ugly child?

The beauty of a child has nothing to do with his physical body, it comes from some inner strength. Within him, his lamp of love burns brightly and its rays emanate from every pore of his body, spreading their luster all around. Wherever he looks, he looks with love. But as he grows he begins to lose this love. And we help in that process.

We do not teach him how to love, we teach him how to guard himself against it, how to be wary of it. We tell him that love is very risky, very dangerous. We teach him to be suspicious, to be full of doubt. We tell him it is necessary to be like this, that people will take advantage of him otherwise. We tell him there is much cheating, dishonesty and treachery in the world, that it is everywhere, and that unless he is on guard people will rob and cheat him. We tell him there are thieves everywhere. We are totally unaware of the fact that God is everywhere, yet we never forget that robbers abound! And so we train children to be on their guard against thieves.

If you want to prepare children in this way, then you cannot teach them love — because love is dangerous. Love means trust; love means accepting — and being suspicious is keeping a look-out so no one can steal from you; it is being on guard, remaining constantly alert, as if there could be an attack at any moment from any quarter. So, before any attack comes, you yourself become the aggressor. You see this as the best way of protecting yourself. We train our children to be like sentries. And this is how we do it.

When a child learns to behave in this fashion we say that now he has become mature. But by this time his capacity to love is completely lost. Now he begins to see enemies all around him; he looks on no one as a friend. And when he even begins to doubt his own father we say that he is now fit to enter the world. We say that he is now no longer a child and that no one will be able to cheat him. Unfortunately, he will cheat others now.

Kabir has said to be ready to be cheated, but not to cheat. He says that you lose nothing when you are cheated, but that all is lost when you cheat others.

What does Kabir means by "all"?

As you practice deception your ability to love diminishes. How can you love someone you are deceiving? And if you are afraid of someone then the flower of love will not be able to bloom in you. It cannot happen because fear is poison. If you are full of fear how can you love? Has love ever been born out of fear? Only hatred is born out of fear; only hostility grows out of fear. And it is because of this fear that you begin to protect yourself.

As a child grows he becomes involved in protecting

himself — with money, with a house, with all sorts of things. He makes every possible arrangement to secure himself from attack, no matter from which quarter it might come. But in the midst of all these arrangements we forget that we are closing all our doors, that we are even barring the entry of love. Our protection may now be complete, but it is the same security as that of the grave.

A certain emperor once built himself a palace for his safety and protection. Emperors certainly live in greater fear than others — they have such great material wealth, there are many threats against their lives. They have riches, power, authority; it may be stolen at any time — and their fear is in proportion to their wealth. So, in the palace the emperor built, there was only one gate. There were no windows, no doors; there was no way for an enemy to gain entry.

The king of a nearby kingdom came especially to view the palace. He was very impressed; it was so safe and so well-guarded no enemy could possibly get in. There was only one door, and that was guarded by a carefully selected group of guards who had been especially chosen in order of seniority. After all, can a guard really be trusted? One might be tempted to kill the emperor in the night. So they had been hand-picked according to seniority, and each guard had to keep a keen eye on his junior. The other monarch was so impressed he said, "I shall also have such a palace built."

A beggar sitting by the side of the road overheard the two rulers talking and began to laugh loudly. Shocked, they turned to him. The beggar said, "Pardon me, but there is just one thing you have overlooked. I have been sitting here begging, and I have watched this palace being built. There is only one flaw, but it might prove costly one day. If you take my advice you will go inside and stay there; then you will remove this one door and replace it with a wall instead. Then there will be no flaw, and no danger whatsoever."

The emperor said, "you idiot! I understand what you are saying, but I would be as good as dead inside there. The palace would be my tomb."

The beggar replied, "It has already become a tomb. The grave is always the last door to remain open."

We are all in the process of dying, and the degree to which we step up measures for our security is in direct proportion to the progress we make in digging our own graves. The reason you look so lifeless is because you have made so many arrangements for your safety.

To be insecure is to be alive.

Life's mantra is to live in insecurity. And, of course, living like this there is no safety. A stone is safe and a flower lives in danger — but a stone is dead and a flower is full of life! If a storm comes, the flower will fall but the stone will remain where it was. Mischievous children may come and pick the flower, but the stone will remain where it was. When the sun sets in the evening the flower will wither, but the stone will remain unaffected, will remain in its place. Would you prefer to be a stone simply because it is safe from such dangers? That is the condition you have chosen! You have become like stones. The flower is always in jeopardy. Love is a flower. And there is no greater flower, no more important flower in this world than love. There is also nothing that is in greater danger.

Love is life. Love means that your doors are open, that you are standing beneath the open sky. There may be great danger being in such a position, but this is the essence of life. Exposed like this, two things can happen — one, an enemy can attack you; two, a friend can come and embrace you. But if you protect yourself from the enemy you are also protecting yourself from the friend. If you build a wall around yourself it means you are building your own tomb. You will always be uneasy in it; you will always feel you have lost something. You have not lost anything. It is just that the flower of your heart has not opened; it is just that you have not been able to love.

We prepare children to live so-called "safe" lives, and the result is that love starts to wither. Then we teach them to be dishonest, and love withers even more. Then we show them how to be egoists, and love dies. There is only one way to be full of love, to be loving, and that is to love oneself. And we teach our children to save themselves; we never teach them to lose themselves, to let themselves go. We tell them it is a question of one's name, of one's family, of one's community, of one's nation.

Once Mulla Nasruddin's eldest son ran away from home. The Mulla was very unhappy, but after a while he heard that his son had joined a theatrical company and had become a great actor. Now the Mulla began to praise him. After some time it was announced that the drama company was coming to the town where the Mulla lived. He bought a dozen first-class tickets and invited all his friends. He invited me as well. The Mulla wanted everyone to see what a great actor his son had become. He was very excited; it was a great occasion for him.

On the night of the play we all went to the theater. The play began, but by the time the first act was almost over there was still no sign of the Mulla's son. The Mulla was perched nervously on the edge of his seat. The first act finished and the second began. The son was not in the second act either. Now the Mulla began to get a bit upset; he became quite dejected. When the third and final act opened his son was still not on the stage. Near the end of the play, when it was almost time for the curtain and the audience was getting ready to leave, the Mulla's son appeared on the stage with a gun in his hand. He was playing the part of a sentry. He walked back and forth across the stage in front of a gate. Then the curtain began to fall! He had not spoken a single line! The Mulla could not take this. He stood up and cried aloud, "You fool! You may not be allowed to say anything, but at least fire your gun! The prestige of our house is at stake!"

We educate our children in the ways of prestige, pride and vanity. We admonish them never to do anything that might endanger the prestige of the house, of the family, of the name. How pleased you are when your son comes first in his class! You teach him not to love, not to be loving, but when he comes first at school you receive him with kindness and distribute sweets to your friends and relatives.

Do you know what you are doing? You tell your son to try always to be first. But only they who know how to be last receive love. You tell him to compete, to fight, to be ambitious, always to be first no matter what the cost. You are teaching your son politics; you are making him into a politician. And now throughout his life, come what may, he will always try to be first. But one day he will realize that he may have stood first, but that he has lost the real thing: he has lost the ability to love; he has lost the greatest thing in life.

A politician cannot love anyone. He has no friends. He cannot have any friends. Do you think Indira Gandhi can have a friend? How can one who has power and authority have a friend? All who are near are enemies, awaiting her downfall, always ready to throw her out. That is why Indira Gandhi makes changes in her cabinet so often. It is dangerous to keep a person in the same post too long because he will become too sure of himself. Being sure of his position, he will trip her up whenever he gets the chance and knock her down. This is the tactic used by everyone who has ever risen to the top. How an there be love in politics? Politics is full of hatred, conflict and competition. When you want your son to be competitive you are indirectly teaching him hatred, antagonism and hostility.

You also want your son to amass great wealth — piles and piles of rupees. But don't you know that the lives of those who acquire great stacks of money are devoid of love? Their lives are empty of love. Those who have real love in their lives have so much genuine richness they are not crazy enough to pursue this other so-called wealth.

Try to understand this point clearly and carefully. Wealth is a substitute for love, and so you will never find love in the life of a miser. He is a miser because there is no love in him. His substitute for love is his wealth.

If love exists in your life then you know you have spread so much love around that those who have received it will care for you if some difficulty arises in the future. And if there is so much love in your life that it takes the form of prayer, then you know that God will look after you. You will think, "If He takes such good care of the birds and plants, why should He be displeased with me?"

But if there is no love in your life then you know that there is no one but your bank balance to look after you. Then your only friend is your wealth. If there is no love in your life who will worry about you in your old age? Who will massage your tired feet? Who will help you? Who will support you in your old age? If there is no love in your life, no one will. Then you will only have your money. It will be your only friend. In a miserly, loveless life there is no support, no help but wealth. So you will find that the heart of a rich man is as lifeless as his grip on his wealth is solid.

Love's nature is to share; hoarding is difficult for love. The man who hoards does so because he does not have the courage to share. He has no heart, no feeling for sharing. Love is giving away; love is charity itself. Love means sharing with all.

You prepare your son to earn money, to reach a high position in the government, to be a man of prestige, to be an Alexander or a Napoleon or a Birla. You are doing all you can to see that he does not become a man. None of the things I have mentioned are possible if he becomes a man in the true sense of the world. If he becomes a man, then how can he become a Napoleon or a Birla or the president of the nation? If he becomes a man, then all these doors are closed to him. All these doors lead to inhumanity, to savagery, to animalism; they do not lead to the human attributes, to becoming humane. To open these doors, hatred and violence are the keys; love leads to the door of God.

And so love is lost. By and by, a child's relationship with himself is broken; by and by, his relationship with his heart is cut off. He begins to live without roots; he begins to wander here and there looking for what is missing in his life. But he himself does not know what is missing. He has no knowledge, no awareness of what it is he has lost or when he lost it. He was very small, very young then. When you trained him to move away from love he had no idea at all what you were doing. He trusted you. He believed what his parents said. He began to conform to the society, to the culture; he followed the advice of his elders and of his teachers. He did not know what was happening. In his ignorance, his relationship with himself was cut off; in his unconsciousness, his roots were severed.

In Japan, gardeners give a particular shape to certain trees, and Swami Ram was surprised to see them when he first visited that country. He could not imagine how such trees could exist. The trees were two to three hundred years old and only six to eight inches high! It was hard for him to believe a three-hundred-year-old tree could only be six inches high, so he asked the gardeners to tell him the trick, the secret. The tree increased in size but did not grow high at all! Its trunk thickened but it did not rise upwards at all!

The secret, the gardeners told him, was to keep cutting back the roots. The tree is planted in an iron pot with a broken bottom, they explained. The roots are not allowed to go deep; their tips are snipped periodically.

When roots do not penetrate deep into the earth, trees do not grow high. They grow older and older, their trunks increase in size, they look old and withered, but they cannot grow in height. The only remedy, the only way for them to grow tall is to allow their roots to go deeper and deeper into the earth. A tree grows upward in proportion to the depth of its roots; the ratio is the same. How can a tree grow tall if its roots are trimmed regularly? It will remain stunted. This art,

Tale Of Love, Untellable

this trick of stunting trees, is very much in fashion in Japan. That day, Swami Ram noted in his diary that Satan was playing the same trick on man.

The whole human race has become stunted, as if someone were continuously pruning its roots. The trees do not know what is happening to them; their roots are hidden in the earth — but the roots of your love have been severed and if you do not take steps to correct this mischief you will never be able to reach those roots again. And then, even if you visit temples and mosques, even if you worship and pray and perform all sorts of religious rites, nothing will come of it. It will all be to no avail. No matter how hard you try, your prayers will not reach God. Only a prayer of love can reach to Him. If love is present, it is not even necessary to pray. Then, even if you say nothing, you are heard. But if there is no love, nothing whatsoever reaches Him.

Now let us try to understand these sayings of Kabir.

Each and every word is invaluable. Before Kabir the Upanishads lose their luster. The Vedas look pitiful and second-rate before him. Kabir is singular, unique. Although he is illiterate he has succeeded in extracting the essence from the experience of his life. He is not a scholar; he has expressed this essence very briefly, not at all in great detail. His words are like seed mantras:

Love's not grown in gardens'
Love's not sold at market.

He who wants it, king or commoner;
Gives his head and takes it.

In the world of love there is no distinction between king and commoner. Where love is concerned there is no question of poverty or of nobility. In love, the beggar and the king are on the same level.

There is only one way to obtain love. The man who wants love, *Gives his head and takes it.*

The man who wants love will have to lose himself, will have to sacrifice himself for it. He will have to sacrifice his ego, his pretense, his false show, his feeling of "I." This is what Kabir means by "head." He will have to sacrifice his head. Love will not be born in you as long as you are not prepared to lose your head.

Go into this a bit more deeply. There are two dimensions to this giving of the head. One aspect is that your ego must fall, must disappear, must go away. Your ego is contained in your head. This is why you often admonish others to hold their heads high. And when you have insulted someone, you will say how you showed him you were somebody, how you made him bow his head. The head has become the symbol of the ego. That is also why you lay your head at the feet of the one to whom you have surrendered. Why the head? There are other limbs to the body, but it is because the head represents the ego. So you bow down and lay your head at the feet of the person to whom you have surrendered yourself completely. And when you become angry with someone you hit him on the head with your shoe. The head is synonymous with the ego. This is its domain.

Kabir says that if you give up the ego it makes no difference whether you are poor or rich, white or black; he says that you can fill yourself with love, that you can take as much as you want.

You cannot purchase love in the market because then there

would be a difference between the poor man and the rich man, because then the rich man would be able to buy it but the poor man would be left out. Love is obtained unconditionally; there is no question of paying any price.

There is only one condition to be fulfilled. There is only one barrier. The mind, filled with the ego, thinking it is everything, feeling it is the center of the world, cannot fall in love. It cannot be in love with anyone because the very meaning of love is to make the other the center of one's life. The other becomes so important that he becomes the center and you remain on the periphery. The man who is full of love says, "I will live and die for the other; I will breathe in and out for the other, and if necessary I will sacrifice myself — but I will save the other."

Love means the transformation of the center. An egoist considers himself to be the center. He says, "I must be saved even at the cost of the whole world. Even if it is necessary to destroy all, I will save myself." The ego is aggressive, and so when the egoist shows his love for someone he destroys him; he tries to destroy the other's individuality. In this kind of false lovemaking countless people have lost their individuality.

You say you love your wife or your husband, but everything you do is geared to curbing the other's individuality. The husband tries to destroy the wife's individuality, tries to destroy her freedom, her very self. He tries to make his wife his shadow, something to be used whenever he desires, something without its own will, without its own freedom, without its own strength. And the wife tries to do the same thing. Each plays the same political game. All the time the wife is busy trying to make her husband a slave, henpecking him.

In America, a certain woman filed suit against her husband. Her finger had been chopped off in a car accident and she was claiming a million dollars. When he heard the amount asked, even the judge was shocked. He said, "I agree you should receive something since you were not responsible for the accident, but, even considering the harm that has been done to you, the amount seems exorbitant."

"I used to make my husband dance on the tip of that finger," the wife replied. "It was not an ordinary finger at all!"

Wives try to henpeck their husbands and husbands try to keep their wives in control. This is why they are always quarreling. You will never find a bigger quarrel anywhere in the world than marriage. And it is perennial. All quarrels come to an end at some point or other — even peace treaties are eventually singed and wars finally end — but the quarrel between husband and wife goes on and on forever. It never ends.

Once a policeman arrested a priest for driving without his lights on. When he appeared before the magistrate the priest said, "I did not know the lights were not working, so please forgive me. As I explained to the policeman, there must have been some mechanical failure. Everything worked fine yesterday, so I did not bother to check today."

The judge replied, "This is not a very grave offense, and I believe you. Yet I also believe the policeman. Do you think the policeman arrested you because he didn't like you? Has he ever had any trouble with you before? Have you ever done any hard to him?"

"I cannot remember any other harm I might have done him," the priest said, "except that I performed his marriage three years ago. Maybe he is taking revenge on me because of that!"

The institution of marriage has become a sad affair, an affliction, because it is a conflict, a constant quarrel. And what is the cause of this quarrel? It is because one desires to become the other's master, because one desires to control the other. The desire to become the other's master is a form of violence, and this desire has no relation whatsoever to love.

You are not able to love, and yet children are born to you! And then the same old game of ownership goes on — this time over them. You suppress them; you dominate them. You are engaged in killing them, in suppressing their selves. You think that children should not be allowed to be free, that it is dangerous. You insist that they obey you, because you think that whatsoever you say is true. But you don't know what truth is at all! You have no knowledge whatsoever of what is right and of what is wrong. Your own life has been a waste, and yet you claim dominion over a small child?

You say to him, "I am your father, so whatever I say is right and you must accept it as such." What is your motive? What do you mean by asserting yourself like this? You simply want to turn him into an object, into a thing; you want to kill his sense of freedom, his self-respect.

It generally happens that children who are lifeless, dull and lethargic are praised by their parents for their obedience, and children who are full of life, who are active, who jump up and down, who run here and there are complained about. Then it comes as a great surprise to parents when obedient children turn out to be worthless, and the mischievous ones shine. They shine because they have energy, vitality. They shine in spite of your whole clever conspiracy to control everything around you, to be the master of all.

The seed of love cannot sprout because of this burning desire to be the master, to be the be-all and the end-all. Love is the art of dissolving your ego. If you really love your son you will place your ego at his feet. Then you will not be an egoistic father. Then you will marvel at how your son will reciprocate. As soon as you set your ego aside he will set his aside. Now you will be cooperating with each other.

Before now the son has been feeling sad and troubled; he has just been waiting for the chance to be free. He has been telling himself that soon the opportunity will come, that as time advances you will become weaker and weaker and he will still be a strong young man. Your son will harass you; he will take revenge on you. Then you will think that he has gone astray. But in fact you have only reaped what you have sown. When he was weak you harassed him; now that he is strong and you are weak, he is harassing you. This is the unalterable law of karma — you reap what you sow. If you are not egoistical with your son there is virtually no possibility of his being egoistical with you when you are weak, when you are old.

We have invented beautiful ways to harass one another. On the outside they are very attractively painted, and we disguise them with nice names. We destroy and murder in the name of love. We kill in the name of discipline; we murder in the name of obedience. All this shows is ego.

He who wants it, king or commoner,
Gives his head and takes it.

Whosoever desires love should bear in mind that, whether

he desires it or not, he is still going to remain as empty as a clay jug. He will only be filled with sorrow and weeping; he will not be filled with life. Without love, no one has ever attained to joy, to celebration. Nor will he ever. This is a perennial rule of life.

So the first meaning of *Gives his head* is that a man gives up his ego. Whenever love is present the ego yields. Even if the person is younger than you, even if he is your son you will yield — because when love is present the ego no longer remains. Even if a woman is your wife you will not set yourself up before her, full of ego; you will not set yourself up as her lord and master, as her *pati-devata,* as her husband-deity — you will yield. And this phenomenon of love is such that neither the wife nor the husband cowers before the other; in fact, both bow to the god of love. No one bows and submits to anyone, but both are yielding. If you like you can say they are yielding to each other, or you can say they are bowing to an invisible god of love that sits within their hearts.

The first meaning of the word 'head' is ego; the second, thoughts.

Whether they are relevant or irrelevant, your head is a collection of thoughts. Your mind is nothing but a vast crowd of thoughts. And it is a very busy and active crowd indeed. Because of it your whole energy is wasted, and you have no energy left for love. The head is an exploiter. It drains you to such an extent that the flow of energy is unable to reach your heart. It is all expended in thinking. And ninety-nine percent of your thoughts are useless; they have no substance whatsoever. No harm at all will be done if you stop thinking.

But you do not live in consciousness; you are not aware. When you are sitting quietly, do you ever observe what you are thinking about? Have you ever watched the rubbish that goes on in your mind? What do you hope to achieve by permitting all this rubbish? It goes on during the day and at night when you are asleep, in your waking hours and in your dreams. It runs in circles all the time. And bear in mind that even the most trivial thought consumes energy. Scientists have come to the conclusion that the amount of energy you would expend in one hour digging a pit in a field is the same as the amount you would expend in fifteen minutes thinking and worrying. This means mental activity requires four times more energy than physical activity.

These days, man's physical activity has decreased, but his mental activity has increased and continues to do so. The head has become an exploiter; it does not allow the energy to flow anywhere else. The head consumes all of the energy itself. The heart is not aggressive. It waits. And because the heart can wait, it does without. Your heart will remain as dry as a desert until the supply of energy that goes to your ego and to your thoughts is cut off. The flow of water will never be able to reach your heart. The seed of love is lying there, and it will only bloom when the water reaches it.

Try to grasp the meaning of the phrase, *Give his head*. When thoughts and ego disappear, the head disappears. Then there is a possibility for love; then love will be able to bloom. Now you have removed the obstacle that smothered the seed of love. There is no other impediment but your head. It sits there like a stone, blocking love's flow.

Studying great books many have died.
None ever become learned.

Tale Of Love, Untellable

Two letters and a half in love,
Who studies them is learning.

Kabir says many people simply spend their lives reading and reading. They read countless books and scriptures and finally they die, but they do not attain to wisdom. Wisdom has no relation whatsoever to information. As you keep on reading and listening and accumulating facts your memory becomes very full indeed, and you will know much without really knowing anything. Because of this great burden of words you will be under the illusion, under the false impression, you are a man of wisdom.

According to Kabir, a man of letters, a man of information, is a scholar who has only read about love. The Hindi word for love is *prem,* and in the Hindi alphabet it is made up of two and a half letters. Kabir says to read these two and one-half letters in a book is meaningless. He says they must be experienced through the book of life, that a man must enter the university of life, that he must attend the college of life. This is the only place words like this can be learned.

Although the word 'prem' is made up of two and one-half letters, Kabir also wishes to indicate another, deeper meaning. Only when a person falls in love with someone do the two and one-half letters of *prem* become complete. One letter is for the lover, the second letter is for the beloved and the half is for that something unknown that exists between the two.

Why does Kabir call it half? He could easily have called it three. There is a beautiful reason for calling it half, for indicating that it is incomplete. Kabir says no matter how hard you try, love never becomes complete, never becomes completely full. You are never totally contented with love. You never feel it is enough; you never feel fully satisfied. No matter how much love you feel or make or show, love always remains incomplete. It is like God. God keeps on expanding and expanding, becoming fuller and fuller, and yet His expanding keeps continuing, keeps going on and on and on.

The fact that love always remains incomplete is also an indication of its everlastingness. Remember, whatsoever attains to completion, dies. Completion is death, because then nothing remains to do, nothing remains to be. There is no more movement, no further progress. Anything that becomes complete is certain to die. What else can it become? What else is left? Only something that lives forever is always incomplete, always half — and no matter how hard you may try to fill it, it will remain incomplete.

To remain incomplete is love's nature. You can strive as hard as you like after satisfaction, but you will see that each satisfaction only makes you more dissatisfied, only makes you crave for more and more. The more you drink, the more your thirst increases. This is not the water that quenches your thirst when you drink it, this is the water that kindles your thirst more and more. So a lover is never satisfied and his joy is endless. His joy has no end to it, because joy can only come to an end when things reach completion.

A sexual person can be satisfied but a lover cannot. A sexual act has an end to it, a limit, but love has no end, no boundaries. Love is beginningless, just like God. Love is God's representative in this world. Love is the gateway to that dimension beyond time. Love is the penetration of superman into the world of man.

Love is the symbol of God in the world, and the nature of love is like the nature of God. God will never be completed. If He were to become complete, our world and our universe would be finished. God's perfection is like a very subtle imperfection. The Upanishads say that even if you remove the perfect from that perfection He will still remain perfect, and if you add the perfect to that perfection even then He will be the same as He was before. He is what He is. With Him, neither increase nor decrease is possible. And the same is true of love. Love will be the same in the end as it was in the beginning.

The love that becomes exhausted, that wears out, is not real love at all. It can only be a strong and violent desire for sexual enjoyment, and that relates to and culminates in the body alone. Anything related to the soul has no end, no point of termination. The body dies, the mind dies, but the soul continues to be. Its journey is infinite; it has no resting place. If it had a resting place that would also be its conclusion.

Kabir says that the word 'prem' is composed of two and one-half letters, and pointing to these two and one-half letters of 'prem' he makes a deep and significant statement about the incompleteness of love. Between the lover and the beloved there is an invisible flow, an invisible bridge uniting the two into one.

Narrow is the lane of love.
Two will never fit.
When I was, the Lord was not.
Now He is; I am not.

The path of love is very narrow. No other is as narrow. And two cannot walk together there.

In the beginning, in the first meeting between lovers, there are two and one-half, but finally the other two disappear and only love remains. The lover feels he is lost, that only the other exists; the beloved feels she is lost, that only her lover is — but in fact both are lost, and only love remains. Both heads disappear and only the one in the middle remains. Only love remains. And so the meeting between God and man never takes place. It cannot. When the moment of meeting comes the man is dissolved; as long as the man is, the moment of meeting never comes.

Look at the whole phenomenon in the following way — if you let a drop of water fall into the ocean it will maintain its own identity only as long as it does not actually touch the ocean. It may only be for very short distance, but the drop still exists as it falls. There is the ocean and there is the drop. This is exactly what is meant by *two letters and a half in love* — the drop, the ocean and the fall. The drop is on its way but it is still the drop. It still has its own identity; there is still a short distance between the two. That distance is filled with love, filled with attraction. The drop is in the act of falling but the meeting has not yet taken place. No sooner does the meeting take place than the two are one. Then there is no longer the ocean and the drop. Then the drop will be the ocean and the ocean will be the drop.

In one of his couplets Kabir says how very surprised he is to see the drop merging into the ocean, to see that the drop has now become the ocean:

Seeking, seeking, long sought.
Now how to find Kabir?
The ocean fell into the drop.
How to take it out?

You have to understand Kabir's point of view. He is speaking from the standpoint of the drop — from your standpoint. And in yet another couplet he says he is surprised to see the ocean merging into the drop and asks how the ocean can be removed again. Here he is looking through the eyes of the ocean.

There are two points of view. One is of the drop — I am lost; only the ocean remains. The second viewpoint is of the ocean — I am lost; only the drop is. The drop has become vast and the ocean has merged into it.

If you understand this correctly, if you can look at this from the viewpoint of the half, then you will see that neither the ocean nor the drop remains. The ocean was the tiniest bit less before its meeting with the drop. It was less by one drop. But that tiny amount is not at all insignificant. The drop may have been very, very tiny before it met the ocean, but the whole ocean itself was less. Now the drop and the ocean are no more as they were. Now both are lost. Now only the merger remains, now only love remains, now only the half remains. The lover is lost, the beloved is lost, the devotee is lost, the Lord is lost, Kabir is lost, God is lost. And only love remains.

How can one experience that infinite and immortal love from the scriptures? How can you grasp this love from the Vedas, from the Koran, from the Bible? How can the master even explain it to you? then what can the master do? He can only do this much — he can give you a push so that you can experience it. Unless you experience it for yourself there is no other way for you to know love.

Narrow is the lane of love.
Two will never fit.

When I was, the Lord was not.
Now He is; I am not.

People say they want to seek God. They say, "Where is God? We want to find Him." They also ask for proof that God exists. They do not understand what they are saying at all. There is only one way to seek God, and that is to lose yourself. You will not have the experience of God as long as you try to save yourself, as long as you try to retain your own identity. You can only have the experience of God when you are not. You will never have proof of God's existence; you will only have it when you are lost, when you are not.

Whosoever searches for proof that God exists will come to the conclusion that He does not exist. You can only obtain atheism from the scriptures, not theism. From the words of the scriptures you will only be able to conclude that God is not. From words, you will never conclude that God is.

Omar Khayyam has said that he went to many learned men to obtain true knowledge. He says they were very well-read, that he listened to their learned discourses, to their discussions and to their arguments for and against, but that he returned empty-handed, that he obtained no glimmer of true knowledge whatsoever from them. You can never get anything from them. Even if you memorize their words nothing will come of it; you will always come home empty-handed.

Is anything more lowly than a word? Yet it is very interesting that a man with nothing more than a vast storehouse of words is so proud of them and considers himself to be a man of knowledge. It is interesting how such a man thinks he really knows something. This is sheer foolishness.

Studying great books many have died.
None ever become learned.
Two letters and a half in love,
Who studies them is learning.

And then:

Kabir says: clouds of love
Came on me showering;
Soaked the heart,
Greening the inner jungle.

Can there be rain from word-clouds? And if rain could pour down from clouds of words would they make your garden green? You cannot cheat the trees. They will not be deceived by a shower of words; they require real water to flower. The water of experience is the real water.

Kabir says: clouds of love
Came on me showering...

No sooner do you do away with the head than the rains come. The clouds will begin to shower on you as soon as your ego disappears. The clouds of love are always hovering above you. They have not forsaken you, not even for a moment, because love is your innermost nature. Love is the nature of your soul. It is not something you amass on the outside and then distribute to others. Just as heat is the nature of fire and freshness is the nature of water, love is the nature of the soul. But your eyes are not focused on the clouds of love. Your gaze is always downcast. The clouds hover about you, and sometimes you hear their call but your mind is such that you give some other interpretation to what you have heard.

In one of his famous poems, Rabindranath Tagore tells of

a huge temple served by one hundred priests, of a temple where hundreds of thousands of rupees were regularly spent on food and on various rites. One night the chief priests had a dream in which the temple deity said he would visit the temple the following night and that preparations to receive him should be made.

When the priest arose in the morning he said to himself, "A dream is just a dream after all. It cannot be true." In general, priests never have any faith at all in the deity of their temple, although the devotees who go to the temple may. The priests of the temple have no faith because they see their calling as a profession. Such people never have, nor can they ever have, any faith in the temple deity. And yet the chief priest was somewhat nervous. He began to wonder if perhaps the dream might come true after all. If no preparations to receive the deity were made it would be terrible; if nothing were ready when the deity arrived he would be in great difficulty, so he decided he had better tell his fellow priests about the dream. He called them together and told them what had happened.

"It is only a dream," he said. "You don't have to believe it, but if it does come true we could be caught unaware." The other priests said, "There is no problem. We will make the necessary preparations and if the god does not come we will enjoy the food ourselves." This is what the priests have always done. They prepare food for their gods and then eat it themselves. They also decided that since the temple had not been cleaned in some time it had better be done as well. No one really had any faith in the dream, and they all kept remarking to each other, "Have dreams ever come true?" In any case they cleaned the temple and made the other

Tale Of Love, Untellable

necessary preparations. They lit lamps, burned incense and decorated the temple with flowers.

When evening came there was no sign of the god's arrival. Evening turned into night and still he did not come. At last the priests began to murmur among themselves, "We have been very foolish. We believed this dream too. Let's enjoy the food and then go to bed." They were quite tired after the day's activity, so they ate their dinner and went to bed.

The god's chariot arrived at midnight. The rumble of the wheels resounded throughout the temple. One priest was awakened from his sleep by the noise and it seemed to him the chariot was coming nearer and nearer. He called to the other priests, "Listen! Wake up! It sounds as if the god's chariot it approaching the temple!"

The other priests replied, "Stop all your silly chatter. We are exhausted. There is no chariot. It's only the wind knocking against the door." And so, dismissing the whole thing, they fell asleep again.

The chariot stopped at the gate and the god began to mount the steps. The sound of his footsteps could be heard clearly. And then he knocked at the door. One of the priests said, "Listen, it sounds as if he has arrived. Someone is knocking at the door."

When he heard this, another priest became a little irritated. "Can't you see we are tired from the day's work?" he said. "Stop talking nonsense. Have you ever know a dream to come true? There is no sound of knocking; it is just the rumbling of thunder. Go to sleep and be quiet!"

When they arose in the morning they saw wheel-marks running up to the steps of the temple. They saw that someone had climbed the steps, that the footprints of the god were there. But as Tagore says, it was too late. They had missed the opportunity.

The clouds of love surround you on all sides. Those who have real vision can seen them, but you cannot. Your head is the barrier; it stands in between. And the clouds are unable to shower upon you; and even if there were a shower, the drops of rain would not be able to reach your heart. Your head is like an earthen jug that has been coated in grease and so the drops would scatter everywhere. The rain would be unable to reach your heart. You heart is the jungle about which Kabir is speaking:

Kabir says: clouds of love
Came on me showering;
Soaked the heart,
Greening the inner jungle.

The heart is wild, like a jungle. Intelligence is polished, refined by society, but the heart is a jungle — primitive, uncultured, uncivilized. It is like the wild animals, like the trees, like the clouds in the sky. But the hand of man has not been able to touch his heart; it cannot reach there. Society cannot move beyond the head; only God can reach your heart. The man who gives up his head, his ego, his thoughts, is drenched by the shower from the clouds of love, Kabir says. The soul is drenched and the jungle becomes green.

A heart dry of love;
God again untasted.
Thus is man in this world:
His arising wasted.

At the time of your death, Kabir says, you will find that

your life has been wasted. If your lips have not uttered the name of God and if your heart is not filled with His love, at the end you will realize that you have missed. Then you will open your door and see how often His chariot has tried to reach the temple of your heart. You will see His footprints on your steps, you will realize that He has knocked many, many times but that every time you have misinterpreted all the signs. "It is the rumbling of the clouds," you have said. "It is the blowing of the wind. It is the sound of some wanderer." One by one you have missed the opportunities. And all of this you will realize at the hour of your death.

At the moment of death you will find people weeping, dejected, in anguish. But this anguish is not because of death. It is because people realize they have wasted their lives; it is because they feel that life has been wasted. The opportunity was held out to them but they have let it slip through their hands.

No one is really afraid of death. How can you be afraid of something about which you know nothing whatsoever? You have never encountered death. How can you be afraid of it? How can you fear a stranger? Has death ever harmed you? Has it ever done anything to you to make you weep and tremble and cry aloud? No, the real cause is something else altogether. You realize for the first time that you have wasted your entire life. Then you think, "What can I do now? Now there is no time. Now death is standing in front of me." This whole feeling of helplessness is nothing but the outcome of an unsuccessful life.

Those who have lived a righteous life; those who have known the secret of life; those in whose lives there has been godliness; those whose innermost throne has not been vacant; those whose lives have been full of love and whose lips constantly form the name of God, welcome death joyfully. The man who has known the secret of life knows no death. Such a man sees death as a resting place, as a place of deep rest that follows the exertion of life. But you will be afraid. You will be afraid then because at present you are wasting your lives away.

A heart dry of love;
God again untasted.
Thus is man in this world:
His arising wasted.

Never stop looking to see whether or not your heart has become filled with love yet. Time is fleeting. You cannot stop it; no one has ever succeeded in reversing the clock. Time flows on continuously. Every moment life slips through your hands; every moment you move closer and closer to death. Death may come at any moment. And death shows no one forgiveness or mercy. No matter how hard you plead with it, you cannot hold death off a single moment longer.

So keep on searching your heart to ascertain whether or not it has yet become filled with love. And if you find that it is still not filled with love, that it is still a desert where the rain has not yet fallen, then be quick to get rid of your head, to get rid of your ego. This is what meditation is; this is what prayer is. The art of severing the head, of getting rid of the ego, is yoga. No sooner does your ego disappear, no sooner do your thoughts go, than love begins to pour into your heart. God showers continuously, but your head has blocked the access to your heart.

Tale Of Love, Untellable

A heart dry of love;
God again untasted.

And the name of God automatically springs to the lips of the man whose heart is filled with love. This does not mean you have to keep repeating the name of God, it means that your mouth, your lips, your tongue savor the taste, savor the flavor hidden in His name. Your palate will enjoy no other taste so much. The taste of that name will roll on your tongue constantly, just as a sweet held on the tongue melts slowly, sending its sweetness vibrating through the body. The name of God has a kind of sweetness; it has a particular taste of its own.

There is no point in simply repeating God's name, nor is there any point in putting a sheet on your bed with the word 'God' printed on it so that others can read it. This will serve no purpose whatsoever. The name of God has to send thrills pulsating through your whole body.

Roused, ecstatic with His name,
Love-drunk, overflowing,
Reveling in His vision.
Why bother with liberation?

Kabir is saying something very unique here. He is saying that a man who becomes saturated with the taste of that name becomes so aroused, becomes so ecstatic from having drunk so much, that he begins to overflow. You will only be able to love others when you become so overwhelmed by the love of God that it begins to overflow from your very being. This is the state of an ecstatic man. A moment comes when you have so much love you will go mad if you do not share it, when you are so filled with love you will be in great difficulty if you do not empty yourself. In another poem Kabir says to empty yourself with both hands.

But your present condition is quite the opposite. Each of you is like an empty bowl. You wander about like a beggar, beseeching others to fill your bowl with love. You are beggars. You ask everyone you meet to toss you a scrap of love. Your eyes are desperate for love; they are begging for love, and even if someone bestows a little smile on you, you are thrilled. There is no end to your beggarliness. If someone tosses a stone in your begging bowl you think you have been given a diamond.

Among yourselves you beg love from each other all the time. You clamor after it. And bear in mind that those from whom you are begging are as empty of love as you. They can only give you consolation; they cannot give you love. Even if they want to give you love, they cannot. You are beggars standing before other beggars with your begging bowls.

Every beggar is an egoist; every beggar thinks he is an emperor. But inside he is still a beggar. He speaks of giving only so he can get. You give a little love to someone else, but you only do so because you want love in return. It is a bargain. The other is only trying to barter in love; he is only trying to exploit you too.

In this world everyone begs love from someone else — the son from the father, the father from the son, one friend from another — and not one single person sees that the person from whom he is begging has also come to him to ask for love. That is why their kind of love is a failure. Initially, this sort of deception can work for a few days, but how long can any deception last? Very soon you will realize that the other is also a beggar, and then you will be in difficulty.

You see a woman and you think she is full of love; a woman sees you and she thinks you are full of love too. Each of you tries to deceive the other. It is all a deception. The whole thing is like putting a lump of dough on a hook to catch a fish. The dough is just an outer covering; there is a hook inside. In such a situation, love between two people can be considered to have lasted a long time if it lasts two or three days, because no sooner do two people get close than each quickly realizes the other is also a beggar. Both of them have spoken of giving love, but in fact each has approached the other begging for love. Everyone keeps on promising he will give love.

You even ask for love from small children! There is no limit to your beggarliness. A mother looks at her newborn child and wants him to smile, and so she teases him into smiling. Smiling is forced on the child. The mother tries to teach the child to smile, and so in a few days he begins to learn the art of politics. He will soon understand that it is advantageous to smile. He will learn that if he smiles his mother is pleased, and that if he does not smile she is displeased, and so he will begin to smile more often. But that smile will be forced, just a put-on smile, just a show.

Under your influence, young children soon become clever and cunning. It is a kind of *satsang,* a kind of learning not unlike that of disciples who learn just by being in the presence of the master. And when children smile they are doing so out of selfishness. They smile because they want something from you. When they do not want anything they will not smile, no matter how much you try to make them. "What is the point of smiling if I don't want anything?" they think. You must have observed how cleverly they can flatter you when they want something from you. Then they try to please you in every possible way — laughing and dancing and looking very happy.

Everyone is a beggar. And everyone will remain so as long as he has *a heart dry of love*. But when a man knows himself, when he knows his situation accurately and is able to rid himself of his thoughts and of his ego, it is a different matter.

What is so difficult about ridding yourself of your thoughts and of your ego? What have you ever attained or achieved through them? You have achieved nothing whatsoever, and yet you cling to them! You are like a drowning man clutching at a straw. And if you say to such a man, "You fool! That is only a straw; it will never save you!" he will shut his eyes. If he sees it really is just a straw his only hope will be shattered. People live in hope. You all think something may happen and so you hold on a little longer. Your hopes have not been fulfilled so far, but you say, "Who knows? Some miracle may happen tomorrow and my hopes will be fulfilled."

If your hopes have not been fulfilled today, how will they be fulfilled tomorrow? You will have to transform yourself. You have not transformed yourself thus far and you have seen that nothing has happened; you have not transformed yourself thus far and although you have tried to fulfill your dreams for countless births you have failed. You simply go on repeating the same foolishness from birth to birth.

Roused, ecstatic with His name,
Love-drunk, overflowing,

Reveling in His vision.
Why bother with liberation?

But the man who loses his head, who drops his ego, is filled with ecstasy — king or commoner. He is filled with delight. And love begins to radiate from every pore of his body.

Why bother with liberation?

Such a man does not even ask for liberation. Nor does he pray to God to grant him freedom, to give him *moksha*. He says, "Who cares about liberation! I couldn't care less. I simply want to see you!" Devotees of God do not demand liberation, nor do they ask about it. They simply say, "We only wish to see You. We only want to see You once to be totally satisfied. We are not concerned with liberation at all. We have no desire for liberation whatsoever!"

This must be carefully understood, because it is quite possible for the desire for liberation to become a subtle form of ego. In ninety-nine cases out of one hundred this is what happens. When you say, "I want to be liberated," it is the "I," the ego, that desires liberation. And then your liberation, your *moksha*, becomes just an extension of your ego. In this instance you want to save your "I." You are prepared for the body to perish, but you want to preserve your "I." You call this "my" liberation. But bear in mind there is only one kind of liberation, and that is liberation from "I," liberation from the ego itself.

There cannot be any such thing as "my" liberation. How can "I" be liberated? "I" is the bondage! "I" can never be free. There is no liberating "I," there is only liberation from "I." That is why devotees often achieve the liberation yogis are unable to attain. A yogi says, "I want liberation. I desire to be liberated," but his liberation is linked with his "I." It seems to be the last desire of the "I." But no matter how purified it may be, it is still a desire. Chains may be forged of gold, but they are still chains.

Roused, ecstatic with His name,
Love-drunk, overflowing,
Reveling in His vision.
Why bother with liberation?

Such a man says, "I care nothing about liberation; I do not even ask for it. I only want to see Your face." Such a man is even ready to forego liberation, and in so doing he becomes liberated. That is the only liberation — when there is no desiring at all. The desire to be liberated is not present in such a man. He only desires to see Him; he only desires a glimpse of Him. A devotee is satisfied with very little, and so he receives everything. But a yogi demands all. Bear this in mind — as you become satisfied with less and less you will receive much more. But when you become satisfied with whatsoever you are...

I say to you, do not even ask to see His face. You should not even say, "I only want a glimpse of Your face." Why should you even hold on to that desire? Only say, "Whatever Thy will may be it is fine with me. If I get a glimpse it is okay; if I do not, even then it is okay." That very moment you will be liberated.

Tale of love, untellable.
Not a bit's ever told.
The sweets of a dumb one —
He enjoys...and smiles.

Tale Of Love, Untellable

These sutras are filled with love. Kabir says that whosoever gives up his head attains love, that clouds of love shower down on such a man, drenching his soul — so much so that it overflows into an abundant sharing with others. He also says love is such freedom that not even the desire for liberation remains. Love is the highest kind of liberation, and when one achieves love even the desire for moksha, for ultimate freedom, disappears.

It is difficult to put what Kabir wishes to express into words. It is virtually impossible. Only he who knows, knows. Only he who lives in love knows. It is a matter of personal experience. That is why Kabir says love is like a sweet tasted by one who is dumb. When a man who is dumb eats a sweet, he simply enjoys it and smiles. If you ask him, "What is the matter? Why are you smiling?" he cannot express his feeling in words, he can only keep on smiling. And so the man who has drunk pure love also smiles. He is also dumb; he is also at a loss to express his joy. He is so filled with the taste that even the experience has disappeared. If you can understand his smile then you will know it is the only way he can indicate his feeling of great joy.

Go to the enlightened ones, to the men of wisdom. Don't worry too much about what they say, but be alert and thorough enough to see what they are. Their very beings are indicative. What they are is not something that can be put into words. The enlightened man is like the man who is dumb and eats a sweet; he simply smiles after he has tasted it.

To sit at the feet of the enlightened man, at the feet of the masters, is the only meaning of the word *satsang*. You should sit at the feet of those who have tasted that sweet, who have tasted the sweetness of love. Their lives are filled with ecstasy; their lives are in flower. You should inhale their fragrance; you should drown yourselves in their taste; you should merge totally into their joy. Don't be too concerned about what they say. Be alert. Understand what they are. And perhaps you will understand their secret. If you are able to understand them, you will be able to progress, you will be able to move forward.

2

TELL AND STILL IT'S HIDDEN

*Knowledge of inner experience
Many come asking for.
Struck dumb savoring the sweet,
Whose mouth will tell the taste?*

*The sign of the dumb
Only the dumb understand.
Likewise, the joy of a sage
Only a sage knows.*

*Not of written words
But of experiencing:
When the bride meets His embrace
The guests all fade away.*

*That which sees cannot speak,
Which speaks cannot hear,
That which hears cannot explain.
Why tongue, eyes, ears?*

*What's full empties out;
What's empty fills up.
Empty, full — neither to be found.
The experience is this.*

Such a wonder! It's never told.
Tell, and still it's hidden.
Koran and Veda couldn't write it.
If I say it, who will listen?

Let us go deeply into the meaning of each word. There is a saying about "containing the ocean in a pot." Kabir has done that. He has managed to contain the unlimited in very small words, in words we use every day. But Kabir has given them a unique meaning. You may think, "But this is all known to me!" When you hear them; you may understand the surface meaning of the words, but you are not acquainted with their depth. And each word is so powerful it can set you off on an infinite journey.

Knowledge of inner experience
Many come asking for:
Struck dumb savoring the sweet,
Whose mouth will tell the taste?

Information about objects can be collected, but this is knowledge you have obtained from outside. You perceive objects from four sides; you can walk all around them. For example, when you go to a Hindu temple you walk around the idol of God, but this walking only happens outwardly and so it has become phony, a mere ritual. No matter how much you may know about something from the outside, your information about it is never inner, never from your own experience.

As long as we do not enter the depths of something our information about it will always be surface. It is like going to see the ocean and coming back home simply having glanced at the waves. The real ocean, the depths and the treasures of the real ocean, are hidden beneath the waves. On the surface there is only foam; on the surface there is only conflict, competition, enmity. In the waves, only mischief and upheaval exist. The real ocean is hidden beneath them. There is only one way to know that ocean and that is to dive deeply into it. And there is only one kind of diving, the diving into yourself.

No matter how deeply you penetrate the inner reaches of another, you will never be able to touch his soul. Your journey will be just an orbiting on his outer boundary. So if you want to know the ocean through and through, then even diving into it is not enough. Then you have to become one with the ocean, just like a lump of rocksalt that is thrown into the sea dissolves and becomes one with it. Then and only then will you know the infinite depths of the ocean.

The experience of knowledge can only be of one's own self, and never of another's. We always remain a tiny bit removed from each other. Even when we make love we are still unable to reach the other's innermost depths — even then we remain on the circumference. And this is the problem for lovers. Lovers feel they come very close to each other, but their actual experience with each other reveals to them that they always remain far away. As they come nearer and nearer to each other they begin to realize it is impossible to be really close. A distance always remains between the two. That is why love for another is never satisfying.

Love will only be satisfying when it is established in God. God is you; He is not someone else. And there, with God, the distance disappears completely. Kabir calls such an experience knowledge. Such an experience can be only of the self. Self-knowledge is the only knowledge; the rest is all information.

Knowledge is only that which a man has tested for himself; it cannot be achieved without experience.

There are many things in this world that can be known through others, many things that can be known with no personal experience. Whatever we know about this world, whatever information we have about it, for the most part is given to us by others. Scientists give us information about the various sciences; experts in geography tell us where the Himalayas are and where Tibet is, and this is how we gather information. This information received from others about the world can be accepted, but you cannot accept information from others about your self.

Whatsoever another tells you about yourself will be untrue. No matter what you have learned about yourself from the Upanishads, from the Vedas, from the Koran, from the Bible, from the saints, from the scholars — give it no credence at all. After all, you are not a stranger to yourself! The idea that someone else can show you what you are is outrageous. What greater impotency can there be than your powerlessness even to know your self! What greater blindness can there be than your inability to know your self!

Are you so enveloped in darkness that you need someone else to show you the light, to show you who you are? If you need someone else, then it is quite clear you have no concept whatsoever of your being, of who you are. And how can another person give you that knowledge? There is no other way to achieve that experience than for yourself.

The master can indicate to you how to dive into yourself, but he cannot show you anything, he cannot tell you anything about your self. He can lead you to the bank of the river, but

Tell And Still It's Hidden

you will have to drink the water. And when you drink the water your thirst will be quenched. But that will be your own experience.

I can tell you everything there is to know about water — its whole chemistry, how it is composed of oxygen and hydrogen, its different properties, at what temperature it becomes vapor, at what temperature it turns into ice — but that will not quench your thirst. Your throat will remain parched and dry. No matter how great or how complete the information may be it will not quench your thirst. Mere information about the chemistry of water will not help you.

Understand what the master is indicating first — then go in search of water and drink. Then you will have the experience of water for yourself. Then the dryness will disappear and your throat will feel cool; then the fires of deprivation and of uneasiness will vanish, and a kind of peace, a kind of satisfaction will well up within you. No one else can give you this experience, but you are quite capable of having it for yourself if you want to.

So far you have tried to obtain this experience from someone else. You do not even wish to exert yourself enough to drink. It is your thirst, so how can my water help you? You will have to find your own water. This is why all the enlightened men, all those who know, say there is no knowledge except that which comes from experience.

So free yourself as quickly as possible from whatever knowledge you have gathered, from whatever information you have accumulated that is not from your own experience. You will never start out in search of that spring of fresh water as long as this burden is on your head because you are under the illusion you have known, without really having known; under the illusion you have drunk, without really having drunk; under the illusion you have acquired something, without really having acquired anything. This is an impossible situation.

Kabir is saying that you have read a lot, that you have accumulated much information, and that many people are satisfied with this kind of knowledge.

Kabir lived in Kashi, a place abounding in scholars. They believed it was enough to read, to accumulate knowledge from books. They were well-versed in the Vedas, in the Upanishads and in the other scriptures, and they looked upon Kabir as ignorant, as an illiterate man. In one sense, you can say Kabir was illiterate. If you consider a scholar as literate, as a well educated man, then Kabir was definitely illiterate. But of what value is the scholar's knowledge? A scholar will go on and on about the immortality of the soul, but when death approaches you will find him trembling and weeping and wailing. All this talk of immortality will crumble into nothingness because he has not known it. He has only read about immortality; he has only heard about it from someone else. It may be someone else's experience, but it is not his own.

When you possess the pure gold of your own experience you will be fully prepared to face the rest of life, but the gold of another's experience will turn to clay in your hands. It will not help you face life at all. The knowledge you gain from others may help you to obtain a university degree, may earn you the world's respect as a man of letters, but you will know inside yourself that you have not attained true knowledge. Inside, the lamp will be unlit; inside, there will be no flame.

Scholars and pundits can deceive others, but how can they deceive themselves? Their so-called knowledge is like this story Buddha used to tell about a villager who sat at the door of his house, counting the cows and buffaloes of the other villagers as they passed by his door each morning and evening. He could tell how many cows and buffaloes there were in the village, but all of his activity never provided him with a single drop of milk. Buddha used to warn his disciples not spend their lives like that villager.

All scholars are like that villager. They keep the accounts of others — what the Vedas say, what the Koran says, what the Bible says. They spend their whole lives counting the cows and buffaloes of others without ever getting a single drop of milk to drink. The experience must be your own.

Knowledge of inner experience
Many come asking for.
Struck dumb savoring the sweet,
Whose mouth will tell the taste?

The great difficulty is that the man who has known the truth cannot give it to you even if he wishes to. You have no comprehension of the affliction of the wise. You only know one affliction, the affliction of the ignorant. The enlightened man has known the real thing. He knows. He sees you groping in the dark and he wants to give you all that he knows, but he is helpless. That is his affliction.

Struck dumb savoring the sweet,
Whose mouth will tell the taste?

He has already tasted the sweet and he sees you still wandering all over in search of it. He sees you becoming more and more downcast, more and more entangled in your problems, in your cares and sufferings. He wishes you could have the taste too; he wants the door of heaven to open for you as well. He wants to help you. He wants to cry out and say, "It is so very sweet!" But just as a man who is dumb is unable to cry aloud, the throat of the enlightened man is blocked; his lips cannot form the words. He is in the same position as the dumb man.

But the difficulty of the enlightened man is even greater than that of the man who is dumb. A remedy for dumbness may be possible, but for the enlightened man there is no way out. If the difficulty were physical some cure could be found, but his predicament is his inability to express what he has known. His dilemma arises out of the very nature of the experience of self-knowledge. If you also attain to that knowledge you will understand this quandary as well.

And even if the awakened man tries, his attempts are all unsuccessful. Not only are they unsuccessful, they can create the wrong impression. He wants to say one thing but has to say something else. He wants to say something definite and precise, but words are unable to express what it is he wants to say and they carry him somewhere else. He wants to lead you to a particular spot, but when he looks at you he sees he has led you to some other place, he sees you have misunderstood him.

This is why so many religious sects exist in the world. The enlightened preach religion, pure religion, but it branches off into sects. What the enlightened men have said has not been understood correctly. As it travels from them to you, truth becomes untruth and is misconstrued. No sooner do you hear something than you become involved in it and your mind gives it its own interpretation. You implant your own interpretation, your own meaning; you twist it to suit yourself. This is the distinction between real religion an sects.

The enlightened man tries to see that religion reaches you, but what actually happens is that it becomes distorted into a sect. He wants to make you free, but what happens is that you become even more tightly bound. And then a new difficulty arises. He wants love to manifest in your lives, but when he looks at you he sees you ready to fight in the name of love. Take the example of the Christians. Jesus used to say, "God is love," and yet no other people have waged as many wars as the Christians. He said to turn the other cheek to the one who strikes you, and the Christians have killed hundreds of thousands of people. And do you know why they have massacred these people? With a sword in one hand and a Bible in the other they did this to bring them religion!

The rishis of the Vedas and the Upanishads say, "There is the same Brahman in all. He alone resides in all. He is spread throughout; He exists in the smallest particle." And what the Hindus have done is quite the opposite. The scholar who quotes the sutras of the Upanishads so often is not prepared to touch the lowborn, the untouchables. This proves he considers Brahman as untouchable. If Brahman is in all, then who can be looked upon as untouchable? Then who can be deemed unholy? But this has happened in this land of the enlightened. Not only was the untouchable not to be touched, he was punished if ever his shadow fell on a brahmin! His shadow! Can a shadow be unholy? The shadow is a shadow; it is nonexistent, completely unsubstantial! Suppose a brahmin were sitting somewhere and an untouchable passed by. If his shadow fell on the brahmin he would have been thrashed, beaten, perhaps even killed — the crime was considered punishable by death. What an inconceivable thing! This so-called knower-of-Brahman, afraid of a shadow!

Why were the minds of those who said Brahman was all-pervading so diseased? How did this happen?

Those who said that Brahman is all-pervading were perfectly correct, but those who heard it interpreted it in their own ways, in quite different senses. Words travel very short distance between the master and his disciples, but even in that short distance everything is perverted. This perversion is not because of anything related to the body, memory or mind — if it were it could be corrected — but it is nonetheless quite natural. The nature of this sort of discourse, of this sort of transmission, is such that we can only say exactly what it is we wish to say to those who have had similar experiences, to those who exist at the same level of experience. That is why Kabir says:

The sign of the dumb
Only the dumb understand.
Likewise, the joy of a sage
Only a sage knows.

The master is speaking from a particular level and the disciple is hearing at another level, at a different one. So how is a dialogue possible between the two? The master stands on a high peak of consciousness and the disciple is floundering in an abyss of darkness. How can there be any dialogue between the two? The words of the master, spoken from the golden peak, have to descend into the dark abyss — they are polluted with darkness before they enter you. In their journey to you the words are lost, and only darkness reaches you.

Tell And Still It's Hidden

Kabir says you will never truly understand until you and the master are both on the same level. One dumb man understands the language of another. If one wishes to say to another, "It is very sweet," he will be able to do so by hand-signals. They share the same language. They are on the same level; they have the same experience. This means that a dialogue, a communication is possible between them.

Until our experience is on the same level, discussion is possible between us or criticism, but there cannot be a dialogue. If I say something to you, you may immediately begin to discuss in your mind whether what I have said is right or wrong; you may give reasons for and against it, but there will not be a dialogue. When there is a dialogue, no sooner is something said by one person than it is totally understood in the same sense by the listener — with nothing whatsoever missing, with not the slightest difference at all. This is only possible if you are at the same level as I am. This is only possible if two individuals — the speaker and the listener — are standing at the same level. Then there is no distinction.

Only the enlightened can explain to the enlightened — but then it is quite useless because then there is no need. This is a paradox of life. There is no need to explain to one who understands, but it is necessary to explain to one who does not understand. And it is not possible to explain to him.

Then what can be done? How can those who have known distribute their knowledge? How can they share their precious treasure? How can those who have known lead you to that place where knowing happens? How can those who have tasted truth invite you on that journey?

Many ways, many methods have been found. All the techniques of yoga have been uncovered to create a bridge between you and the enlightened men.

Patanjali has said that faith will find a way, that there will be no arguing then, for or against. Faith is the indication that even though you are fully conscious you are not yet ready, not yet fit for truth; it shows you are still standing in darkness. It means you have accepted what has been said to you as gospel; it means you have not begun to discuss, to reason things out, to raise questions. And if you do start to reason and to question, the real meaning of what has been said to you will be lost. Whatever interpretation you give it will be your own, and not that of the master.

Faith has only one meaning. Faith is a device to bridge the gap between master and disciple. You are simply to hear what the master says and accept it immediately. You are not to engage in any inner discussion. Just see that he is giving you an indication and begin your journey. Do not hesitate even for a moment. Do not even stop to think, "Where am I going? Why am I going?" Do not consult your mind at all; just give your mind a holiday. Faith means giving your mind a holiday. Ask your mind just to keep its place, just to be quiet. Tell it, "Let me hear this directly. Don't get in my way. Don't interfere. Don't bring your interpretation in. It is not needed. If it is needed, I will consult you. Do not interfere. Do not offer advice for which you have not been asked."

The mind will try to interfere, that is for certain — that is its habit. No matter what you undertake, it will say, "This is the right thing to do," or it will say, "That is the wrong thing to do." It will say, "I am telling you this for your own good, for your own safety." Such behavior by the mind may be acceptable in worldly affairs, but in moving beyond the world, in moving into spiritual realms, it is a hindrance. How can it be trusted in areas about which it knows nothing at all, or in things it has never tasted? In the beginning the mind will tell you not to trust; it will say you shouldn't trust because this kind of thing has never happened before. And from one standpoint it is right — you really have never experienced this kind of thing before.

Your mind is nothing but a storehouse of things that have happened to you in the past. It is the sum total of all that you have experienced up to now. So, immediately, the mind will tell you that this kind of thing has never happened before, that there is no such taste. It will tell you this man is deceiving you, that this man is trying to ensnare you. It will say, "This kind of thing never happens. It is illogical, irrational. Don't listen to this man. Be careful. Run from him from these things he is suggesting." The mind is telling you these things for your protection. And it is not wrong. Whatever it has known or experienced does not include this taste. It has no knowledge whatsoever of this taste. Then what is to be done?

If you follow the advice of the mind then the doors of the unknown will remain closed to you, then what you have not known will remain unknown forever. The mind is only in favor of what it has known. the mind knows the desire of sex, it knows the taste of sex, but it has no idea at all what *brahmacharya* is, what celibacy is. So if anyone speaks about brahmacharya, the mind will consider it sheer nonsense. The mind has never known what celibacy is. The mind only knows the downward flow of energy, the flowing into sex. The mind only knows the momentary bliss that comes from the downward flow of the life-force. It has never known the upward flow; it does not know it can rise upward. And so the mind will argue. The mind will say it never really flows upward at all; it will ask how something that has never happened before can possibly happen. "If it could happen," the mind will say, "then it would have happened already."

Your mind will tell you that everything has already happened, that everything is already over — but the master says everything still remains to be accomplished, that what has happened so far is practically nothing, is as good as naught. You are now a seed; you are not yet a tree. And yet your mind will tell you that you are already a tree. It tells you that whatever fruit the tree will bear has already been borne; it tells you that whatever the tree can produce has already been produced. It says that all the possibilities are now over, that all is now fulfilled.

That is why the mind is so troublesome; that is why it is so bored. It says that whatever you wanted to taste you have already tasted, that all is repetitious now. It says you have already enjoyed whatever you wanted to enjoy and that now you are only repeating the same thing over and over again. The mind knows perfectly well it moves in circles, that it repeats the same things continuously, but it does not know that this whole existence, this whole universe is much bigger than it is. The unknown is infinitely greater than the known.

The master keeps on telling you that whatever has happened so far is not even the beginning, that you are still standing outside your real home, that you have not even begun to mount the stairs, that your admission to the palace that is your real home is still very far off.

The question now is how to solve this puzzle. If you listen

Tell And Still It's Hidden

to what your mind says you cannot listen to what the master says. If you wish to listen to what the master says you will have to get rid of your mind. That is why Patanjali stressed the importance of faith; this is why he considered it the first step. All the enlightened men regard faith in the same way.

Why was faith made the first step? The reason faith was made the first step is indicated by Kabir when he says:

Knowledge of inner experience
Many come asking for.
Struck dumb savoring the sweet,
Whose mouth will tell the taste?

Next, Kabir says:

The sign of the dumb
Only the dumb understand.
Likewise, the joy of a sage
Only a sage knows.

There is no word in our language to express that ecstasy, not even to indicate it. Your language is your language — it is the result of your experience — but the enlightened man has no language; all of his experience comes from silence, from emptiness, from total peace. His experience does not come from thoughts, it comes from the absence of thoughts.

Whatsoever the enlightened man knows is known in emptiness, is known where there are no words at all. What you will come to know in emptiness you will not be able to express in words either. That which is born out of emptiness can only be experienced in emptiness; only the dumb will be able to communicate with the dumb. But for the dumb, there is no need to tell each other anything.

Buddha and Mahavira often used to stay in the same village at the same time. Once they even stayed in the same inn. Yet no meeting took place between them. There was no need for it. But for the Jainas and the Buddhists this has remained a problem. And they keep on discussing it. "Why did they not meet with each other?" they ask. "They both seem quite egotistical," they say. "When they were both in the same inn they should certainly have met. Who knows what beauty might have flowered out of that meeting?"

I tell you there was no need for them to meet at all. Both had tasted the sweet and both were dumb. What would have been the point of exchanging mere signals? If one of them had made a gesture he would have been considered a fool. If either of them had tried to speak he would have been in error; he would have shown he was unable to see that the other had also arrived. So the meeting did not occur, simply because there was no need for it.

There are three kinds of meetings. The first kind is between two ignorant men, between two unenlightened men. When they meet there is great discussion between them. There is talk and talk and more talk, and no good whatsoever comes of it. It is mere chitchat, going on for hours.

The second kind of meeting is between two enlightened men. There is no discussion; complete silence prevails. Emptiness flows between them. It is as if the two are standing on separate banks of a river and the river of emptiness is flowing between them. There is no noise, no talking, no sound.

The third kind of meeting is between the enlightened man and the unenlightened one. When two unenlightened persons meet there is discussion, but it has no substance to it at all. When two enlightened beings meet there is substance, but there is no discussion. And what usually happens in the third case, in the meeting between the enlightened and the unenlightened, is that the unenlightened man talks and talks and talks while the enlightened man just keeps silent and listens.

Many people come to me. They come to ask some question, to seek some solution, but they soon forget that they have come for some reason and begin to give me all sorts of information about themselves. And when they take leave of me they say, "We are so very pleased we came. You spoke of such nice things."

There was once a saint called Baal Shem. One day a very talkative man came to see him. He talked so much nonsense, and such a lot of it, that Baal Shem grew fed up and began to wonder how he could get rid of him. The man talked nonstop; he didn't even give Baal Shem a chance to say, "Enough, brother! Now I have other work to do."

After quite some time the man began to tell Baal Shem how he had gone to another village to meet such and such a saint. "We spoke of you," the man said, "and he told me a great deal about you."

This was the chance Baal Shem had been waiting for. He immediately shouted, "This is totally untrue, completely false!"

The man was quite surprised. He said, "I have not yet repeated what the saint said about you, and you tell me it is totally false?"

Baal Shem replied, "Certainly I say it is false. You probably didn't even give him a chance to open his mouth! So how could he say anything about me? From my own experience with you I can clearly see he never had a chance to say a word!"

The third kind of meeting is like this — the unenlightened man goes on talking and talking and the enlightened man listens. This is what happens in most cases. The enlightened man listens out of compassion. He thinks it may lighten your load if you can give vent to your feelings and to your thoughts; he feels you may obtain a little relief from your cares and tribulations. This talking is a kind of catharsis. And so he listens.

In the West the practice of listening has turned into a business, a very flourishing business based on the idea that talking about one's problems is a kind of catharsis. These days a psychoanalyst has the most profitable business. It has become very expensive, and all the psychoanalyst does is listen.

For ignorant people the discoveries of Freud have been a great boon, a great comfort. In the psychoanalytical treatment Freud developed for mentally ill people, the patient is asked to lie down on a couch and the psychoanalyst sits behind the couch and says, "Say whatsoever you want to. Just speak aloud whatever thoughts come into your mind. Don't worry at all whether they are relevant or irrelevant, whether they are good or bad, meaningful or meaningless. Just let the thoughts come; just give voice to them." Sometimes this treatment can go on for three years; it all depends on the condition of the patient. And the whole treatment costs a great deal of money. The time of treatment varies — it may be one hour a day; it may be two to three times a week — and the psychoanalyst

Tell And Still It's Hidden

simply listens. After chattering on like this for three years or so many people eventually become calm and quiet.

The psychoanalyst is a professional listener. He does nothing; he simply listens. You have undoubtedly encountered professional speakers; this man is a professional listener. Even when Freud grew old he worked eight to ten hours a day, listening to the jabber of eight to ten people every day. One of his newer pupils once asked him, "Don't you get fed up? Don't you feel exhausted after listening to two or three patients? I get so tired of it sometimes I feel I'll just die. But you are wonderful. You go on listening from morning until night."

"Don't be a fool!" Freud replied. "Who listens? The patient keeps on talking — that's fine, let him speak. But who listens? If you did listen you would wear yourself out!"

In the West psychoanalysis has become a very thriving business, growing day by day. And there is a reason for it. These days people do not have enough leisure to spend time in conversation, in chit-chat. Who listens any more? The wife does not listen to the husband and the husband does not listen to the wife. There is no leisure; there is no free time, and so people need a professional listener to hear their problems, to afford them some relief, to lighten their loads.

The enlightened man will listen to the unenlightened man, but he only does so to bring you some relief. The opposite should happen. The unenlightened man should listen to the enlightened man. But this can only happen when there is faith between the two; otherwise, the unenlightened man will always mistrust what the enlightened man is saying. No matter what he says, it will create suspicion in the unenlightened man's mind. His mind will protest. It will say,

"This cannot be! It is impossible! Why should I move towards the unknown? Why should I waste my energy? Why should I pay any attention to him?" To be able to set the mind aside you need faith.

The mind will not allow you to move into the experience of the unknown. It will stop you at the shore; it will not allow you to plunge into the ocean. It will ask, "Where is the other shore? What guarantee is there the boat will take me to the other shore? That other shore is not even visible. That other shore is just a possibility; it is not a fact. Has anyone ever reached there? Why do I even want to bother? Those who are supposed to have gone to the other shore have not even returned to say they have arrived! And this one I am supposed to follow, has he a map to show me the way? Is there any real basis to all his talk about this unknown? Has he any real proof?"

No, the master cannot give you any proof. There is no proof. The experience itself is the proof. But when you have deep faith in your heart you can enter into his experience. Your faith must be so strong that you can bridge the distance between you and him, so strong that you begin to obtain not only direct proof but direct sensual perception of his experience as well, so strong that you can also hear the sound of the harmony that rings continuously within him, so strong that you also have an inkling of the taste that fills his mouth, so strong that what has happened to him touches you too, so strong that the darkness within you is shattered by a brilliant flash of lightning and you see for a moment who you are. For this phenomenon to occur you must give yourself the opportunity. And that opportunity will be given to you by your faith.

Tell And Still It's Hidden

Struck dumb savoring the sweet,
Whose mouth will tell the taste?

The sign of the dumb
Only the dumb understand.
Likewise, the joy of a sage
Only a sage knows.

Remember this and remember it well: if you do not approve of a master, of a guru, of a sage, or a saint, leave him at once — but do not make up your mind that he is false, that he is a fake. How can you decide? If you do not approve of him, then just leave him quietly, just say to yourself that his is not the path for you. But do not pronounce judgment on him. Many people turned away from Buddha and declared that he was a fake. Many did the same to Jesus and played their part in placing him on the cross. so don't set yourself up as being so very intelligent. All of these people were intelligent men; they were just like you — and see what happened! They said Buddha was a fake, that what he said was not to be trusted — and they were just as intelligent as you. They had the same minds; they put forth the same arguments as you. They had the same experiences of the world as you do. How could they believe what someone like Buddha said? They had no experience of the world beyond, the other shore was not visible to them. And Buddha was speaking of that other shore.

That other shore is not only unknown, it is also unknowable. Even after knowing it, it cannot be known completely. You have to keep on trying to know it, to keep on trying more and more, and still your knowledge will remain incomplete. Its totality is such that it is always expanding. There is no contradiction in speaking of its totality or of its nontotality. What Buddha was saying was beyond intellect, so many people did not believe what he said. Many people rejected him. But because of their disbelief Buddha loses nothing; on the contrary, it is the disbelievers who miss, who fail to realize the truth. Remember, no one loses anything because of your doubt, because of your disbelief. You are the only loser. And you are the loser because you are hindering your own progress.

So when you feel someone is not completely right for you, do not make any decision about him — just leave him quietly and seek out someone else. What is the problem? There are two alternatives open to you. You can either say, "I am leaving this man because he is wrong," or you can say, "I am leaving this man because his path is not for me." There is a difference between these two statements.

You have come to me. If you feel that what I have to say does not suit you, that you do not approve of what I say, then leave me quietly. Why? Then you will seek out someone whose views suit you better. But if you decide that I am false then your mind will harden, and when you go to the second man you will also decide that he is false. And when you go to the third man you will come to the same decision as well. Eventually this decision you have taken will be like a weight on your mind, and then wheresoever you go it will be an impediment on your path, it will hinder your progress; it will always cause you to find fault with others. And then you will never be able to recognize an enlightened man.

Kabir says:

...the joy of a sage
Only a sage knows.

There is no other way to know Buddha but to become a Buddha yourself. To know Krishna, to understand him, you will have to become like Krishna yourself. Nothing less will do. But we decide things in such a hurry. You are drowning in the valley of darkness and yet you reach monumental decisions about the peaks, about places your vision is not even able to reach — not to mention making up your mind about the journey itself. You make up your minds about things you have not even glimpsed.

There is a reason you make such decisions. The mind decides every master is false because the mind does not want to go anywhere at all. So with this kind of attitude you are definitely going to remain in the dark valley. If you find an authentic master the mind will have to begin its uphill journey, and that it does not want to do, the uphill journey seems painful and arduous. The mind loves to be idle; it loves inertia. It says, "Stay in bed. There is no need to go anywhere today."

The valley is all there is for you. Earning money, having children, seeing your name in the newspaper on and off, having one or two hundred people attend your funeral — all this is enough for you. Then you can say you are a successful man. What success!

The most amazing thing is that you do not believe the enlightened man! You doubt him — yet you never have doubts whatsoever about his mind that makes you so mean and selfish. You never ask your mind, "Is earning money, producing half a dozen children, achieving fame, enough? Is this all? Is this the goal of life? Is this real achievement?" But this is what your mind keeps telling you. When you kneel to pray it reminds you of your shop. It tells you how much you could have earned this hour you are spending praying. It rushes you through your worship, but when it leads you to the house of a prostitute it wishes the night could have been longer. And you never entertain the slightest doubt about your mind?

If you want to doubt anything, doubt your mind! But you do not doubt it at all. You have become so identified with it you have forgotten you are not the mind, you have forgotten you are separate from the mind. You are identified with it; you think it is you. You raise doubts about the enlightened man because to be associated with him you will have to begin an uphill journey, you will have to work hard, you will have to repent. You will be transformed; you will no longer be what you are — and so you find all sorts of excuses not to follow the men who have become enlightened.

Not of written words
But of experiencing:
When the bride meets His embrace
The guests all fade away.

Where can you find greater words than these!

Truth is not something that can be reduced to written form; it is not be found in books and scriptures. Truth is unfathomable. You will not be able to find it anywhere. You may read the Vedas; you can memorize them, but, as Kabir says, you will not be able to find the truth. Truth is not something that can be reduced to paper. Truth has to be seen, to be experienced.

Look at it this way — suppose a blind man were to memorize everything that has ever been written about light; suppose a blind man were to master the whole theory of

Tell And Still It's Hidden

light? Would all his knowledge create a single ray of light? Would it afford him the tiniest glimpse of light? Would it light even a few steps in front of him? There is no way it can happen. Truth has to be seen, to be experienced. One's eyes must be wide open.

And the eyes with which you view the outside world are not the eyes I mean. There are eyes that see within as well. Keep this subtle and deep discovery of yoga in mind — there are as many inner faculties as there are outer ones. It has to be so. A river cannot have just one bank; there must be two. It does not matter whether the second bank can be seen or not. You see the outside world with your eyes, but they have another side, another bank, so that you can see within as well. You hear the sounds of the outer world with your ears, but there are ears for inner hearing too. You touch things with your hands and know them in this way, but on the inside there is also a capacity of touch to allow you your own inner experiences. It would make no sense if we are able to experience all these things on the outside and yet were unable to experience our own selves. It would make no sense if we were able to see everything but our own selves if we were able to hear the hustle and bustle of the whole world and yet were unable to hear our own inner music.

No, yoga says, the sense-organs are of two aspects. One aspect is gross, belonging to the body, moving towards the outer world; the second is subtle, moving within. And about these organs of sense there is no written science for you to read, for you to master.

The Vedas, the Koran and the Bible all belong to the outer world. There is no inner scripture. There is only the soul. Only you are within. And that is the scripture. Kabir says, this phenomenon of seeing the inner scripture is one of experiencing. It happens when you stand in front of your self, when you know your self, when you see your self in such a total way that nothing more remains to be seen.

Not of written words
But of experiencing...

You have already wasted enough time on written words. You have read enough scriptures; you have amassed enough information. What is left to read? You have been wandering in this jungle of words form birth to birth and still you have not awakened.

Words are like the dry leaves the trees discard. These words have come down to us from the enlightened men, from those in whom the fresh green leaves of experience have sprouted, but they have dried and fallen. And you just sit there, collecting them at your leisure. The nights are cold. Burn them. Warm yourselves with them. Their warmth will make you feel good. The man who learns the art of burning words will also be able to learn the art of diving deeply into experience.

Not of written words
But of experiencing...

There is a wonderful story about the Zen monk. Lin Chi. He was sitting under a tree when he became enlightened. He immediately ran into his room and brought out all the scriptures of Buddha, the *Tripitaka* and others, and set fire to them. A crowd soon collected. People thought he had gone mad, that he had gone insane. They could not imagine a greater sin than reducing the priceless words of the Buddha to ashes! And all the time Lin Chi was laughing loudly. Some of the people tried to extinguish the fire so something might be saved, but Lin Chi laughed and said, "Fools! There is no need to save anything! There is nothing there worth saving!"

Later, people asked him, "Had you taken leave of your senses? You threw such priceless literature away!"

He replied, "I realized today there is nothing substantial in the scriptures whatsoever."

If Lin Chi had heard the words of Kabir in those days, he would have agreed with him; he would have said, "Truth cannot be obtained from the scriptures. It is a matter of self-experience." What he did say was, "I have reduced the scriptures to ashes so you may learn from my action, so you may remain aware."

It is not that there is nothing at all in the scriptures, that there is no substance in them — they are the words of those who have seen, of those who have experienced. But their experience is their own; it cannot be conveyed through words. Words cannot express that experience fully; words cannot express that experience totally. Words are like used cartridges, and you are collecting them now that they are of no use. To reach truth you must be free of words, and by becoming free of words you become free of the mind. Becoming free of the mind is taking the first step towards the authentic experience.

When the bride meets His embrace
The guests all fade away.

This is a very beautiful statement. When the bridegroom sets out for the house of the bride he is accompanied by a wedding-party. There is much excitement, much merriment; a band plays all along the way. The procession of the bridegroom to the house of the bride is considered an

important event and guests are especially invited to join it. This procession is composed of all the bridegroom's relatives and friends. Later the bride and bridegroom meet; they sit together and the marriage is solemnized. And as soon as the ceremony is over the procession is the first thing to be forgotten. Then the bridegroom is quite indifferent to his guests. As long as the bride and the bridegroom were as yet unmarried the wedding procession was important, but now,
The guests all fade away.

Kabir is saying that words and scriptures are like the members of a wedding procession. As soon as the marriage has been solemnized the procession ceases to be of any significance. Of what use are the Vedas then? None. When the real thing has been achieve all the scriptures become useless. They were fine before, but then you had not yet reached the door of the bride. If the scriptures can lead you to the door of the bride it is enough; if they fulfill the function of the wedding procession it is more than enough. What bridegroom will care about the procession when he has been given to his bride? Then the guests are unimportant; then the whole affair is over. Who cares about the river or the boat after one has reached the other shore? Who remembers the bridge after it has been crossed? Who keeps carrying a ladder after one has climbed to the top?

When the bride meets His embrace
The guests all fade away.

Then Kabir says:

That which sees cannot speak,
Which speaks cannot hear,
That which hears cannot explain.
Why tongue, eyes, ears?

Tell And Still It's Hidden

Both the anatomist and the psychologist will have to agree with what Kabir says here. Modern science will support him. Kabir says that the eyes do the work of seeing but cannot speak, that the tongue does the work of speaking but cannot hear, that the ears do the work of hearing but cannot explain anything. Then how, he asks, are all these organs united — the eyes, the ears, the nose, the tongue?

Each of the sense organs does its own work, but there must be an inner center where they all meet; otherwise this functioning would not be possible. For example, I am speaking now. You are listening to me with your ears and you are seeing me with your eyes, and somewhere within you it all meets and you know that the person you are seeing is also the one who is speaking.

The eyes and the ears relay their experience to some inner center. And there they meet. They meet in the consciousness, in the self hidden within the organs. Eyes see, ears hear, noses smell, hands touch — all the organs gather their own experiences. And they are assembled in the self; they are brought together as if servants were to carry things from all over the house and lay them at the feet of the master.

The sense organs cannot do anything on their own. A bird may be singing but, the moment it flies away, although the eyes are quite healthy they can no longer see it, although the ears are fine they cannot hear it, and the tongue cannot speak of it because it has gone. The thing that united them has flown away; the bridge that united all the separate functions is gone. It is like the thread of a *mala*. The thread passes through the beads and links them together. Although it is invisible, it is the support. As soon as the thread breaks, the beads scatter. The sense organs are like the beads and the self is like the thread. The self supports the senses; it maintains them.

You are following the servants. You have no idea who the master is at all. You follow whatever the eyes say immediately. If your eyes tell you a certain woman is beautiful you begin to chase after her right away. If your ears tell you a certain piece of music is sweet you immediately stop to listen to it. You follow the dictates of your sense organs without realizing nothing is more helpless than they are. They are absolutely helpless. They only function because of another entity. Their existence depends on another entity; their energy is dependent on another. Someone else hidden within you, is in the driver's seat. This entity is not visible; it is as invisible as the thread of your mala. The beads are visible, but as soon as the life force within takes its leave they will be scattered.

That which sees cannot speak,
Which speaks cannot hear,
That which hears cannot explain.
Why tongue, eyes, ears

Of what use are the eyes, the ears, the nose? How are they useful? Why do you put so much importance on them? Be mindful of him in whose service they are employed. Seek the master of the house. Seek the self.

What's full empties out;
What's empty fills up.
Empty, full — neither to be found.
The experience is this.

Such a definition of experience is rare. Very great and very wise men have tried to define experience, have tried to tell us what experience is, but they have not been too successful.

Tell And Still It's Hidden

Kabir has been quite successful indeed. Try to understand him, go deeply into Kabir's definition.

Life consists of opposites. Day follows night, birth follows death, happiness follows misery, prosperity follows adversity and health follows illness. Each of these things is changing continuously, always moving from one pole to the other. Right now you are perfectly hale and hearty, but in a moment you can suddenly become ill. When you are healthy you cannot conceive that you can be taken ill suddenly, and when you are ill you are sure you will never be healthy again. One moment you are happy and in a good mood, and the next moment you are sad. When you are happy you think how successful you are and you feel that sadness will never come; when you are overcome with sadness you wonder if you'll ever be happy or in a good mood again and you think the sadness will never go away. But if you think about it, if you look back, if you analyze what has happened in your life you will be able to see that every state is eventually transformed into its opposite.

Neither happiness nor misery lasts for long; one state is continuously giving way to another. If you understand this clearly you will not be disturbed when misery overtakes you, because you know that in a little while things will change. Nor will you become so excited when you are happy that you will forget everything else and view happiness as a permanent feature of your life. You will know that in a short while everything will change again. Kabir expresses this phenomenon in these words:

What's full empties out;
What's empty fills up.

There is no escaping this. It is an eternal law of life. One who is young will grow old, and one who lives will die. One who has achieved will lose, and one who has attained success will become a failure. One who has reached the top will topple into the valley.

What's full empties out;
What's empty fills up.

Mountains crumble and lakes are formed. Lakes fill up and mountains rise out of them. This phenomenon happens continuously.

Empty, full — neither to be found.
The experience is this.

So you must try to reach to a state where you are neither empty nor full. Then and only then will there be liberation, freedom, moksha, the ultimate ecstasy. Then there will be no distinctions whatsoever.

The experience is this.

Can you find a state within yourself where you cannot say you are empty and you cannot say you are full, where you cannot say you are miserable and you cannot say you are happy, where you cannot say you are quiet and you cannot say you are restless, where you cannot say you are alive and you cannot say you are dead? Exactly in the middle lies transcendence. One who has attained to the middle of two extremes, who remains unperturbed in the midst of opposites, has achieved what Kabir calls *the experience*. This is the experience of the self. All other experiences are experiences of the mind.

The mind exists in duality. The mind vacillates from one

pole to the opposite, from one extreme to the other. The mind is either happy or unhappy, pleased or displeased, in defeat or victorious. It never stops in the middle. It swings from one extreme to the other like the pendulum of a clock.

But when the pendulum stops in the middle the clock stops working, so when you can remain in the middle, the clock of the mind will stop working as well. From that moment on time will no longer exist for you. From that day on there will be no more birth or death for you; then you are liberated. Remaining in the middle is liberation. In the middle there is no change; nothing is opposite to the middle. This is why Buddha called his path "the middle way." When you are in the middle you have achieved all.

Kabir's way of saying this is quite unique. It is virtually impossible to find a style such as his anywhere else.

To explain truth even the enlightened ones had to choose one extreme or another. The Vedas say, "Be filled with the whole. Be so full that you cannot be empty at all," and Buddha says, "Be empty. Be void. Be so empty of ego that not a single grain remains within you." Buddha indicates truth through his doctrine of emptiness and the Vedas indicate the same truth through the principle of fullness — but both are saying the same thing.

Buddha says to be free from the ego, be empty, and so his doctrine is known as *shunyavad,* as the path of emptiness, of no-self. His stress is laid on emptiness. He uses words like 'void' and 'negation' to indicate freedom from the ego. Buddha does not say that you will become one with God, that you will be filled with God or that God will fill you, he says it will happen of its own accord. He says not to worry about it;

he just says to free yourself of the ego. On the other hand, when the Vedas, Vedanta and Shankara speak of this point they say, "Be filled with God. Do not worry about being empty. When you are completely full your ego will automatically be discarded. When you are filled with God there will no longer be any room left for the ego."

But Kabir is incomparable. Kabir is unique. He is more successful than Buddha and the *Vedas* in defining what the experience is. He has defined it with more precision and with more skill than Vedanta and Buddha have done.

He says:

Such a wonder! It's never told.
Tell, and still it's hidden.

Kabir has realized himself how wonderful this phenomenon is, how unique it is; he has realized it can never be defined, that it can never be put into words. He says it is so wonderful he is keeping it a secret; he says he will only speak of it if he can find a man who is worthy.

Koran and Veda couldn't write it.
If I say it, who will listen?

Kabir says people might possibly believe it if it were written in the Vedas or in the Koran. But the truth is not recorded in either of these scriptures.

Such a wonder! It's never told.
Tell, and still it's hidden.
Koran and Veda couldn't write it.
If I say it, who will listen?

Kabir says he wants to share this wonderful thing; it is in his mind to tell people about it, but he keeps it a secret.

Tell And Still It's Hidden

"Whom should I tell?" he asks. "Who will believe it? Who will have faith in it? It is not written in the Vedas or in the Koran. If it were written in the Vedas at least the Hindus might believe it; if it were written in the Koran then Moslems might believe it. But Kabir knows full well no one will believe him.

The truth is that neither a Hindu nor a Mohammedan will believe anything that has to do with authentic religion. Only a man who is neither Hindu nor Moslem, neither Jaina nor Christian, neither Parsi nor Sikh, will believe something that is in the realm of pure religion, will believe something that does not relate to a specific sect, to a particular religious denomination. Religion has no denomination. No adjective can precede religion. Each sect has a different name, and each sect emphasizes one particular aspect of religion. One sect will stress fullness for example, while another will lay importance on emptiness. Kabir says not to emphasize either of the two — to seek the middle and to remain there, steadfast and firm.

Such a place exists, but how are you going to seek it?

When you are miserable just sit quietly and observe your misery. Don't try to do anything to erase it. Don't fight against it, just let it come. Just let the tears flow; just let the heart weep. Just sit by yourself and keep watching everything that is happening; don't make any effort whatsoever to rid yourself of your misery. If you try to get rid of it, it means you are wishing for happiness.

If you think of misery as emptiness then fullness will represent happiness for you. And when happiness does come to you, just sit quietly and observe it as well. Don't try to cling to it either. Don't try to hold on to it; don't try to make it last. Simply watch it. Be completely indifferent to it. If it comes, let it come; if it takes its leave of you, then let it go. When you make an effort to cling to happiness, when you try to hold on to it, because of the very act of trying your misery will be as great as the effort you spend trying to hold on to your happiness. They are linked together. If you have a greater partiality for one, it will immediately be replaced by the other.

Have you ever watched a tightrope walker? The whole secret of life is hidden there. To maintain his balance the tightrope walker holds a bamboo pole in his hand. There is potential danger in every step. If he leans a little to the left he may fall, so he leans his bamboo pole a little to the right and thus maintains his balance. And still he is in danger, because the maintenance of balance is not a static phenomenon. Balance must be maintained every moment; it must be readjusted at every step. Suppose that now he leans to the right — there is a possibility he may fall to the right so he has to lean his pole to the left. He keeps balancing from left to right and from right to left so that he won't fall. And so he keeps himself in the middle and is able to walk his tightrope. Happiness and misery are like right and left to the tightrope walker.

Just be still within. Just sit quietly, turning neither to the left nor to the right. Just be a witness; just keep on observing. If misery comes, just recognize it. Don't form any judgment as to whether it is good or bad, as to whether it should have come to you or should not have come to you — just be aware that misery is present, just experience it. And do not try to create happiness either; otherwise you will tilt to the other

Tell And Still It's Hidden

side. If happiness comes, don't try to cling to it or you will lean to the other side again, back towards misery.

If you just keep on watching, just keep on observing both happiness and misery, all of a sudden you will find one day that you are separate, that you are quite apart, quite aloof from both. Suddenly you will come to know that both things are only happening around you and that you are beyond them both. This beyondness is the universal soul.

This phenomenon of beyondness, this observing of both and yet not belonging to either, is the moment when you are neither empty nor full. You are neither empty nor full because now you realize you are neither happiness nor misery.

Kabir says, this is real knowledge.

Such wonder! It's never told.
Tell, and still it's hidden.
Koran and Veda couldn't write it.
If I say it, who will listen?

3

DRUNK WITH BOUNDLESS YOUTH

O blessed women,
Sing the wedding songs!
I've come home with Lord Ram,
My beloved.

Body, mind, the five elements,
All loved and offered in welcome.
Ram has come to live with me
And I'm drunk with boundless youth.

The body a pool of Vedas
Brahma himself recites!
United with Ram — round and round.
How fortunate am I!

Gods arrive in millions
And sages in thousands.
Says Kabir: I'm to wed.
And the man's immortal!

Life is a preparation. And the preparation continues every moment. You may or may not be aware of it, but you are moving towards a very great festival. At times you will fall, but you will get up again; at times you will lose your way, but you will find your path again. There is some very powerful destiny, some tremendous pull continuously drawing you towards this great celebration. Something is going to happen to you. In fact, something is already happening to you.

You feel incomplete within, but this is because you are a seed. The seed is groping in the dark, trying to push its way through the earth. The seed breaks through stones, passes through layers of soil and surmounts all obstacles in its upward path towards the sun. But it has no knowledge of what it is doing. If you ask it, "What are you doing? Where are you going?" it will not be able to give you an answer. There is some instinct within it that directs its course. It must reach the sun; it has to touch the sky. There is no other goal. Unless it sees the sun it will never bear flowers; there will never be any celebration in its life.

The tree grows onwards and upwards, spreading its branches to the sky and, when it has done its utmost, flowers bloom. After a time the flowers fall to the ground and become seeds again. Then the same journey begins all over. This kind of repetition is to be found in the life of a tree. The same cycle is present in all of nature.

Man, on the other hand, has evolved to the point where, if he becomes conscious, there is no repetition. But if he remains asleep and unconscious the repetitive cycle will go on and on.

There are a few things that must be understood. Firstly, this infinite universe you see about you, this sun, moon, stars and planets, is not without cause. This whole evolving system exists within a great framework, within a great destiny. Just as flowers are hidden in a tiny seed and bloom from that seed, the potentiality of God's flowering is hidden in the vast universe. Everything in it is moving towards His flowering, towards His manifestation. Everyone is moving towards this, sinner and saint. Some will be late and some will be on time, but it will not make much difference in the end.

There are two kinds of evolution. One kind of evolution is unconscious, and we know nothing about it whatsoever. We neither know what is happening nor why it is happening. Do you really know what you are doing, why you are doing it, what prompts you to act? You cannot even stop doing! You do not even know why you are doing what you are doing; some force, some destiny compels you.

Nature is unconscious evolution and God is conscious evolution. Man is the link between the two; man is how God is linked with nature.

Man is unconscious evolution and God is conscious evolution. Man is the link between the two; man is how God is linked with nature.

Man is a creature of great dignity. Don't toss this dignity off casually. You are the point where nature becomes divine, where nature is transformed into Godhood, where matter is transformed into consciousness, where form becomes formlessness, where shape becomes shapelessness. You are that link; your dignity is without limit.

At present your dignity is hidden in the womb of the future. You are a seed; you do not know your flowers yet. Nature is simply unconscious. It is a blind race, a blind journey. With man a new link begins, but you do not automatically become that link just because you have been

Drunk With Boundless Youth

born as a man. To become that link, to attain to that status, you will have to exert yourself consciously. The way in which you make the effort is through yoga, through tantra, through religion.

What is the meaning of yoga, of tantra, of religion? They mean only one thing. They mean that from now on you will no longer continue your journey blindfolded, that you will now move ahead with your eyes wide open, that you will now be aware of all your conscious activities, of where you are going, of why you are going somewhere. You will breathe consciously; when you walk you will even raise your legs consciously. You are now taking a jump beyond the blind race of nature. All that blind race does is bring you back to the point from where you began your journey.

First the seed becomes the tree and then the tree becomes the seed. You are born, then you die, and then you are born again. It is a circle. The world is a wheel; it keeps on revolving and revolving. But you never seem to arrive anywhere.

Man must awaken; he must make this journey with full awareness. Nature brings you to the human state and now you will have to continue on your own. This is a tremendous responsibility and it worries you. This is why man is always so worried. In nature, nothing is worried. The animals and the birds and the trees and the stones and the streams are not worried. They have no cause for anxiety; they are unconscious of what is happening. Man is anxious because he sees clearly that, no matter what happens, it is inadequate. You feel that whatsoever you are it is not enough, that something is lacking. This feeling disturbs you, stabs at you like a thorn, and unless you become conscious, unless you become aware, it will harass you your whole life long.

Your journey with nature is over, nature has brought you as far as it can — and it has been a very long journey. It has not been an insignificant thing; it has taken a very long time. Assuming the earth were twenty-four hours old, then scientists say man has only been here for two seconds. Man has not been here for very long. Nature is very very ancient, but in a total journey of twenty-four hours only two seconds have passed since the consciousness that is man has been born. This evolution to the human stage is the highest flowering in nature.

The journey through the darkness of nature is over. Man has reached the frontier; he has come to the crossroads. If you go back to nature now you will just be repeating the cycle of births and deaths all over again — this is what humans generally do. Such men belong to the world; such men are worldly men.

The Hindi word for world is *sansara;* it means a wheel. And the man who lives like a wheel, continuously revolving in the same circle, is bound to the world. He repeats the same routine day after day. He gets up in the morning and does what he did yesterday; he spends this afternoon as he spent the one before. Living by the clock — which goes round and round too — he repeats the same routine in the evening and the same routine at night. He is lost in the repetition of his routine. And then one day he is suddenly no more. Then, as a seed, he enters a new womb and the blind journey begins all over again.

The Hindus are the oldest conscious people, the most ancient awakened people on this earth. They were the first to conceive of religion and they have only one great desire, only one great throbbing in their hearts — how to be freed, how to be liberated from this cycle of births and deaths, how to jump outside the circumference of this wheel, how to attain to consciousness and move outside the circle of sansara. The Hindus say, "We have taken this blind journey so many times. We have become seeds and trees and trees and seeds over and over again. It all seems so pointless, so useless."

Now a tension begins; now anxiety is born. No irreligious or nonreligious man will ever become as uneasy as a religious man will. What is there for an irreligious man to worry about? You will find him making merry in a club, in a bar or in the marketplace. Such a man has no worries at all. And even if he does have a few he is easily rid of them. For example, if he does not have enough money it can be earned; his bank balance can be augmented. If he hankers after fame, fame can be found; if his house is small he can build a bigger one. These are not very great problems; they can easily be solved. This is why such a man is not overly concerned. You will find him laughing and enjoying — but do not be deceived by this outward show.

A deep anxiety grips a religious man because he has begun to think, "How long can this repetitiveness last?" This is the beginning of his anxiety. He is anxious to free himself from this cycle of births and deaths. He thinks, "I have gone around and around often enough. It is already late. When shall I awaken" When shall I become conscious?"

So the first stage in the growth of a man of religion will be one of anxiety; the last state will be one of serenity and peace. But this last state is very, very far away; a long journey must be undertaken. Between these two stages, between anxiety and peace, a man of religion has to make tremendous effort.

Bear in mind that, through the process of unconscious evolution, nature has brought you as far as it could. Nature's function is now complete. Now it is your turn; now you have to do something. For a while a father holds the hand of his baby son and helps him to walk. But how long can he do that?

A point comes when the father has to say to his son, "Now walk on your own legs. Now you are ready to walk on your own. Now you are mature. Now you must begin your own journey; now you must take the responsibility for your own life on your own shoulders. Now you must take care of yourself." Maturity will only come to a man, will only grow in a man, when he accepts this challenge. Your ability to look after yourself is in relation to the effort you expend on your own behalf.

Nature is now telling you the same thing a father tells his son. Nature has brought you to the point where you have evolved into a fully grown human being. Now you are able to think, now you are able to discriminate, and when you become anxious about yourself you can now select the path that will lead you out of your anxiety. Nature's job is now over. Now you must take the reins into your own hands; now you must become a seeker.

A seeker is a man who has taken the reins into his own hands; a seeker is the child who says to the father, "This is more than enough. I am grateful to you, I am much obliged to you, but now I will stand on my own two feet." The moment you tell nature you want to stand by yourself you become a young man of maturity. At that moment maturity comes to you for the first time. But from then on you will experience many anxieties because now you are responsible for yourself, because now your *sadhana* begins.

To follow a sadhana is to proceed consciously in the direction of evolution. It is a journey of clarity, it is not a blind race. It is a directing of all one's energy towards a single destination. That is why I always say that if a man's gaze is not directed towards God his whole life is meaningless.

Directing one's eyes towards God is just the introduction, just the preamble; the real thing has not yet begun. Think of a classical musician adjusting the strings of his sitar to bring his instrument to the proper tuning. The recital has not yet begun; this is just preparation. This may take a long time; the audience will often get bored and wonder how long this nonsense will go on, how long this will last — but the musician will not begin to play until his sitar is perfectly tuned. Until you evolve to this point you are in the preparatory stage.

Nature has prepared you by bringing you to the stage of humanity. Now you can sing the great song. Now the universal sound can descend on you; now the sound of the universe can thrill your life. But the tuning of the instruments does not produce any music on its own. If you think the recital is over as soon as the tuning is completed then the whole thing is already finished for you anyway; then nothing more can be said to you. And if the classical musician also thinks the concert is over when the instruments have been tuned, his work is incomplete as well.

I see such incompleteness in you. You have earned enough money, you have built a house, you have a wife and children — your instruments are all in tune — so what more is there to do, what else is there for you to do? You realize now that everything is empty, that the whole effort has been wasted; you see now that you have been caught up in nothing. You had things to do before. You had duties to perform; you kept busy doing this and that — but now? "Now" stands before you like a deep abyss.

Being born as a man was only the introduction; life has not yet begun for you. So far you have only been involved in the preparation; you have not yet begun the pilgrimage — you have only been preparing for the journey. Your luggage is ready — you have arranged all your things very carefully; the trunk, the bedding, the provisions are ready for the journey — but you have not yet set out. Man is at this point, at this stage.

If you want to understand clearly what man is and where he is going, then look at him as a man who has made all the preparations necessary for a journey but is sitting beside his luggage because he has forgotten where he has to go, because he has forgotten why he has made all these preparations. Your condition is the same. All your preparations are complete; you are now a completely evolved human being. Now you can jump into your pilgrimage; now there is nothing lacking in you. The instruments are properly tuned; you only have to start playing your music.

Kabir looks on this as the wedding procession — this is how he sees the preparation that has been going on up to now. But the procession is not the be-all and the end-all, it is simply the introduction to the wedding.

O blessed women, sing the wedding songs!
I've come home with Lord Ram, my beloved.

Drunk With Boundless Youth

If things continue as they have up to now then the whole preparation will be useless, in vain. You will wonder what the point of all this preparation was. You are ready, but you are completely unaware of where you have been preparing to go, of why you have prepared yourself, of who has called you, of what invitation has come to you from the unknown. You have been preparing for so long you are afraid to embark on your journey. You are the kind of person who will unpack his luggage just so he can repack it again. You want to keep busy with your packing. You crave the activity, so the packing continues.

You have prepared for this journey so often. How many times have you done this? And you still have not become a man! You have been in this situation so many times but, each and every time your preparations are complete, you again start to wonder what more there is to be done. Again you unpack your luggage, again you put things away so you can easily find them...then next time you begin to pack. When is the meeting ever going to take place?

The journey will not begin until you become a seeker. And when the journey has been started you are already halfway towards its completion! The beginning is halfway to the end. Once the beginning has been made, the end is not far off.

There is not as much difference between a seeker and an enlightened man as there is between a seeker and one who is not seeking at all. If you can just step out of your house, just once, you will surely reach your goal — no matter how far the place of pilgrimage may be. The real difficulty is getting out of the house — the first step is always the hardest.

Lao Tzu has said that a man completes a thousand-mile journey by taking one step at a time. Who can take two steps at once? When you take a step you can only raise one leg at a time. And eventually, one step at a time, the journey of a thousand miles is completed. As soon as a man takes the first step his transformation begins. Then God takes a step towards him; then divine grace begins to descend on him.

Nature is unconscious evolution, God is conscious evolution, and man is the link in between. Your further evolution is in your own hands. It is as if you are standing at the gate of a house — the whole of nature is behind you, God is in front of you, and you are standing in the middle, at the gate, Nothing in this world is static, and if you grow a little lethargic you are bound to be pushed back. Bear this in mind. If you do not progress you will have to regress; there is no waiting in this world. Even if you want to stand still and wait you cannot, it is not possible. Life is movement; you have to keep on walking.

If you do not move ahead you will be thrown back; if you do not raise yourself up you will be thrown down. Don't ever think, "At least I can remain where I am." Such a thing never happens. Even if you want to stay where you are, keep trying to push ahead. You have to keep trying. Don't stop. If you stop, the flow of life will knock you down.

Have you ever stood in the strong current of a river? If you want to stay where you are you have to fight against the current, you have to work hard, because the rush of the river hauls the sand out from under your feet. The current drags you along with it. In all of existence there is no stopping.

Existence is continuous movement, never-ending motion. Each moment you are either moving forwards or backwards. Don't trust in your belief that you are standing still, this never happens. If you are standing at the gate and looking behind you, the current of nature will drag you back.

You must forget the past. How long do you intend the wedding procession to last? Granted that the bridegroom is in the procession, but he is on a horse in front; he is separate from the rest of the procession. Granted that the procession is on his account, yet he is not part and parcel of it. He is not a member of the wedding procession, he is quite separate from it — the procession has accompanied him, he has not accompanied it. He still has further to go, while the procession is finished the moment the bridegroom begins his new journey. Ass soon as the bride and bridegroom meet, as soon as the marriage is solemnized, the wedding procession is over — but the journey of the bridegroom is just beginning.

Nature has brought you to this door; nature is the wedding procession, and its journey is now over. Just turn and thank it sincerely for having accompanied you so far; it has brought you to the point where you can now stand on your own two feet. So be grateful to the members of the wedding procession, they have brought you to this point. It has been their pleasure; it was not a big thing. Your journey begins when the wedding procession ends.

Yesterday Kabir said:
Not of written words
But of experiencing:
When the bride meets His embrace
The guests all fade away.

Today's sutra is in reference to this. Try to comprehend it. It begins from the point where the wedding procession has lost its significance.

O blessed women, sing the wedding songs!
I've come home with Lord Ram, my beloved.

Then Kabir says:

Body, mind, the five elements,
All loved and offered in welcome.

When one hears Kabir's words about loving the body and loving the mind it is only natural to ask why he does not mention loving the soul. It is important to understand this. Kabir says that he has loved the body and loved the mind, but that the five great elements out of which the body and mind have been created, the five great elements which have brought man to this stage, are now to be sacrificed at God's feet. He does not speak of the soul; he does not mention it at all.

When you fall in love with someone you say, "I shall love you with all my soul," but Kabir only speaks of the body and of the mind. The reason is that the soul is God Himself. There is no distinction. A distinction can only be made up to the level of the body and mind. And sacrifice too can only be made up to this point, up to the point where distinction still exists between things. How can you make a sacrifice when there is no separation between the one who is sacrificing and the one to whom the sacrifice is being made? In the soul, the lover and beloved are one; between Ram and his lover there is not the tiniest space, not the slightest distinction. The who will make love? Then to whom will love be made?

So Kabir says he will sacrifice everything he has now that the lover he has been awaiting has arrived — the lover for whom the preparations were made, the lover for whom the long wedding procession was undertaken. After countless

Drunk With Boundless Youth

births, Kabir says, today his search is finished. He has seen the supreme; he has seen that for which he has been so restless, so anxious. Now he is prepared to sacrifice all.

Ram has come to live with me
And I'm drunk with boundless youth.

There is one kind of youth that is dependent on the body. It carries a certain intoxication with it because youth is a novel thing. Old age, on the other hand, is like a river when the tide has gone out.

Have you ever noticed a river just before monsoon, just before the rainy season? It looks dried up. It is always broken into several tiny stream and a great area of sandy bottom is always visible. It is as if the river itself has departed. There is no trace of the once swollen river; there is only the rubbish it has deposited in its wake. It is as if some event had once taken place but there is no longer any trace of it and everything seems desolate.

Have you ever seen a river flooded by the monsoon? Then there is a sort of mischief in its flow — it is as if it is drunk with wine, as if it is unable to walk straight. A river in flood is intoxicated; a river in flood is in its youth.

The youth of the body is exactly like this. When all the energies of the body are in flood a young man has no faith in God. He seems to have great faith in himself then — he does not worry about anything at all. He contains so much excess energy he is drunk with it. There is no question of bowing down to anyone, no question of surrendering to anybody. In youth a man is mad, blind, but his condition is pardonable, the situation is out of his control; he is in flood.

The youth of the body comes and then it passes on. It is

like the water from the mountains flowing through the riverbeds — the water comes and goes, it does not remain. The energy of the body is like this because the body is a momentary thing, it cannot last for long. It is a miracle the body remains young as long as it does.

It is a mystery of mysteries how a rushing mountain stream can overflow so suddenly and then drop again so quickly. The flood of energy to the physical body will subside too. The light that illuminates the body will soon become darkness; the sweet music of the body will soon become a cacophony, and the beauty of the physical will surely vanish like a dream. The body you saw as a beautiful oasis will turn into a desert. It was all a transitory intoxication, all an illusion you took to be something else. This is why old age is filled with sadness. What was once, has disappeared.

The whole phenomenon of youth is like a dream you see during the night. You dream of becoming an emperor, of possessing huge palaces and great piles of gold coins, of ruling an empire that stretches to far off places — and suddenly you awaken and the dream vanishes. For a moment you hardly trust the sorrowful state you find yourself in — only a moment before you were a monarch with gold and palaces and hundreds of servants. But now all of that has disappeared.

Old people always seem a bit surprised and puzzled; they cannot grasp what has happened. Where has all that energy gone? Where have those sturdy legs gone? Where has all that self-confidence gone? Where has that dynamic personality gone? Their life-energy is at a low ebb; they only see emptiness all around. Old people feel empty inside, hollow within. Only the skeleton of the body remains, and soon the time of departure will come. An old man is standing in the queue, waiting for death.

The youth of the body is transitory. The man who puts his trust in it is heading for disappointment because the death of the body is a certainty. You will be living in deception as long as you put your faith in the body. And you will be filled with sorrow when that trust is finally and positively broken. Youth is the kind of thing that not only torments you in youth but in old age as well. The presence of youth bothers you while you are young; its absence bothers you when you are old. And every now and then an old man's mind will want to go back to the days of its youth.

There is another kind of youth, the kind about which Kabir is speaking. It is the youthfulness of the soul. And there is yet another kind of youth, the youth of the supreme soul — and that is everlasting. There, the river never floods and the water never ebbs, it is always the same. There is no change; there is perpetuity. And the intoxication of perpetuity is altogether different. And the intoxication of perpetuity is altogether different. It is so different, it is of such a different kind, that no matter how you try to understand it in relation to the intoxication you know, you will be wrong. Not only will your idea be wrong, it will be quite the reverse of the real thing. It will not only be different, it will be exactly the opposite of whatever notion you have.

The intoxication of unconsciousness that is associated with the body is exactly like the intoxication caused by wine. This intoxication is caused by your unconsciousness; it is because you are not awake. The intoxication of the soul comes out of total awareness. Then you are filled with ecstasy because you are filled with awareness. The wine is the wine of awareness.

If only such a wine could exist!

There is one kind of intoxication, the intoxication of Buddha, of Mahavira; and there is another kind, the intoxication of Napoleon, of Alexander. This is another kind completely. The intoxication of Napoleon and Alexander will soon wear off, but the intoxication of Buddha and Mahavira will last forever. If the intoxication depends on the body, how can it last? The body itself does not last so very long. If the foundation crumbles, how can the building be saved?

Ram has come to live with me
And I'm drunk with boundless youth.

When the individual soul meets the universal soul a kind of intoxication comes. It comes out of your great awareness. It is a kind of ecstasy that drowns you completely, and yet it is unable to drown you because the lamp of awareness is burning so brightly within you.

Ram has come to live with me
And I'm drunk with boundless youth.

You will be able to understand Kabir if just a glimpse, if only the tiniest taste of this intoxication descends into your consciousness.

At times you feel cool and collected, and you feel like this because no one can be so perturbed and ill at ease as not to have ever had a momentary glimpse of peace. You could not live unless you experienced such moments of peace. In moments of such peace your roots are nourished.

Whenever you feel a little calm or when you feel a little elated, simply close your eyes and look within. In that moment of calmness a rhythm happens between you and existence, between you and God, albeit for a very short time. That is why you are calm. Whenever you are with God you become calm. And whenever you are calm, understand that God is near to you. You should remember this sutra; you should make this your touchstone; you should tie a string on your finger to remind you of it — whenever a tuning, a rhythm, happens between you and Him, you experience calmness and peace.

In America, a very rare thinker by the name of Henry Thoreau existed. When he was close to death an old aunt of his, a religious old lady — though Thoreau was not religious because he never went to church or read the Bible — she came to him and asked compassionately, "Henry, have you made your peace with God?"

Lying on his deathbed, Thoreau opened his eyes and said, "I didn't know we'd ever quarreled. What is there to make peace about?"

Henry Thoreau was not the type of man to quarrel with God. He never went to church because it wasn't necessary. If there is no quarrel, then what is the point of going to court? He never made a mantra of God's name; he never said a rosary. None of this was necessary because a continuous hymn to God was being sung within him. Henry Thoreau was an incomparable flower among men. He was always calm and unperturbed and never quarreled with God. So how could he pray? Whom would he worship? Whom would he adore? The quarrel between you and God disappears when you are at peace; otherwise, you would be in conflict twenty-four hours a day. And the more you are in conflict, the more agitated you will become.

How can a tree that quarrels with the earth remain calm and tranquil? Its roots are in the earth, its roots are buried in the earth! Are you fighting with the earth? Are you fighting with your own roots? If you are, uneasiness will become your natural state. Then you will be disturbed; you will be perplexed and confused. If they fought with the earth the trees would go mad. The earth is the womb.

Just as the roots of the trees are in the earth, your roots are in God. Do you intend to fight with God? You fight with Him twenty-four hours every day! God expects one thing from you and you want something else. The substance of all your prayers is, "Listen to my prayer. Fulfill my desires." What you are doing is wrong; your praying is nothing but giving advice to God. You say, "My son is ill. Make him well." god is the instigator of the illness — who are you to interfere in His work by asking Him to make your son well? In your prayers you say, "I am poor. Give me wealth." God is the giver. God is more sensible than you, so to whom are you praying? If you listen carefully to people's prayers, as I have done, you will discover that everyone says this to God: "Oh God, please do as I ask, but I am not prepared to listen to You." You try so hard and in so many ways to fulfill your desires, and when your attempts fail you approach God with a prayer. But all your efforts are in aid of your own victory and you are busy trying to defeat God. How can you defeat Him? In your very effort to defeat Him you will be defeated. God is your foundation, He is your existence, He is your breath, your life.

No sooner does God come to your door than everything is suffused with calm. A new kind of intoxication pervades your body, your soul, your every heartbeat. The beauty of that intoxication is that it is a thousand times more intoxicating

Drunk With Boundless Youth

than wine, and yet there is no trace whatsoever of the unconsciousness caused by wine. This is its beauty. This is why the Sufis sing songs in praise of this wine.

The songs of Omar Khayyam were translated by Western writers, but were not correctly understood. Edward Fitzgerald, who did an admirable rendering of Khayyam's songs, was not a Sufi. He took the word 'wine' literally, for example. He also took the word 'lover' literally, and did the same with 'wineshop'. He read the *Rubaiyat* and tried to understand it with the help of a dictionary. Omar Khayyam was a Sufi fakir, a Sufi saint. When he speaks of wine he is speaking of the wine about which Kabir is speaking:

And I'm drunk with boundless youth.

Omar Khayyam is speaking of this too. The wineshop is the temple, the lover is the master, the guru, and the wine is none other than the wine of God. Fitzgerald made a great mistake when he translated the songs of Omar Khayyam literally, and many people in the West thought Khayyam was a drunkard and had written these songs in praise of wine.

Many adaptations of the *Rubaiyat* were made from these translations of Fitzgerald's and were published all over the world, and so the wineshop of Omar Khayyam became world-famous. This was a great blunder on Fitzgerald's part. But this was bound to happen, because to understand an enlightened person it is necessary to be enlightened oneself. To understand a madman one must be mad, so if you wish to understand an enlightened man you will have to become enlightened yourself. The sign language used by a dumb person can only be understood by another who is dumb. Fitzgerald did not realize this. If Omar Khayyam were to return to the world he would not be so displeased with anyone as he would be with Edward Fitzgerald. Fitzgerald made Khayyam's name famous throughout the world, but he did it in a very wrong way.

Ram has come to live with me
And I'm drunk with boundless youth.

Whenever you are a little quiet, a little calm, and you feel elated, don't miss that moment. It means the greatest guest possible is close to you, is hovering somewhere about you. And that is the reason that all of a sudden you begin to experience that elation, that feeling of pleasantness. Close your eyes in that moment. Turn that moment into meditation. Generally you do the opposite; you sit down to meditate whenever you are miserable. But that is the time when there is a great distance between you and God — and that is also why you are miserable.

How can you call Him when the distance is so great? How will you be able to recognize Him? People remember Him in their misery and forget Him when they are happy. In your moments of happiness He is nearest to you.

Happiness is not building a big house — it does not necessarily follow that building a big house will make you happy. Happiness is not winning a big prize in a lottery — there is no certainty this will make you happy either. It may do the opposite; it may increase your uneasiness — and this is generally what happens. What that moment of happiness means is that now you are able to say, "Whatever is, is fine." This is the definition of happiness, when your mind tells you that whatever is, is all right. You have no wish to improve it; whatever is, is all right. At such a time there is a harmony

Drunk With Boundless Youth

within you, a feeling of all-rightness, and you are satisfied with it. It is a particular feeling we call *tathata* in Hindi; it means that everything is fine just as it is.

At such a moment a harmonious note vibrates within you. Make that moment a moment of prayer, of meditation, of worship. There is no need to go to any temple; you are the temple and God is sitting there, hidden within you. The lover is hidden in the beloved. The path is the goal; the seeker is seeking himself.

Close your eyes and try to be silent, try to go deeper and deeper into the silence. Set all your restlessness aside; the man who is restless remains on the surface. Take a dive into that inner peace and you will be able to glimpse, to experience a new kind of youth.

This is a youth that can never be extinguished; it is a youth that can never become old; it is a freshness that will never grow stale. It is a morning which is everlasting, a morning never followed by evening. It is a birth beyond which there is only life and more life and nothing but life; it is a birth beyond which there is no death. It is birth that is not followed by death; it is a morning that is not followed by night.

And then there will be no more nights for you. Then, all of a sudden, you will begin to dance. And in that dance there will be awareness — rather, awareness itself will be the dance. In that dance there will be the kind of wisdom and awareness Buddha and Meera had. You will be like Buddha; you will be like Meera. In Kabir, both Buddha and Meera meet. Kabir is as silent as Buddha and as dancing as Meera.

The body a pool of Vedas
Brahma himself recites!

United with Ram — round and round.
How fortunate am I!

Kabir says his body will become the altar. The guest has already arrived at the door and Kabir is preparing to welcome Him. Any offering less than the body itself would be unseemly, so Kabir says his entire body will become the altar for the sacrifice. He is sacrificing his body; he is surrendering himself completely. In the sacrificial fire he is offering his body to God.

Brahma himself recites!

This is rare. When you surrender your body as an offering in the sacrificial fire you will not have to invite any brahmin, any priest, to recite the hymns from the Vedas; that day, God Himself will sing them.

This symbol is of very deep significance. Hindus say that Brahma created the universe, and so when you offer your body in the sacrificial fire then it is not necessary to invite a brahmin to perform the rites. All other sacrifices are false, and the mere recitation of the Vedic hymns is of very little value. And who will sing the hymns? Some brahmin you have hired? Under conditions like these the Vedas are false and the brahmin is false; it is all self-deception. And since both are false how can the recitation of the Vedas be authentic?

So when you make your body the offering, Kabir says it is not necessary to invite an ordinary brahmin. Kabir says that Brahma himself, that the creator of this whole existence will himself sing the Vedic hymns. The whole of existence will be filled with the music of the hymns. The whole of existence is elated, filled with ecstasy, when someone surrenders himself completely. And then the whole of existence sings a song of thankfulness, of gratitude.

Brahma himself recites!

Existence is not disjointed. Existence is whole, undivided. Somewhere the English poet, Tennyson, has said that if you pick a flower you will shock even the stars that are millions and millions of miles away. If existence is one whole, then how can that not happen?

Last night I was reading a book by Ugovetti, an Italian dramatist, and I came across a sentence I liked very much. Like the words of the Vedas, it is of great significance. Ugovetti said that if there was even one drop of water less in existence the whole universe would feel thirsty. What he means is that not even a tiny drop of water is separate, that the whole universe needs even the tiniest drop of water to quench its thirst.

Existence is completely full as it is. Nothing can be taken from it; nothing can be added to it. Whatever it is, it is full. When your mind is in this state — when you experience the fullness of the whole existence, when you feel that nothing can be better than it is, when you say with all your heart, "This is the real fullness" — then God comes to your door. At that moment Brahma, the Brahma that is hidden in existence, the Brahma that is the highest existence, the Brahma that is the greatest consciousness, comes and knocks at your door. From that day on you are totally at rest; from that day on the guest is always standing at your door.

The body a pool of Vedas
Brahma himself recites!

Kabir says, "I shall light the sacrificial fire in this body of mine. I shall offer Your presence in this body as a sacred offering. I shall welcome You."

The Hindus prepare an altar when the marriage of the bride and bridegroom is to take place. The sacrificial fire is lit, offerings are made to the deities, and the couple circles the altar seven times.

This altar is false and this circling is false! Whether the couple circles the altar seven times or seventy times makes no difference. Until you sacrifice your life, until your whole energy burns like fire, this whole show is false! Who do you think you are deceiving with this farce? You are only deceiving yourself with this show! And until you understand this, your hired brahmins will keep on reciting the hymns from the Vedas. The Vedas are books; and they can be purchased in the market. Remember what Kabir has said:

Love's not grown in gardens;
Love's not sold at market.
He who wants it, king or commoner;
Gives his head and takes it.

Nothing less than this will do. You have been haggling for love for so long. How much longer will you keep on trying? You will have to offer your head.

The body a pool of Vedas
Brahma himself recites!

When a man transforms his body into an altar the whole of existence begins to sing the Vedic hymn. Then the whole of existence is filled with the sound of *Aum*, as if Brahma himself were reciting the Vedas.

United with Ram — round and round.
How fortunate am I!

Kabir says how fortunate he is to circle the sacrificial fire as the bride of Ram.

United with Ram — round and round.
How fortunate am I!

There is no greater fortune then to have Ram as your lover and to be His beloved.

Why does Kabir choose to consider Ram as the lover and himself as the beloved? The position can also be reversed, and this is what the Sufis have done — the Sufis call themselves the lovers and God the beloved. Both types of devotees have their own reasons and both are worth understanding.

Kabir calls himself the beloved because he believes that meditation is absolute nondoing. Woman is nondoing, nonaggressive by nature man is active. Man is aggressive and woman is submissive. That is why no Indian woman will ever say, "I am in love with you." She will not say it in so many words. Even that much of a declaration would be considered aggressive.

No woman in India ever runs after a man, she simply sits and waits. She invites but makes no sound; she indicates but her signs are indirect. She may use the language of the eyes, but she will not seize the lover's hand. To take the lover's hand would be to go against her feminine nature. The kind of woman who would grab at a man would not be considered pleasing or attractive. Such a woman would be thought of as rude and uncivilized; she would be considered aggressive, a bit manly. That is why a woman in India never extends a direct invitation, but shows by her feelings that she is waiting.

As far as courtship is concerned, no blame can ever be

attached to the woman; the wife can always accuse her husband of having been after her. The young lady has never presented herself at the door of her husband-to-be, and so that husband can never say to his wife, "You were chasing me." Such a thing simply does not happen in India. It is the man who frequents the house of his beloved; it is the man who makes all the fuss about love. It is the man who declares his love. The woman only does one thing — she accepts him or she rejects him. A woman never takes the initiatives.

Kabir is asking, "How can I take the initiative? How can I seek You? — I do not eve know your address. I am like a beloved who can only wait and wait. So when You feel like coming, please come," he says. "You are welcome."

According to Kabir, the devotee waits and God goes to him. Even if the devotee wanted to go to God, where would he go? Where would he look? So the devotee simply sits and waits, calling to God with heartfelt emotion, weeping for God from the depths of his heart. His whole life becomes tears of devotion; his whole life becomes a waiting. This waiting is feminine. And God comes. God is male; God seeks out the devotee, enters his body, goes deep into it, penetrates to the farthest reaches. Then the devotee cries: "How fortunate am I!"

Then the supreme union takes place; then Brahma recites the Vedic hymns to celebrate the occasion.

Sufis have done the same thing in reverse order. They call God the beloved and consider themselves as lovers because their whole sadhana, their whole search, is aggressive. They see God as a woman, sitting there, hidden by a veil. God is to be sought; God's veil is to be removed, and to accomplish this much effort is needed. God is playing hide-and-seek —

He will not reveal Himself of His own accord.

To seek Him out you will have to hunt in many different places. You will find many places empty and you will have to wander here and there, but you will just have to keep on searching. You will have to be manly; you will have to behave like a man. You will have to be like the lover who surmounts any obstacle that stands in his way. You will have to seek as Majnu sought Laila, as Farhad sought Shirin. These are characters from Sufi stories. Majnu is devotee, a seeker, and Laila is his God; Majnu is seeking her.

If your sadhana is aggressive, the Sufi analogy will appeal to you; if your search for God is nonaggressive, you will prefer the symbology of Kabir.

Ram has come to live with me
And I'm drunk with boundless youth.
United with Ram — round and round.
How fortunate am I!

When the five great elements of the body have been left behind, when nature has been left behind, when the stages of unconscious evolution have all been left far behind and your body becomes the sacrificial altar, in that deep valley of the heart the whole of existence begins to sing the Vedic hymns to celebrate your acceptance, your offering, your penance, your sacrifice, your gift.

In that inner valley where Brahma himself performs the Vedic rites, where existence itself begins to sing the Vedic hymns, the ceremony of encircling the sacrificial fire takes place. This is the meeting between the devotee and God; this is where the lover and the beloved become one. Then there is no duality; then the lover and the beloved are one. Then who is the devotee and who is God? Then there is no distinction. Before this, before the ceremony took place, the distinction was still there.

Not only is this ceremony, this *saptapadi,* this seven circles around the sacrificial fire, prevalent in this country, it is also a reflection of an inner activity. Have you ever wondered why the fire is encircled seven times? The great yogis have asserted that when the inner ceremony takes place it happens at each of the seven centers. The energy travels through all the seven centers of the body; it passes through each of them.

You may have observed a whirlpool in a river at some point. No outward cause is apparent, but some source of energy is causing a certain part of the river to revolve in a circular motion. In the current of your bodily energy there are seven such whirlpools. At seven places the river of your bodily energy moves in circles, and when the divine energy descends in you it does so in each of these seven spots, one by one. That is why we speak of seven centers. And because of this inner phenomenon, the husband and wife make seven circles of the sacrificial fire at the time of marriage. Although these are happening in the outer world they are symbols of an inner phenomenon. When this inner event occurs Kabir says:

How fortunate am I!

There is no greater blessing than this. This is man's destiny. Now one has reached where one has wanted to reach. The seed has achieved the ultimate; the seed has flowered in beauty. Now there is no returning. All has been achieved; one has arrived home. Now is the moment of eternal rest.

You will only attain to this rest when this *saptapadi,* when this circling of the sacrificial fire happens between you and

God. Until then your journey will continue.

Gods arrive in millions
And sages in thousands;
Says Kabir: I'm to wed.
And the man's immortal!

Kabir is speaking of the moment when the Sita within you will meet the Ram of the outer world, when the inner woman meets the outer man, when you meet existence. What happens at that moment? At that moment the whole of existence celebrates. We are linked to each other; we are joined together. When all of existence remains thirsty if there is even one drop of water less, then just imagine how the whole of existence will dance the day you achieve godhood. And it will dance!

Your fulfillment is also existence's fulfillment. Existence is one; it is a combined thing. Existence is a complete entity. It is not disjointed, it is not divided into several parts. We are not separate like islands in a sea, we are all joined together. That is why, when a buddha is born, doors open immediately and thousands of others are able to become buddhas as well.

Gods arrive in millions
And sages in thousands.

This means that the whole of existence participates in this great event. The original Hindi sutra speaks of thirty-three *crores* of gods, because in the days of Kabir the population of India was thirty-three crores, three hundred and thirty million — and the Hindus said there were thirty-three crores of gods because every person is ultimately going to become a god, because there is a hidden god in everyone. Today's number is much greater.

The figure is symbolic; the phrase means that the whole of existence in its entirety was present. Those who were partly awakened came, but those who were asleep remained behind because they had no idea what was happening. Those who were partly awake — godhood is only a part of consciousness, of existence — came. And the buddhas, those who were fully awake, came as well. All gathered to witness the great event.

When something great occurs you will only go to witness the event if there is some awareness in you. When a buddha is born not everyone will go to witness the happening; only those who were fully awake, came as well. All gathered to witness the great event.

When something great occurs you will only go to witness the event if there is some awareness in you. When a buddha is born not everyone will go to witness the happening; only those whose hearts respond to that mysterious attraction will go there. They will be dragged there, as if they were unconsciously pulled by some great magnet. It will be impossible for them to resist. Thousands of obstacles may stand in their way, but they will surmount them and go. They may have thousands of responsibilities resting on their heads, but they will all be ignored, set aside, thrown away. Their awareness will be gone then. They will be in a kind of hypnotic state, as if some great force is calling them.

Kabir says that when this great event took place within him millions of gods and thousands of sages, of buddhas, came to witness the occasion. There is no greater happening than this; there is no greater celebration.

Says Kabir: I'm to wed.
And the man's immortal!

Drunk With Boundless Youth

Now, Kabir says, his marriage to the immortal is to be solemnized; now he is in a state of eternal rest. At that moment you enter into eternal rest the whole of existence feels grateful, ecstatic and tremendously blessed — because you are the child of existence, the son of existence itself.

When you are to marry, your parents seem to be even more pleased than you are. They are very excited; their joy knows no bounds. Those who have given you birth feel filled with great blessedness.

Parents are always anxious about the marriage of their sons. They worry about when the son will marry and whether or not he will agree to the bride they have chosen, and they always feel incomplete until the marriage has taken place. This feeling of incompleteness is always there — even with the fathers of buddhas — and parents are only content when their son marries.

If worldly parents, if those who are merely related to your body are so keen for your marriage, for your joy and happiness, then is there any wonder that existence — your real mother and father, this earth and sky where you live, from whence you have come and to which you will return — begins to dance and sing when you achieve the highest state of blessedness, when you marry Ram, when you marry the immortal, when you marry Him?

Bear this in mind — through your blessedness the whole of existence is blessed. And remember this also — in your helplessness and wretchedness, the whole of existence is helpless as well.

4

A TRUE LOVER NEVER DIES

Dying, dying, all go on dying.
None die a proper death.
Kabir met with death,
Never to die again.

Dying, dying, all go on dying
Without a second thought.
Only mine's an artful death.
The rest die and rot.

Die you must, so die!
All whirlpools fall away.
Such is death. So why die
Hundreds of times a day?

When there's fear of death
Love cannot be felt.
The abode of love is far away.
Understand this well.

Nothingness dies, the soundless dies;
Even the infinite dies.
A true lover never dies.
Says Kabir: know this.

A True Lover Never Dies

Death — the whole world fears.
Death — my heart overjoys.
When will I die and give myself
In ecstasy complete?

Only yesterday Kabir told us:

Ram has come to live with me
And I'm drunk with boundless youth.

Says Kabir: I'm to wed.
And the man's immortal!

Today Kabir is talking about death. Love and death are deeply related. The man who does not know death will not be able to know what love is, and the man who has experienced love knows no death. Understand this correctly. Move into these wonderful words of Kabir and try to understand them.

Love is the deepest of deaths. The bud of love will not open, will not flower, until you are no more. How can love exist as long as "you" are there? There is no love as long as the lover exists. Your ego is the impediment; your I-ness stands like a dam in between. And so love's spring will not well up in you; it will not be able to spill forth. The only barrier that stands in the way of love is you yourself.

People think love will come to them when they find a lover, a beloved. This is an illusion. The beloved is already found. He is there every moment. The beloved is present everywhere, but the meeting will not take place until you are no more. How will your ego allow you to encounter Him? How will it allow you to see Him? How will it allow you to recognize Him?

You have wandered in search of love from birth to birth,

and you have never found it. Many times you have deceived yourself thinking you have found love, but each time you thought you found it you discovered your hands were really empty. Many times you thought you had found a rare drop of nectar, but in the end you discovered it was just an ordinary drop of water because it did not turn into a pearl of love in your heart.

You have deceived yourself like this many times. Even now you are behaving in the same way; even now you are hoping what you feel may be true love and not a deception. You have only had dreams of love, you have not experienced real love itself. You have made love in sleep, not in awareness. Only one who is wide awake is willing to face extinction.

The ego is the only impediment. And to drop the ego is a worse death than death itself. In death one only leaves the body. One soon takes another body — and there is not much time involved in this transfer — while you, your mind, remains intact, untouched. "You" are not scratched at all. Your mind, your ego, remains whole. Only the clay vessel is broken. And that is not very costly affair; you simply get a new jar to replace the old one. It will be fresh and strong and will last a long time. You simply leave your dilapidated old house and occupy a new one instead. "You" lose nothing. When you die, your mind, your ego, your desires all go with you, but "you" remain whole. Death does not take anything away from "you" at all.

But dying to love will take your mind away; dying to love will take your ego away. The feeling of "I am" will vanish and a kind of emptiness will spread throughout you. A deep, complete stillness will engulf you, and you will not be able to find yourself even if you try. Of course, the beloved will be

A True Lover Never Dies

seen, but you will be lost. You will experience the meeting with the beloved, but you will cease to be. The beloved will be there, but you will not. That is why Kabir has said:

When I was, the Lord was not.
Now He is; I am not.

Even in the life of an ordinary sort of man the ability to make love is only there when he is able to lose himself. Even in your daily lives you are unable to make love, unable to show love — so what can be said about divine love? Divine love is very far away. As Kabir says, *The abode of love is very far away.* You cannot even make the kind of love that is so close to you, the day-to-day love between individuals, between husband and wife, between friends. This ordinary, day-to-day kind of love is very close to you — this house of love is in your neighborhood — and yet you are unable to enter it. Your ego is your handicap.

You ask, "How can I surrender? How can I yield?" But I ask, "How can you fill your jar without bending?" You may be thirsty, and you may be standing on the bank of a river or you may be standing in the middle, but even though the water is flowing, the river will not jump up to reach your lips. It is you who are thirsty, not the river. But you stand there — erect, in your ego. How will you quench your thirst if you do not stoop and fill your cupped hands with water? You will have to bend — you will have to stoop down to the level of the river, to the surface of the water.

The current of love flows in every heart, and anyone can drink. But what about bending? Being unable to bend is the real obstacle. For thousands of lives your back has been cramped and now you are unable to bend, you are suffering from paralysis. And whenever the question of bending arises something happens in you to create difficulty. Your ego says, "I? Bend down? I would rather die!" Your ego tells you it is better to break than to bend. This is the lesson that is taught, the advice that is given — break but do not bend. This poison has been injected into your bloodstream. As if this were the yardstick of a brave man! As if this were being heroic!

In fact, this fear of bending, this fear of losing one's prestige is the fear of a coward. Why should a brave man be afraid to bend? He is not going to lose anything. When a storm comes, big trees may fall but the small plants yield. And after the storm has passed the big trees are unable to stand erect again, but the small plants bounce back easily. They know the art of yielding. They know how to be humble. The big trees that stood erect and fought against the storm were defeated and broken; they were unable to stand up again.

Lao Tzu said to behave as the plants do; he said, if a storm comes, yield. Who are you going to fight? What are you fighting? You will find that the storm cleanses you, washes away your dirt, and that after the passing of the storm you will again stand erect — fresher, greener.

Don't always remain erect; learn to bend. Don't be an egoist; learn to be humble. Remaining stiff and erect is really a sign of old age, while bending, yielding, is a characteristic of childhood, of freshness. An old man cannot bend — his bones have hardened, have become stiff. A child is soft and bends easily. A child often falls down, but he stands up again just as quickly. Why do you want to be old? Why do you want to paralyze your inner life? Why don't you want to be like a small child? When a man falls in love he becomes a child again. Again he learns to yield; again he becomes soft. Then all the fear and paralysis disappear.

Do you know what this fear is? Do you know why you are afraid to yield? It is because you ask, "What will happen to my prestige if I bend, if I yield?"

The man who is concerned with protecting his prestige really has none to begin with. The man who is unsure of his success is the one who is afraid of defeat, and the man who has been defeated within is the one who tries to make a victorious show on the outside.

You have always been told a man does not yield, a man does not bend, a man does not give in. The so called brave man is nothing but an egoistic coward. Cowardice exists within him, he is afraid that he will lose his prestige if he yields. But a man who is afraid like this cannot possibly have any prestige, and the man who really has prestige is not afraid to lose it. Bear in mind it is impossible to fear losing something you really have; it is only possible to fear losing that which you do not have at all. This seems paradoxical, but it is the truth.

You are afraid of losing something you do not have; you are afraid of giving away the thing you do not possess. That which you really have you give away in abundance — you know you have it, you know it will not be exhausted. The fear of losing something only exists in relation to that which you really do not have but wrongly suppose to be yours.

The person who is truly fearless never enters into conflict with the flow of existence. Not only is it someone else's existence, it is his own existence too. The storm is also yours.

It is not against you, it is also on your side. A truly fearless man is convinced the whole of existence is his.

No sooner do you learn to bend, to stoop, to be egoless, than the flow of love descends in you. And if you are unable to experience that flow in relation to your neighbor, how do you expect to experience it in relation to God? This is the final surrender, the final yielding; there is no further arising. And then there is no return. Reaching there, you attain to your real self but you do not return. It is an evaporation into the supreme, a melting into God; it is becoming one with Him. If you only knew how to lose your self, if you even dared to lose your self just once, you would be a truly brave man. You would have given up your fear and your habit of being egoistic, and you would have attained to a life that is ageless.

*Ram has come to live with me
And I'm drunk with boundless youth.*

You would be able to sing this along with Kabir. You would be able to say that God has come to your door and that a youthfulness of spirit has been born in you — the kind of youthfulness that is never born, that just is, that is eternal. At such a moment you are no more; at such a moment you make room for God.

Readiness to die is sannyas. To learn to die is sannyas. And for ultimate fulfillment, death is the condition. Love is the great death. People who die ordinary deaths return to the world, but those who die in the achievement of this love do not return. Nothing is left to achieve. There is no cause, no reason to return. They have achieved all.

*Says Kabir: I'm to wed.
And the man's immortal!*

A True Lover Never Dies

Why should he who is to marry the immortal return? The man who has found his beloved does not see her face in his dreams. We only dream about those things we have not achieved. A poor man dreams of wealth, a beggar dreams of becoming an emperor, a hungry man dreams of food — this is how we console ourselves in dreams. A dream is false, deceptive, a consolation, an illusory contentment.

No man can fill his stomach with dream-food, but at least he can sleep soundly, without a break. You may have gone to sleep without food and you may be hungry during the night, but then you will dream you have received an invitation to dine in a palace. That food will neither satisfy your hunger nor nourish your body, but at least you will be able to continue sleeping without interruption. Your mind will assure you that you have eaten. Now you will be satisfied; now you will go on sleeping quietly. A dream helps sleep.

When you wish for something you do not have, that desire will go on troubling you as long as it remains unfulfilled. So when all desires die, why should a person return to the world? But you return because you die unfulfilled, and this happens many times. You are still interested in worldly happiness, there are still desires, and they shout at you, "Where are you going? Come back!" No one sends you back into this world, you come back yourself because of your desires. You return yourself; you travel over the bridge of your own desires. The body is left behind, but you come back with your same mind and start your journey once again. You enter another womb, you repeat the same routine all over again.

The death that becomes the means for another birth is not, in fact, real death. Kabir says it is an incomplete death, an immature death, one that is not fully ripe — you have not grown up yet. You have not yet become wise and died a mature death. You have not yet attained wisdom and died a mature death.

Wisdom does not necessarily go hand in hand with old age. Hair turns grey in the natural course of things, but there is a great difference between attaining wisdom and having one's hair turn grey. Wisdom is attained only when one's desires grow old and crumble, only when one's desires exist no more.

Animals grow old, trees grow old, and you will also be old one day. And one day you too will die. But the man whose desires grow old, the man who knows what desires are, the man whose desires die, is the man who attains to wisdom. The death of such a man is totally different. Kabir dies, Buddha dies, and you will also die, but there is a qualitative difference between your death and that of Kabir, between your death and that of Buddha.

Try very carefully to grasp each of these sutras. Once you have fathomed their meaning correctly you will be able to understand that qualitative difference.

Dying, dying, all go on dying.
None die a proper death.
Kabir met with death,
Never to die again.

Kabir says everyone in this world dies but that no one dies in a right and proper manner. He says, as all the other enlightened men have also said, that dying is an art.

You may never have thought of death in this way — you do not even consider living an art. You live like a log floating on the river, being dragged wherever the current pulls it. Your life is a tragedy; it has not become an art. Before you take a step you do not even stop to think. If someone asks you, "Why did you do that?" you really have no answer. Although you prepare an answer and give it, inside you know very well it is no answer at all. You live as if you are groping about in the darkness. Your life has not become an art. That is why, up to the end of your life, you do not know what beauty is, what truth is, what bliss is. You do not experience any of these things. You feel as if you have spent your whole life wandering in a desert; you feel as if you have achieved nothing at all in your life.

But this is all quite natural, because your life has not become a work of art. If it had, you could have made your life into a beautiful sculpture. You could have given your life a definite shape — you could have cleaned it and polished it and brought out its intrinsic brilliance. If you had burned all the rubbish in your life you would have achieved the purity of gold by now. If you had chipped away all the superfluous stone, each limb of the statue would now be sheer artistry. You could have created a beautiful sculpture of your life, a beautiful work of art. But no, in spite of the fact you have done many things in your life, you have achieved nothing substantial.

Your life is not art, it is not art through and through — and Kabir says that even death must be total art. Death is as much an art as life is. And death is the test. If you have lived rightly, you can die rightly. If you have not lived rightly, you will not be able to die rightly. Death is the final offering. It is the highest; it is the crowning, the peak. Death is the essence, the flowering of life. How can your death be right if you have spent your life wrongly? How can your death be full of meaning if your life has been a waste? How can a tree whose roots are rotten bear sweet fruit? It is impossible.

What is the secret to the art of life? The secret is this: Live in full awareness. Don't grope in the darkness, don't walk in sleep — walk in awareness. Whatsoever you do, no matter what it is — even if it is as insignificant as opening and closing your eyes — do it thoughtfully, do it with awareness. Who knows, everything may depend on that tiny action, on opening and closing your eyes! You may be walking along the road and see a woman, and you may spend your whole life with her. Even opening and closing your eyes, stay alert.

Buddha used to tell his disciples not to look more than four feet in front while they were walking. "For walking, it is quite enough," he used to say. It is not necessary to look around, to keep checking on all sides. When you complete the first four feet you will see another four feet in front of you. It is enough. You can travel thousands of miles in this way. What need is there to look about? Don't keep on looking all over the place. Such a journey never ends.

If you examine your life you will be able to see that whatever has happened in it has been accidental, has happened by chance. Something happens accidentally, and because of that accident the course of one's entire life is changed. You were walking along the road on your way to the temple, for example, and a woman smiled at you. And, instead of reaching your destination, you arrived somewhere else. You married that woman; you begat children. You were anxious to marry her, and so you were caught in a huge wheel that turns round and round. Has it never occurred to you that all of this was caused by chance, by an accident? Had you followed Buddha's advice to his disciples, perhaps none of this would have happened.

To acquire the art of living, remember this — never act in unawareness, never act in sleep. Never allow anything to happen of its own accord. First see it properly. First consider it rightly. Look at it firmly, with discretion and wisdom, before putting it into action. If you do this you will find that your life acquires a kind of beauty, a certain elegance. You become like a sculpture; you become like the situation in which the sculptor and the stone are not separate. You yourself are the sculptor, you yourself are the statue, you yourself are the stone, you yourself are the chisel — you are everything, you are all.

If you live in awareness you will find that the chisel has done its work well. It has cut away the useless stone; it has not allowed anything worthless to remain. The chisel has chipped away the superfluous and gone right to the essence. And then, one day, you will find you have reached the temple, that you have become the divine sculpture itself; you will find you have achieved a kind of beauty, that you have attained a deep consciousness.

If you remain awake and alert until death, you have lived rightly. And then you will be able to meet death in a right manner as well.

Dying, dying, all go on dying.

Kabir says that everyone in the world dies, that death is a daily occurrence, that it happens every moment. He says we are surrounded on all sides by the sea of death. The whole is drowning in it continuously.

None die a proper death.

No one dies in a correct way. Kabir is saying no one dies in consciousness.

Kabir met with death,
Never to die again.

This is the art. This is the verification that there is no death any more. If you do a thing correctly once, you will not have to do it over again. You only have to do a particular thing again when you have been unable to do it correctly before. God gives us opportunity after opportunity to live rightly. He is not in a hurry, He has plenty of time to spare. And as long as you keep on making mistakes you will be thrown back into the world.

You will only be caught in His net when you can go to Him with full and complete experience of this life. You are just like a child who is sent back to the same class again and again until he makes a passing grade — we tell him he will not be allowed into the next class until he completes this one. The abode of love remains closed to you in the same way until you are through with life.

The art of life is getting through life successfully. And the man who gets through life successfully has nothing more to learn in this world. He has learned all that can be learned in this world of matter. He has passed through the ordeal of longings, through the fire of desires. Now the door to the higher grade opens for him; now he is admitted there. He has learned everything there is to learn here in this world so this door is closed to him. Now he cannot return.

Kabir met with death,
Never to die again.

Live in such a way that there will not be another birth, and die in such a way that there will never be another death. If there is birth, then there will certainly be death; death will follow automatically. So live in such a way that there will not be another birth — and then there will be no more death either.

Everyone wants to be saved from death. Can you find a man who does not want to save himself from death? Then why are these people not saved from birth. Birth is the other end of death. If you say you want to be born over and over again forever you are speaking nonsense. All this means is that you have not understood a very simple rule of arithmetic — that birth is one pole of life and death is the other.

The man who is born will have to die. The thing that has begun will also have to end. But if there is no end, there can be no beginning either. So if you want to save yourself from the end, never wish for the beginning. Do not long for the beginning if you want the beginningless, if you want the infinite. Just try to save yourself from the beginning.

Even the small experiences of life will be helpful to you in this effort. People come to me and they say, "We want to save ourselves from feeling angry. What should we do?" I tell them to stay alert right from the beginning. If anger has already caught hold of you it will be very difficult, it will be almost impossible to avoid it, to free yourself of it. You will have to pass through it. It makes no difference whether you go through it quickly or slowly, you simply heave to pass through it. It may take time, but whatever has begun is sure to end at some point.

If you want to be saved from anger, be alert from the very beginning. Be aware before the wave rises up in you. It may not have come yet, but it may well come later on. Suppose someone abused you and you were not angry right away —

it will catch up to you and you were not angry right away — it will catch up to you. So this is the right moment to be alert, to be fully awake. Anger is on its way to you. Then you remain the master. You have stopped anger from entering your house. You are the master as long as anger is not born in you. But if it is already born in you, you will have to pass through the whole process. To stop anger after it has been born is an impossibility — there is no way to end it. You have to be alert at the very beginning of the thing you wish to halt.

You want to save yourself form death, but you do not even know when death begins. People think death begins in old age, when the body becomes incapacitated, when medicine is no longer effective, when physicians become helpless. If you think like this, you are in the wrong. Then you will have to die over and over again; then you will not be able to understand the truth about life.

The beginning of death happens with birth. And if you go deeper into this phenomenon you will also see that death happens along with conception. When you are born you have already been dead for nine months, because for nine months you have already lived in the womb. Those nine months must certainly be included in the journey towards death that begins at the moment of conception. You are already nine months old at the time of your birth. That much old age has already overtaken you. Your birth actually begins from the moment your essence enters the womb, and that moment is also the beginning of death. You are dying every day. It is not an event that takes place at the end of your life. Death is not a miracle; death is not a magic trick. Death is a process. You are slowly dying, dying ever so slowly every day, and a day will come when this process of dying will cease. Death is the

A True Lover Never Dies

finale of this process. Death is the end of the beginning. And it has lasted a long time, nearly seventy years!

If you want to save yourself from death, then try to save yourself from entering another womb. And if you do not want to enter another womb, then go deeper and deeper within yourself. As you do this you will come to realize, you will come to understand the true art of life and death — you will come to know what life and death really are. If you do not want to enter another womb you will have to save yourself from desires, from desiring.

An old man who is dying — who is on the verge of death but still attached to life — will say, "If only I had a little more time, I could complete all my unfulfilled desires. My house is not finished yet, and I still have to see my son married. There are so many other desires yet to fill. And only recently have I begun to fulfill them. Is it just or proper that I am to be dragged away from the world? Only lately have I been able to organize things better. And I was planning to take a little vacation. Now that the children are grown up and have started earning their own living, I was thinking I might devote some time to worshipping God, to going to church and singing hymns."

No one ever does this. Yet when death approaches a man always thinks, "Had I had the time I would have spent it worshipping God. It seems to unjust that God is taking my life away without letting me fulfill my desires."

This is the difficulty at the time of death. A man's desires are not fully satisfied and the body is ready to leave him. So those incomplete and unfulfilled desires will immediately seek a new birth. They must be fulfilled. You cannot be free of the world before that. Your desire for a little more of life, to live a bit longer, is the cause of another birth.

Therefore, understand well that the beginning of death is not really in the womb, it happens before you enter another womb. This chain of death started when you desired more life at the time of your previous death. As you go deeper and deeper into the phenomenon you will find that desires are the links in the chain of deaths. Whether someone is young or old he has desires he wants to fulfill — and that is the cause of the series of births and deaths. Buddha said continuously: "Be free from desires and you will be free of *sansara*, free of the world. So don't entertain any desires whatsoever. Be happy with what you are. Be satisfied with what you are. Then there will not be another birth for you."

You should be content — as if you have reached your goal; as if there is no further journey to be undertaken; as if there is nowhere else to go. No matter what may be achieved, it should be more than enough. There should be no thought whatsoever of achieving more than you already have. If this happens to you, how will you be born again? You will die fully satisfied. And the man who dies completely satisfied has no reason to come back again. Such a man has known the art of death. The man who dies in desirelessness knows the art of death.

Kabir met with death,
Never to die again.

Kabir says:

Dying, dying, all go on dying
Without a second thought.

Kabir is saying you have never stopped and given a

moment's thought as to why you are still trapped in this web of life and death — despite the fact that you have lived and died countless times.

Only mine's an artful death.
The rest die and rot.

Kabir says he first attained wisdom and then he died, but that you die in a condition of helplessness. This is the difference between you. This is the difference between the death of an enlightened man and the death of an ignorant one. The distinction is qualitative: a physician would never be able to see the distinction.

If Buddha, Kabir and you were dying in a hospital, and someone were to question the physician as to the nature of your deaths, he would not be able to point out any difference at all. The doctor would say, "There is no difference whatsoever." He would have to say that the heartbeat in all three men was slowing down, that the breath was becoming more and more shallow and that the circulation of the blood was slowly stopping. He would have to say that all three men were dying in the same way. He would have to say there was no qualitative difference whatsoever.

But try to understand the phenomenon. There is a definite qualitative difference between your death and that of Kabir. That is what Kabir is saying.:

Only mine's an artful death.
The rest die and rot.

Having attained wisdom, having become fulfilled, Kabir dies. He dies having known reality, having known truth. And you are dying without knowing it at all. You are dying without being fulfilled, without being awake, without wisdom. Having grown old, you die; having attained wisdom, the enlightened ones die. This is what Kabir is saying. You die in a state of helplessness, crying for someone's help, weeping for doctors and medicines.

In America, dead bodies have been preserved. It is a a very costly experiment and only multimillionaires can afford the expense. The experiment has been undertaken because scientists believe that soon they will have found medicines that will make it unnecessary to die. One man who died in California in 1950 made arrangements to have his body preserved, because he thought only a period of thirty years was involved. The medicine was supposed to have been found by 1980 and he believed that if his body could be preserved until then he would be revived and able to live again. Ten thousand dollars is being spent every day so the body does not rot, so the brain cells and the tiny blood vessels are not damaged. To achieve this they air-conditioned an entire building, and the body is kept in a special deep-freeze. If the electricity stops even for a moment the body will be finished, then and there. So very elaborate arrangements were made to preserve the dead body. All possible precautions were taken in preparation for the arrival of the year 1980.

Man dies — but he does not want to die; he dies because he is helpless. You try so many tricks not to die. You believe in the false assurances given to you by the astrologers and the so-called holy men. Some people even wear amulets in an attempt to save themselves from death. You try all sorts of things to save yourselves.

To grow old does not mean to grow wise. Attaining wisdom means you have realized there is nothing worth achieving in this life and there is nothing worth saving. Attaining wisdom means you have explored all your desires and found them to be without substance. You have made love and found it to be nothing but lust; you have found that nature simply uses you as a means for the procreation of the species. You have earned money and found that even though it is considered valuable by society it is nothing more than soiled pieces of paper. You have attained a high position and hundreds of thousands have looked up to you with awe and respect, but you have realized that your position has not brought you any contentment, that your mind has remained in discontent. You have scaled the heights of the ego and found that there too only meanness and pettiness are to be found. You have lived in palaces, but your inner beggarliness did not disappear.

You may have earned everything, you may have achieved everything, but only when you realize that all this acquiring is really nothing but losing do you become a wise man. Only then do you realize there is nothing worth achieving in this life. In spite of the fact you have searched in every nook and cranny you have found that there is nothing of substance in your life.

You learn this from your own vast experience. It is not by listening to someone, not by reading Kabir's words or by listening to me that you realize this whole game of life is played in ignorance. You realize this through your own testing, through your own experience.

In this world there is no place for the enlightened man. Here, there is nothing for the enlightened man to do. This world is a child's toy — children are playing in it; children are engrossed in it. When you are enlightened you will laugh;

then you will also see it is just a toy. Then you have known. Then you are enlightened you will laugh; then you will also see it is just a toy. Then you have known. Then you are enlightened. And the moment you realize this, the chain of desires will be broken. This condition is called *samadhi* by Patanjali. He calls it *nirvikalp Samadhi* by Patanjali. He calls it *nirvikalp samadhi,* samadhi without ambiguities. Then there are no alternatives — neither "Should I do this?" nor "Should I do that?" No "Should I get this?" No "Should I get that?" All alternatives have disappeared.

The word 'Samadhi' is very beautiful. As well as for the condition of supreme knowledge, we use the word 'samadhi' for the grave of a sannyasi. There is a hidden meaning in the use of the same word for the two conditions. We give the name samadhi to the grave of a man who became enlightened before death, who gave up all his desires before death, who forsook even the desire to live, who died before death.

At the time of death you do your utmost to save yourself. You are terrified and you tremble. You are an ocean of uneasiness and agitation. You are dragged into death; you do not want your life-force to leave your body. You cling to the body as hard as you can. And you are forcibly separated from it. you die weeping, you die in anguish. You die a defeated man, in total helplessness.

Sit near a man who is dying and see what frantic efforts he makes to cling to life. Do this, because you may not be conscious enough to see all of this at the time of your own death. The dying, man is trying to grab at any straw to stay alive a bit longer, to remain in this shore a little while more. The call to go to the other world has come — the boat is waiting a the shore for you, the oarsman is beckoning you, calling you to make haste, saying, "Your time is over," asking, "Why are you still clinging to that shore?" — and you say, "Please, wait a moment. Let me have a little more happiness. I have not had any in my life." You have been unhappy throughout your life and yet you want to live just a moment more in the hope of attaining a bit of happiness. This is the tragedy.

You die unsatisfied, you die thirsty. You have drunk water from several streams but your thirst has not been quenched. Your hunger was insatiable and you were unable to satisfy your tastes, and so your desires have remained what they were. Even though you have gone through all sorts of experiences your desires have remained. They have even continued to disturb you up to the moment of your death. This sort of death is the death of an ignorant and foolish man.

If, after you have undergone all sorts of experiences, your desires begin to disappear and you begin to laugh; if you realize that trying to squeeze happiness from this life is like trying to extract oil from sand; if you see that there cannot be any kind of authentic relationship in this life, that there is no way to obtain happiness in this life; if you see that you have been wandering in vain, that you have been traveling in a dream — if you become conscious of all this, then you have become a wise man. Become wise before your death. You have already died so many times.

Dying, dying, all go on dying
Without a second thought.

Think about this. You have not done so up to now. If you die again without thinking about it, you will simply go through the same fuss, the same slavery all over again. So this time, before you die, think about it first. Death is still a little way off, so before it comes to you live thoughtfully, live consciously. Learn the art of thinking; become used to remaining alert.

When death comes to your door for you, go with it in full consciousness; accompany death as an enlightened man would. Don't go weeping and crying and shouting like a child whose toy has been snatched away from him. Don't be childish at the time of your death. Die with a smile on your face. Say to death, "You are welcome. I am ready for you." And when you say this, not even the tiniest bit of regret should remain. In actual fact, if you have really known life there will be bliss and ecstasy in your voice — and no sorrow whatsoever.

Die you must, so die!
All whirlpools fall away.
Such is death. So why die
Hundreds of times a day?

Kabir says, when death is certain, when there is no doubt of its coming, one should die as an enlightened man dies. Then the entanglement of this world is left behind forever; then there is no question of ever returning to this world again.

Such is death. So why die
Hundreds of times a day?

The death you encounter is the death of an ignorant man. It happens hundreds of times every day. Whether you are aware of it or not, inwardly you are only afraid of one thing, of just one thing, twenty-four hours every day. And that fear is that death is standing nearby, that death is immanent. The shadow of death is always on you. There are various faces to fear, but the base is one. Whenever you are afraid the obvious reason may be anything whatsoever, but if you look deep within yourself you will find that the real cause of your fear is death.

You become nervous when you lose money. Ponder this. Look deep within to see whether the fear is actually because of the loss of the money or if there isn't some other cause. At first you will feel you are afraid because of the loss of the money because you have gone bankrupt or are going to go bankrupt; but search within. You will find that the real cause of your anxiety is your hidden fear of death.

Money helps you in life; if you have money you have the means of supporting yourself, of saving yourself. If you cannot get the best treatment and the best medicine here in India then you can go to America — provided you have the money. But if you have no money you have no remedy. Then you have no way to save yourself. Then your helpmate has disappeared and you will be helpless when death comes knocking at your door. The fear one feels at the loss of money, or even at the idea of losing money, is nothing but the fear of death.

When the wife is on her deathbed the husband is upset. His wife's death is also the death of part of him. He saw her as half of him, and her death will take something away from inside him as well. With her death some inner part of him will also die. He will never be the same as he was before.

A wife is even more upset and frightened when her husband is about to die. She has no choice but to live a lifeless sort of life, while a husband can quickly find another wife to fill the vacancy left by the death of the first. A widow is a woman whose husband is dead, a woman who has now to live a dead sort of life. Nearly ninety percent of her is dead; only ten percent carries on. Such a life is very pitiable. It is really neither life nor death, it is nothing but dragging things out.

This was the reason wives used to die with their husbands, the reason a wife used to burn herself on her husband's funeral pyre. She used to do this because she thought it was better to die along with her husband than to lead the life of a widow. Leading the life of a widow was considered tantamount to dying a hundred times a day, so it was better to die now, to die once and for all.

How many times in a day do you die? How many times a day are you afraid? You are dying every time you are afraid — whenever you are afraid the shadow of death falls on you, the stench of death hovers about you. Kabir says that because death is certain you should die only once, but that you should die in the right manner so the entanglement of this world can be left behind forever. He is saying that no matter what you do, do it so perfectly there is never any need to do it again.

A novice singer once came to a town mainly populated by musicians, and the whole town gathered to hear the new musician who had just arrived. He was really a beginner; he was just learning. He hardly knew the ABC's of music, yet he was in the habit of visiting places where no one knew anything about music and so his scanty knowledge had always been considered great. But there were experts in this town; classical music was in their blood.

Hardly had he sung his first note when everyone cried,

"Again! Again!" He misunderstood. He thought, "How nice these people are! They really are great lovers of music! They are everything I had been told they were." So he sang again. And once more the whole hall cried out, "Again!" And so it went, seven or eight times more.

Now his throat was beginning to ache. He was becoming exhausted. He finally said, "Friends, I am deeply touched by your love, but please pardon me. No more! My voice is at the point of breaking."

Then the whole audience shouted, "You will have to keep on singing until you can sing it correctly."

All this time the novice had thought the cries of "Again!" had been in praise of his singing. But the people were experts. "If your voice breaks," they shouted, "then let it break, but you will have to keep on singing until you can sing it correctly!"

You are often sent back to sansara, back to this world, but don't think it is because you are so important, because you are so valuable. The fact that you are sent back is God's message that you will have to keep on singing until you learn to sing life's song correctly. You need this practice, this repetition, because you always return to Him without having become complete. God does not accept incomplete things; only the complete is accepted by Him. That is why Kabir is so full of ecstasy. That is why Kabir rejoices that he is going to Him, that he is going to marry the immortal.

Die you must, so die!
All whirlpools fall away.
Such is death. So why die
Hundreds of times a day?

Then Kabir says:

When there's fear of death
Love cannot be felt.
The abode of love is far away.
Understand this well.

Love will not be born in you as long as you are afraid of death. Love is the door to God. As far as Kabir is concerned, 'love' is the ultimate word; there is nothing above it or beyond it. It is prayer, it is meditation, it is worship, it is adoration, it is penance, it is yoga, it is tantra, it is the mystic mantra — all is included in love. And what Kabir has said about love is without comparison in this world.

As you move more and more into Kabir you will realize that no one has ever sung of love's greatness as he has. Love is the quintessence; love is the ultimate accomplishment.

When there's fear of death
Love cannot be felt.
The abode of love is far away.
Understand this well.

Understand well that for you the abode of love is still very far away. Whatsoever you have known as love up to now is false. It is not love; it is just something you call love. It may take thousands of shapes and forms, but it is not love at all.

The man who has known love has known God. For the man who has known love, nothing remains to be known. And the death of the man whose life has become filled with love is the final death — he will not have another birth. The man who has learned the lesson of love has no reason to come back to this world. He has known love. He has learned the song of love.

*When there's fear of death
Love cannot be felt.*

You have to be prepared to efface yourself completely at God's door. As you are you wish to possess God, but such guile on your part will not do at all. People come to me and they say, "We wish to seek God." I tell them, "Don't speak about that with me. Don't bring that up for discussion. You should be asking me how to efface yourself."

All this talk of seeking God is useless, there is no substance or meaning in what you are saying — and there is no end to it either. For you, where you are, it is enough to know how to efface yourself. When you are not, you will find that you are the lover and that you are standing at His door. On that day you will see that God Himself has answered your knock, that He Himself has opened the door to you. But as long as "you" are there you will not be able to seek Him. That is why, no matter how hard you try to seek Him — in temples, in mosques, in Kashi, in Kaaba, in remote mountain caves, through renunciation or through yoga — you will not be able to find Him. Your penance will simply enhance your ego, your renunciation will simply bring you status, your charity will simply bring you fame. Whatsoever "you" do will strengthen your ego.

Real charity only exists when you are not; authentic renunciation only exists when you have been blotted out completely. That is why love is the ultimate for Kabir. He says, no matter what you do you cannot attain to God while "you" are there. He says, "Give up this fear of death." He asks, "What is the point of dying so often? What is the point of dying a hundred times in a day?" It is better to die just once, to break the entanglement of this world once and for all.

The abode of love is far away.
Understand this well.

The distance is in proportion to the size of your ego. That is the distance. If you have a thousand-mile ego the distance is a thousand miles; if your ego is the size of an inch then the distance is one inch, but if you have no ego at all there is no distance whatsoever.

On its own, the abode of love is not far away at all. Don't think it is far, otherwise you have misunderstood Kabir's meaning. The abode of love is only far away because of your ego. So measure your ego. Size up your ego accurately, because the distance to the house of God is in direct proportion. You don't have to find God's house, what you do have to do is diminish the distance. So, if you wish, even though you are sitting in your own house, you can enter the temple of God.

Kabir has said he did not seek God, that he did not wander about in search of Him, that he remained in his own house and yet achieved Him. There is no question of going anywhere. In actual fact there is no such thing as path, no such thing as a pilgrimage. The only real obstacle is your ego. Even if you travel from one holy place to another, nothing will happen to you as long as your ego accompanies you.

Once the Hindu mystic, Eknath, was going on pilgrimage. His brother said to him, "You are lucky to be going on a pilgrimage. I have no time to go with you. But since you are going and you are my brother, it is enough for me. Take this gourd with you Dip it in holy water in all the holy places. It will become pure. And then I will eat it."

Eknath laughed, but still he kept the gourd with him and

he dipped it in the water of all the holy rivers in which he bathed. On his return he gave the gourd back to his brother. The brother cut a piece and tasted it. He found it to be very bitter. "Your gourd opened my eyes too," Eknath said, "and I attained true knowledge. I shall never go on a pilgrimage again. Since all those holy waters could not turn a bitter gourd into a sweet one what is the point of bathing in them? If the holy waters cannot remove the bitterness of a gourd, how can bathing in them remove a man's inner bitterness? Those places of pilgrimage now hold no more meaning for me. I shall no longer seek Him there."

As long as the ego exists there will be bitterness within. The ego is the poison. And no gourd can be as bitter as you are! When an insignificant thing like a gourd can defeat the holy places, then you will certainly defeat them also.

Although you visit temples and shrines and holy places, you remain you; you return as you left. Actually you may return even worse off, because then you return as a pilgrim and you have become even more egoistic. You are in the habit of enhancing your ego. You even do it with religion.

When there's fear of death
Love cannot be felt.

Efface yourself. That is the only way to achieve Him.

Then Kabir says a great and revolutionary thing, something that will even surprise the enlightened ones:

Nothingness dies, the soundless dies;
Even the infinite dies.
A true lover never dies.
Says Kabir: know this.

Everyone will be startled to hear this. Kabir is wonderful; he is a great, courageous, outspoken man. His desire to tell the truth is so keen he does it directly. He neither cares nor thinks about who might be adversely affected by it. He says, *Nothingness dies.*

The enlightened ones have said that when one attains to that emptiness, one has achieved Aum, one has achieved the sound of the universe. They say when you have become nothing, when you have become empty, when you experience that emptiness you have achieved the ultimate. Kabir says that emptiness will also die, that the unutterable will die too.

Nanak has said — and the Sikhs believe — that when Aum is achieved, that when the universal sound is achieved it is such a mantra that it is not uttered by you but just goes on by itself. The Sikhs say you have then achieved the ultimate. Nanak has said the sound of Aum, the sound so highly praised by the Vedas, is the only true word. But Kabir says that even Aum will die.

Even the infinite dies.

The Sufis have called the infinite *anahad*. It means the limitless; it means without limits. They say if you experience this you have experienced everything. But Kabir says that even the infinite will die, that even anahad will die, that all this will die.

A true lover never dies.

But, says Kabir, the man who has achieved the love of God does not die. This must be understood in a bit more depth. This statement is not only very deep, it is also very revolutionary in meaning.

A True Lover Never Dies

Nothingness dies, the soundless dies;
Even the infinite dies.

There is not even going to be the experience of emptiness. If you have become silent, if you have achieved samadhi, if you have known that everything becomes nothingness, then this emptiness, this nothingness itself will also become an experience. "You" will be separate; the knower will be separate. The emptiness will also be an object of knowing, a matter of information. Who is there to know that you have become nothingness. Who is there to experience this condition? You, the knower, will still be standing a little distance away. There will still be duality. And as long as there is duality there is death. That is why Kabir says, *Nothingness dies.*

The great enlightened ones have also said the same thing. Buddhists could not grasp it, for example. Lin Chi was a great Buddhist seeker, and he once thought he had achieved the ultimate knowledge. There was nothingness in him. There were no thoughts; there was no mind at all. When this happened he ran to his master and said, "I have become emptiness." The master replied, "Throw this emptiness away and then come to me. Emptiness and things like that are not needed here."

What did the master wish to convey? He was telling Lin Chi the same thing Kabir is saying to you. He is telling Lin Chi, "You are still separate from the experience you are having. And if separateness exists, there is duality." The moment you say, *I'm to wed, and the man's immortal,* the ultimate has not yet come, there is still some distance. The emptiness is there, but you are also there. The knower is there and the thing that is being known is there. Both subject and object are still there.

Nothingness dies; the soundless dies...

Who will hear the sound of Aum? You will hear it. Granted the noise of the marketplace is gone; granted the sound of Aum, the universal sound is being heard instead of the noise of the bazaar, but who is the experiencer of the sound? You are still separate.

Even the infinite dies.

If "you" know it, that infinite has a limit, becomes limited. Knowledge creates limits. When you say you have known the limitless, it cannot be true limitlessness, it cannot be the infinite. Knowing can only be of the limited. Kabir says this is the point at which all experiences die.

A true lover never dies.

Only love does not die, because in love the lover dies first. And then true love is born. This is Kabir's hidden indication that the first condition of love is that you must die, that you must be no more. And a moment comes in love when neither you nor God is there, when only love is there. Then there is neither Ram nor His lover, there is only love. Both the shores disappear and only the everlasting flow of love remains.

A true lover never dies.

And then Kabir says:

Death — the whole world fears.
Death — my heart overjoys.
When will I die and give myself
In ecstasy complete?

The man who has known the truth of life will be filled with joy at the coming of death because he will soon be free from the entanglement of sansars, from the entanglement of the world. Soon this useless carry-on will be over; soon this childish toy will be put away. Now such a man is worthy to journey to that place from which there is no return.

Jesus said that a fisherman throws his net into the water to catch fish, and that the tiny fish escape from the net without any difficulty but that the big ones are caught. Jesus said that God will continue to throw His net out for you until you become a big fish, but that before then you will always keep slipping back into the ocean of the world.

Kabir says:

Death — the whole world fears.
Death — my heart overjoys.

God's net is coming for you shortly. You think of death as the end of life — Kabir sees it as the beginning of the highest kind of life. You are afraid, because to you death is the end of life — Kabir is ecstatic because it is the moment of ultimate life. The temple for which you have been searching through countless births is now very near to you. The insignificant distance that still remains because of the body will soon be gone. And then there will be no distance at all.

Death — the whole world fears.
Death — my heard overjoys.
When will I die and give myself
In ecstasy complete?

Kabir says he will meet God when he dies. Those who have known life look upon death as a meeting with God, as an encounter with Him. For them, death is the greatest fortune. For them, death is a marriage, a union. For them, death is the ultimate, the perfection; the supreme flowering of love. For them, the face of death is transformed.

From the angle at which you look at death you think it is the end of everything, that all will be destroyed. What you have taken to be real is nothing more than a dream. But the angle from which Kabir is looking will open the door of truth, will remove the useless and usher in the bountiful.

You consider death as the blackest night, but to Kabir it is the morning, the dawning of the greatest promise. As the night gets darker and darker and death comes nearer and nearer, Kabir is filled with joy. It means the sun is about to rise.

If you live correctly, you can die correctly. The right kind of life is the basis for the right kind of death, so the man who dies in the right way has to face death no more.

Look for the key to dying only once. You have slipped through the net many, many times; many times you have fallen back into the ocean of sansars, back into the ocean of the world. Before His net descends on you this time, make yourself worthy to be chosen by Him.

5

ONE WHO WALKS ALONE

Confused, choosing for and against,
The whole world goes astray.
Choiceless and celebrating God;
He is a true sadhu.

People all bound together
As donkey tied to donkey.
Who has inner vision,
He's authentic man.

One who walks alone,
He alone finds truth.
Heart absorbed in love
Never again comes back.

Wholeness is total vision;
Everything is holy.
Says Kabir: it can't be understood.
This is something unwritten.

All that we know and achieve is going to die. There is no question that one's worldly riches will disappear, but the wealth that we store up within ourselves will also disappear.

The enlightened ones have always said not to amass

worldly wealth, but Kabir says that even one's inner wealth will also die. He says that inner wealth will disappear and that you alone will be saved; he says that experience itself will die and only the experiencer will remain.

It is easy to grasp what he means as far as the riches of the outside world are concerned. We see people dying, leaving wealth, buildings, palaces and kingdoms behind them, but Kabir is saying that one's inner riches will also have to be left behind. This is a bit subtle, and it is also final. It is the final statement; nothing more remains to be said. So it is important to understand it deeply.

No sooner do you experience something than duality sets in. As soon as you say, "I am pleased," you become two — the pleasure and you. A distinction has been created. First there is the happening, and second, there is the person to whom it has happened. But no distinction can enter into God; you alone can enter there. You cannot take anything with you. You cannot even take your spiritual experience.

Nothingness dies, the soundless dies;
Even the infinite dies.
A true lover never dies.
Says Kabir: know this.

Your meditation, your *samadhi*, your *kundalini* — all will die. All your spiritual experiences will die. You will go alone. So do not cling to these experiences, otherwise you will create a new world for yourself. Before you were amassing wealth; now you are collecting experiences.

People come to me and they say they have experienced light within. It is enjoyable; the inner wealth is very subtle. They say they have experienced the awakening of the kundalini and it is thrilling; they say they experience great peace and happiness within.

Don't cling to these experiences either, because they are also on the outside. All experiences belong to the outside; an experience is always an experience of the other, of the outer. Don't cling to ecstasy or peace or freedom, because as soon as you cling to something you create *sansara,* the world. Clinging is what sansara is. Don't cling to anything. Only bear in mind that you are a separate entity, and no matter how near and deep an experience may be it is still far away. The experiencer is always aloof, afar.

You are separate from whatsoever you know, so you cannot make God your experience. God can never become the object of your experience because whatsoever becomes an object of your experience is certain to die.

Nothingness dies, the soundless dies;
Even the infinite dies.

If you say that you have experienced God then that experience will also die, that God will also die. The only man who will be saved is the man who does not create any duality, who does not know what duality is.

God is not separate from you. God is your very existence, your innermost being. He is your very self, your soul. He is the hidden sound lying deep within your being, he is your own song. And just as a dancer is not separate from his dancing, the experience of God is not separate from you. It is not even proper to call it an experience. That is why the Upanishads say that he who says, "I have known," has not really known Him at all.

How will you know God? To know means there is some

distance between the knower and the object that is known. To know a thing some distance is needed — I can see you because you are a little away from me; you can see me because I am at a little distance from you. But how will you see yourself? To see a thing you need some distance.

When you look into a mirror you stand a little away from it; if you go close and put your face against it, it will be difficult for you to see your own face. And if you are able to see a bit of your face it means your eyes are still a tiny distance from the mirror. If your eyes touch the mirror, if they become one with the mirror, then nothing whatsoever will be seen. You may experience a dim figure perhaps, because you and the mirror can never be one; there will always be some distance.

In your deepest depths you are one with God. There is not the slightest distance, not even the most minute space between you and him. That is why the enlightened man says that as long as he was there God was not there, and that when God was there, he was not there. Deep down within you, you and God are one.

All experiences will die and only you will be saved, so do not cling to experiences. Even yoga and meditation are to be left behind. But remember that you cannot give something up before you have possessed it. Kabir says that nothingness will die, but first you have to become emptiness, first you have to achieve nothingness. Kabir says that *Aum* will die and that even the infinite will die, but you still have to become infinite first. How can something that is not, die?

So after listening to this discourse do not be under the impression that it is necessary to meditate, that it is unnecessary to attain to Aum, that it is necessary to become limitless. Don't say, "All this is going to die, so why bother trying?" You have not achieved them yet. You have to achieve them first. These words are spoken to warn you against your ego, otherwise the tiniest, most subtle experience will give birth to sansara, to more worldly attachment. And you will be caught in that entanglement once again — subtly so, but trapped nonetheless.

This is what is meant by the Hindi word *yogabhrasht*, meaning one who has fallen from yoga. Such a man has achieved samadhi, but has then fallen in love with it. He has achieved the highest peak of meditation, but has become attached to it. He has failed to reach to nonattachment. He has experienced ecstasy, but he has desired to hold fast to it so as not to lose it. He needed to take one step higher — to leave yoga behind, to leave samadhi behind. Such a man is a yogabhrasht. Kabir is referring to that last step:

Nothingness dies, the soundless dies;
Even the infinite dies.
A true lover never dies.

Why? Love is the only experience which is not separate from you, the only experience in which you are the experience itself. When you are in love you do not feel that you are experiencing love; in a moment of ecstasy you do not feel you are experiencing ecstasy. Understand this a bit more deeply. In the moment of love a person does not feel that he is experiencing love — he only becomes aware of it when the love has gone. Then he feels that he has experienced love.

How can a man be aware in that fiery moment of love? Love is such an intoxication, and the feeling of ecstasy is so deep and so extreme that no one can stand apart and think about it, no one can be aloof from it enough to look at it. As long as it lasts one is not conscious of it, but when it passes one is surprised and only then becomes aware that something was there but has now gone. Then you remember it. Then you say, "That was love." But in the moment of ecstasy itself one is not conscious one is experiencing it.

The experience of love is like the experience of perfect health. Only when you fall ill do you remember that before you were perfectly well and healthy. You only become aware of health during sickness. If there were no illnesses in the world people would not know what health is, they would simply remain healthy and in ignorance about it. Becoming ill reminds you of health. Only when you have a headache do you become aware of your head. When it is fine you never think about it. When the body is perfectly sound a state of bodilessness happens of its own accord and you do not remember the body at all.

When love is profound you have no idea at all what is happening; then you are in some other world. But it is not a world of knowledge or an experience, it is a world of existence. Then you are not a lover, then you are love itself. Then who is there to know this state? There is no one to stand apart, to remain aloof.

This is why Kabir says that only the lover of Ram does not die. The lover of Ram does not mean the devotees of Ram one sees here and there, Kabir is not talking about this ordinary kind of devotee. Kabir is talking about a true lover, in the authentic sense of the word. In real love there is no longer any Ram nor any lover of Ram; there is neither God nor devotee — there is only the manifestation of Ram. When the duality is gone, when the devotee and God are both lost, then there is neither worshipper nor worshipped. The devotee and God are both lost, and the river that flows between, touching both the shores, is the love of Ram, the love of God. That love cannot die because all that is perishable is already dead and gone. With any kind of experience a very subtle ego would have lingered, but that too has gone, that too has died.

In reality, the devotee has nothing at all; he has neither yoga, nor samadhi, nor miracles. He is totally helpless, totally blank, totally empty. There is not even emptiness, because even the experience of emptiness is gone. Through weeping and crying and emptying himself, through effacing himself, he is totally lost. No trace, no sign of him is left behind. That is why Kabir says that the whole world dies but that no one knows how to die rightly.

The man who dies in the right way does not have to die again. Only the death of the true devotee — only Kabir's kind of death, is the right kind of death. And it is a wise and correct death, because first he knew and then he died. He saw death as a step forward; he turned death into a ladder to reach the last point on the journey of life. Just as the drop loses itself and becomes the ocean, we become one with Him whey we die.

The man who has surrendered himself at the feet of God is a true devotee. Although he is alive, he is as good as dead, because he has said, *"Now only You are. Now I am not."* And in such a man the voice of the ego no longer arises because his own existence is lost, because he has killed himself, because he has killed his ego. Then there is no death for such a man. Then he is not — so who is there to die?

The yogi will die because he is full of ego as he practices his sadhana. He undertakes penances, learns techniques, practices tantra, repeats a mantra — and so he creates an enormous paraphernalia around himself. This simply means he is still there. But the devotee has already gone. The yogi reaches in the end, but the true devotee arrives with the first step. And a yogi can fall.

We have spoken of the word 'yogabhrasht', meaning one who has fallen from yoga — but have you ever heard of *bhaktibhrasht,* of one who has fallen from devotion? There is not such a word as bhaktibhrasht! It is possible for a yogi to fall back because he has to take the final step at the end of his sadhana. Before this, there is always the possibility of a fall. But for a devotee there is no possibility of a fall, the devotee has to take the final step in the beginning — the yogi will drop his ego when he completes his sadhana.

But what guarantee is there the yogi will be able to give up his ego? As the ego becomes finer and finer, more and more subtle, it becomes proportionately more enchanting and pleasing. And the more subtle it becomes, the sweeter its net becomes. Your ego is bitter and still you are unable to let it go, so how will you be able to drop it in the final stages of yoga when there is a continuous showering of ecstasy on all sides? You did not drop it when it was poison, and now it will be as sweet as nectar. So in the final stages of yoga a moment comes when the yogi has to make a decision to drop the ego which, until then, has been the basis of all his happiness. That is why people fall from yoga. No one falls from devotion. A person on the path of devotion cannot even take the first step if there is a possibility he will fall. And if he falls, he will immediately turn his back on that path. For a real devotee there is no question of turning back, because the first sutra of devotion is to die, to die once and for all. As Kabir asks, *So why die hundreds of times a day?* Die only once so that you can be saved from the world's entanglements. From the very first step this is the insistence of the path of devotion.

Whether you choose the path of yoga or the path of devotion you will have to drop your ego. The only difference between the two is that yoga will try to purify you first. When your consciousness is on the point of becoming totally pure, when there is only a faint smoke-screen of ego but the fire is bright and shining, when only a few particles of dust remain, then yoga will ask you to drop the ego. Yoga will purify your ego first and then ask you to throw it away.

The path of devotion asks you to throw away the ego at the beginning, because no matter what you do you will remain impure as long as you continue living with the ego. The ego is poison, so whatever you touch will be polluted. You cannot pour nectar into a contaminated vessel, because then the nectar will be turned into poison as well. And so Kabir says:

A true lover never dies.

In these sutras of Kabir, the name Ram has no special significance. Even if you have never heard the name Ram you can still be a lover of Ram. The Sufi fakirs are lovers of Ram, although they have nothing to do with the Ram of the Hindus, and the Jewish Hassid mystic is also lover of Ram. In this connection do not think of Ram as the son of Dasharatha. Kabir's use of this name has no relation to Hindu mythology whatsoever; he uses the name of Ram only to indicate the supreme, to indicate God.

Why can you not attain to the state where you can surrender yourself completely at the feet of God? Why does this not happen to you? Kabir says:

Death — the whole world fears.
Death — my heart overjoys.

Why does this not happen to you? Why are you not overjoyed at the prospect of encountering the death the whole world fears? No one is safe from the clutches of death, everyone has to die. Even if you run away, even if you hide yourself somewhere, at the end you will surely face the jaws of death.

Since death is such a definite part of life why not accept it in an easy and natural fashion? Why can't you see the joy in death? Why are you running from it? Stop running.

There are some very subtle reasons why this does not happen. The first reason is that the mind is accustomed to dividing a thing in two and then looking at it. The mind is unable to look at the whole. This is the limit of the mind, that it is only able to look at part of something. If I give you a small stone you will not be able to look at it at once in its entirety. At first you will only see one side, and when you turn it over you will see the other side — but then the first side will be hidden from you. You are not even able to look at the whole of the tiniest particle of sand at one time. The capacity of the mind is such that it is only able to see a thing in an incomplete form.

The mind also clings to the part it has seen. It becomes attached to the part it has seen and rejects the other part in fear it may be opposed to the part to which it has already become attached. Because of this difficulty you pass your whole life in tension and unease. You cling to life and try to avoid death. You want to live; you do not want to die. You do not even realize that life and death are just two aspects of the same coin, and so you remain as bereft of life as you are afraid of death. But they are just two sides of the same coin! You spend your time trying to save yourself from death, but at the same time you are missing the chance to live life properly.

You will never be able to live life in its true sense in this way. Look at your past. Have you enjoyed life up to now? Or have you lived in fear? Have you lived properly, or have you just been busy making arrangements to live well in the future? If you had learned how to live properly and had lived accordingly, you would most certainly have seen that death is an inevitable part of life, that there is no way to escape from it. If you want to live, then death is definitely going to be part of your life.

The mind looks at things in opposition; it sets one thing against another. The mind says that day and night are two separate things. It says that the night is dark and that the day is bright, that there is sun during the day and no sun at night. Day and night are one. The day becomes night and then the night becomes day. But you are afraid of the night and want to cling to the day.

The mind looks on love and hate as opposites, as separate. This is a mistake, a false belief, an illusion. They are but two aspects of the same coin. You want to hold onto happiness and avoid misery, but they are two sides of the same coin as well. And so you are perplexed; you are in a great dilemma. But this state of perplexity is not because of the world, it is because of your mind. The way your mind looks at things is partial, biased, prejudicial.

And what Kabir says today is relative to this. If you can see the whole, you will be liberated. Then you will be willing to meet death, because life and death are just two different names for one and the same phenomenon. They are two banks of the same river. The man who is not attached to life is not afraid of death. Such a man knows how to live and he knows how to die. He harvests joy and happiness from life and from death as well.

In asking this question, Kabir is saying he has gathered as much nectar as possible from life, that life has given him nectar in abundance:

When will I die and give myself
In ecstasy complete?

Kabir says the taste of life is unique and that the grace of God is also unique. He says now he has achieved both, now he knows them both, and that he is now ready to experience the taste of death. And if the taste of life is unique, the taste of death will be even more unique because it comes at the end of life. Death is the highest climax in life. It is the highest peak, the Everest of life. And when a man can attain such happiness in life, when he can uncover so many secrets from so insignificant a life, then at life's final peak what doors will open to him!

Confused, choosing for and against,
The whole world goes astray.
Choiceless and celebrating God;
He is a true sadhu.

The whole world looks at things incorrectly. Everyone divides everything into pros and cons, you divide the world into parts. You say, "I am in favor of this," you say, "I am not in favor of that." You think of happiness as being in your favor and of misery as being against you. This is the mistake you make.

*Confused, choosing for and against,
The whole world goes astray.*

The whole world suffers from this complexity. Be neutral, look at both sides. But to be neutral you have to be apart from the mind, outside the mind. The mind is always partial, the mind cannot look at the whole. The mind looks at one part first and then considers the unseen part as its enemy. Then it becomes involved in fighting against the part it cannot see.

There is no way for the mind to look at the whole, to look at the totality. The mind is like a flashlight, like a torch; it has a focus. When you light a torch only one specific area is lit up; the surrounding space remains in the dark. The mind is not like a lamp that brightens an entire room — consciousness is like a lamp; the mind is like a torch, like a flashlight.

As long as you look through the mind you will see two parts of one whole — you will see the bright side and the dark side. And you will always think of the dark side as your enemy simply because it is the opposite of the bright one. Heraclitus has said, "God is day and night, winter and summer, war and peace, satiety and want," but you can only see this when there is no mind, when you become neutral. Then you will see that god is both birth and death, that God is both happiness and misery. Then you will also be able to dance in your misery, because misery is God as well. And you will also be able to bow to Satan, because Satan is also God.

If you can dance in your misery, who can make you miserable? If you can bow to Satan then who can cheat you? If you can see good in bad, if you can see life in death, then there is transcendence; then you have gone beyond both. Now nothing can harm you. Now there is no need for you to pass through the cycle of birth and death. Now your lesson is over, now you have learned what was to be learned. Now there is nothing more to learn, now there is no need to return. This is one meaning of these words of Kabir.

Confused, choosing for and against,
The whole world goes astray.

The other meaning, the second meaning, is that you have even created *for and against* in relation to truth. You say that someone is a Hindu, that someone is a Mohammedan, that someone is a Christian, that someone is a Jaina, that someone is a Buddhist — but God exists in all of them at one and the same time. And if, clinging to one aspect, you try to go to Him, to Him who is neutral, to Him who is hidden in all aspects, you will find yourself caught in a great dilemma. You will be caught in a web of your own words; your principles and your scriptures will have become your chains. If you look deeply into yourself you will find that the Vedas, the Koran and the Bible are hanging like dead weights about your necks. You are being crushed by this burden.

Existence is neutral and you are biased. You say, "I am a Hindu," but existence does not know what "I am a Hindu" means! These are all mental tricks, intellectual devices. You have created your own ideas about God — and all ideas and suppositions are of the mind! You can only meet God when there is no mind. And when there is no mind how can you be a Hindu or a Christian! People have totally missed truth,

Kabir says, because of this complex web of principles, opinions, dogmas and prejudices they have woven for themselves.

Choiceless and celebrating God;
He is a true sadhu.

Real hymns of praise to God will only begin when you have become neutral, Kabir says. So bear in mind that authentic hymns of praise cannot be the prerogative of any particular religious sect. But you have made it this way. You say you are a theist, a believer, and another says he is an atheist, a nonbeliever. You say you are a theist and so you praise God; another says he is an atheist and does not praise God. To praise God cannot be the sole right of any religious sect.

You only become a devotee of God when you belong to no sect, when you are neither theist nor atheist, neither Hindu nor Mohammedan — when there are no sects, when there are no adjectives, when you stand naked before truth without prejudice or opinion, when you do not cry aloud who you are. How can "I" be given up while you can still say "I am this" or "I am that"? That "I will remain as long as you can assert "I am Hindu" or "I am a Mohammedan"; "I am a Christian," "I am a brahmin" or "I am an untouchable"; "I believe in this" or "I believe in that."

When "I" is gone, who is there to care about scriptures and principles? You can only reach to God when you are naked, when you have no prejudices whatsoever. And the only man who can reach to God is the man who belongs to no sect. Everyone else will remain behind, wandering aimlessly.

Here Kabir is telling us a unique thing:

Choiceless and celebrating God;
He is a true sadhu.

Kabir is saying that the man who worships God without belonging to any sect is a true seeker. He is neither a Hindu nor a Mohammedan, neither a believer nor a nonbeliever. The true seeker has no beliefs or prejudices, he is simply a man who knows nothing but love. He is not interested in academic discussions, he is not guided by intellectual decisions, he lives by the dictates of his heart. No one has ever reached God with the help of his intellect. And now we shall try to understand the reason.

The man who reaches God does so with the help of his heart. As I have told you, the intellect can only see half of a thing, only a part — the heart can see the whole. God is whole, total; if you only see half of Him you have missed. God is total, perfect, complete, and you can only see Him through the heart. The total is only seen in its totality through the heart, that is why this is a matter for love.

Only a man who is neutral can truly worship the Lord. Do not divide yourself by beliefs. Don't say "I believe in this" or "I believe in that." Only say this much, "I am ignorant; how can I believe? Only the enlightened ones can have beliefs. I am ignorant; how can I assert what truth is? I shall be able to see when I know truth." Just say this much.

Bear in mind that those who know never state they have a particular belief or hold a particular opinion. The man who has achieved truth has no need for opinions. This is the difficulty. How can someone who has not achieved truth form an opinion of it? The man who has attained truth is beyond any opinion, and the man who has not achieved truth should not form any. An ignorant person cannot have an opinion because to have an opinion means that you know something, that you believe in something, that you have proven something and that now you believe it. Say this much only, "I am ignorant. How can I have an opinion? I do not know and so I am seeking. If I knew why would I seek? if I knew I would be silent." Say only this much.

This is why so-called learned men do not even seek — they simply think they know. They have committed the scriptures to memory and repeat them like parrots. They already think they know it all, and so any possibility of search is thwarted. If you want to stop looking, then just hold fast to an opinion.

An opinion can never be complete. How can the opinion or belief of an ignorant man be complete? His opinion is like a house built on sand; it is in danger of toppling at any moment. His belief is like a palace built of cards; it will tumble down at the slightest gust of wind. And so you remain afraid to come face to face with any opposition to your beliefs. You avoid people who might shake your foundations, who might undermine your faith, who might threaten the beliefs you cherish. Of what value are such beliefs? They are not even worth two paise.

The faith that is afraid of being shaken is, in fact, no faith at all. That is why you refuse to listen to any discussion of views that are contrary to those you hold. A Hindu will not read a book on Mohammedanism and a Mohammedan will not read a book on Hinduism. That might create complications. Their faith in their beliefs might be shaken; their faith is not solid enough. Such faith is of no value at all. Let it be shaken! Let it crumble! It is good to be without belief, to be without faith, but it is important to be true, to be sincere. A shaky belief is something that has been planted in you forcibly. It is a false thing — it is not real faith, it is not true belief.

When you abandon sects you become religious. Religion is born where sects leave off. And this happens because when there are no more thoughts the heart becomes active. Love manifests when the intellect is undisturbed, when it is calm, at peace. About the manifestations of this love, Kabir has this to say:

Choiceless and celebrating God;
He is a true sadhu.

Seeker after seeker exists, sadhu after sadhu exists, but it is difficult to find a true seeker. The world is such a wonderful place that even seekers after God become entangled in supporting various religious sects! Even they take sides.

There is one seeker who comes to me often. He says, "I am a Jaina sadhu." Can a sadhu also be a Jaina? Such an attitude could be understood if something like a non-sadhu existed. Another man comes to me and says, "I am a Buddhist sadhu." Look at the beauty of this — the sadhu also professes to be a Buddhist! Please leave something for those who are not sadhus!

It is understandable that a non-sadhu can be a Buddhist or a Jaina or a Hindu or a Christian — this we can tolerate. We can say, "This man has no sense, he does not know the truth" — but these men are claiming to be sadhus as well. They have renounced the world, their homes, their wives, their children, their wealth — they have forsaken everything — but they will not give up their religion, whatever it may be.

Whether such a man goes to the jungle or to the Himalayas he remains either a Jaina or a Hindu or a Mohammedan. There is no change in him at all. Kabir says that the sadhu who has no *for and against* in him, *He is a true sadhu.*

Kabir is a rustic, a rural man, and so he uses the symbols found in the villages. He says:

People all bound together
As donkey tied to donkey.
Who has inner vision,
He's authentic man.

If you have some experience with donkeys you will understand Kabir. There were a number of donkeys in my native place and so I know what it is Kabir wants to say. If you tie a donkey to a peg stuck in the ground it is possible the donkey may run away carrying the peg along with it; if you tie one donkey to another donkey then neither of them goes anywhere at all. What happens? They cannot run away because one donkey is pulling the rope towards the left and the other is pulling it towards the right.

People all bound together
As donkey tied to donkey.

The donkeys go nowhere at all. They stand there the whole night — one moving to the left, one moving to the right. They are donkeys after all; there is no way they can go away together.

I saw this in my native village. At first I was also perplexed and could not understand why the donkeys were tied to each other in such a way, but after a while I understood that this was the easiest way to keep them safely in the shed. They might pull out a peg, so why even bother to hammer one into the ground? After a hard day's work the potter used to come home in the evening and tie one donkey to another. This method was satisfactory; it was enough. The donkeys would never go anywhere, he would still find them there even if he didn't return for a long time. How could they run away? They were pulling each other in opposite directions.

You may have heard the story of a very rational donkey that lived in ancient Greece. He was a great philosopher and a great logician. All donkeys are philosophers and logicians; to live by the intellect is to live like a donkey, to be stupid like a donkey.

Once this particular donkey was very hungry and a mischievous man, deciding to have some fun with him, placed a pile of grass on each side of him. The donkey was standing in the middle and both piles were at equal distances from him. There was no rope about his neck, he was free, unfettered. But he was a rational donkey, and so he began to consider whether he should go to the right or whether he should go to the left. No rational donkey or man will take a step without thinking about it first.

His hunger grew very acute, but still he was unable to reach a decision. Both choices seemed equal; both piles were the same distance away. First he would take a step towards the right, but then he would think, "What's wrong with going to the left?" He would take a step to the left and then argue with himself, "What's wrong with going to the right?"

And so the donkey could not decide. He just stood there thinking and arguing with himself. But hunger won't wait for you to think, to make up your mind, and at last his hunger got the best of him and he collapsed — but he kept on thinking.

It is said the donkey died hungry. The piles of grass remained untouched, remained as they were, and the donkey remained in the middle. He could not decide.

Confused, choosing for and against,
The whole world goes astray.

Your condition is the same. God is piled high on both sides of you, and yet you are dying of hunger because you cannot make up your mind. You are wavering. You ask, "What should I do? Should I be a Hindu or a Moslem or a Christian or a Buddhist? In whom should I believe? Who should I worship? Which scriptures should I follow? Which temple should I attend?" Life is fleeting, and you are unable to reach a decision. But the decision will never happen because the intellect's speciality is its inability to reach a decision.

The intellect is exactly like the parliament of India. If something has to be decided there, it never gets done at all. Whenever the intellect decides upon something, one part of it keeps on rejecting the decision. It will be a majority decision; it will be a decision that has not been approved by all. If there were a country called Intellect and one hundred members were in its parliament, sixty would give their consent to a proposal and forty would oppose it. The forty would set forth all sorts of arguments, declaring the approval of the proposal would be harmful to the country.

All decisions of the intellect are parliamentary decisions. And the majority cannot be trusted here either, the balance of power keeps fluctuating. Today's majority may be a minority tomorrow and again the proposals will change.

The intellect can never move beyond doubt. To be definite is not a characteristic of the intellect, it is not in its nature.

On the other hand, to be doubtful is its very nature. How can doubt ever reach a decision? How can doubt ever arrive at a definite conclusion? No matter what decision is reached it will be a temporary one. There will always be an upset after a time because the opposition is forever trying to canvass votes on its own behalf, and will end up being the majority by and by. And the decisions of this new majority will not last forever either. They will meet with the same fate as those of the party that was in the majority before.

The intellect can never reach a unanimous decision, only the heart can do that. The intellect functions in division, in parts, and not as a whole. And those parts are always in opposition to each other. Whenever you decide to do a certain thing there will always be a thousand alternatives in front of you. But you can only act upon one decision at a time, and so, no matter which decision the intellect makes, there is always some repentance involved.

Let us take an example. You have come here to listen to me. By now you could have opened your shop and done some business. You could have caught a big customer in your net, you could have made a handsome profit. But you have missed that. When you go back to your shop your neighbor will ask, "Where were you? Mr. So-and-so was here. He had some purchases he wanted to make and he inquired after you." When you hear this you begin to regret that you came here to listen to me. Perhaps it would have been better had you gone straight to your shop. You begin to ask yourself what profit there was in hearing about Kabir. "I missed a wealthy customer," you will say. "Who knows how big the sale might have been?" you will ask yourself.

Now suppose you had not come here and were doing

business in your shop as usual. A man, returning from this discourse, runs into your shop and says, "What are you doing sitting here? All your goods will still be here when you have gone! We have just come from hearing a discourse on Kabir. It was as if nectar poured down upon us from above. Our hearts were filled with ecstasy. What are you doing here? Why are you wasting your life?" When you hear these words your mind will immediately begin to repent once again.

There will always be alternatives, and time is limited for you. Time is very short, and there are thousands of things worth doing, so you will have to make a choice. But no matter which choice the intellect makes you will repent it, because you never know what would have happened had you chosen one of the alternatives. The intellect always says, "I wonder what would have happened had I done this," or "I wonder what would have happened had I not done that." The intellect is always scratching its wounds and repenting.

So no matter what you do, you will regret it. Whether you marry or do not marry, you will repent. Many married people come to me. They say they are caught up, entangled in the institution of marriage. "We don't know how to get out of it," they say, "It is a problem for us." And those who are not married tell me they feel it is necessary to experience married life, otherwise they will never know what marriage is like. But they do not know how to move into a marriage. Young people ask me whether they should get married or not. I tell them that no matter what they do they will repent it. Whatsoever you do, this is guaranteed: the intellect always repents.

Why does this happen?

This happens because the half that was rejected is waiting for the opportunity to say, "See, I warned you not to do that. You ignored my warning and did the opposite. Now you are repenting. In future, follow my advice." You will continue to repent until you reach a decision in which you are total. Until then your life will be nothing more than repentance. This totality is only achieved when you become neutral.

Confused, choosing for and against,
The whole world goes astray.
Choiceless and celebrating God;
He is a true sadhu.

The man who has given up all taking of sides, who has dropped all divisions, and who has merged in love is the only seeker who becomes enlightened. This merger can only happen in love, because love has no relation whatsoever to the intellect. This is why the intellect says that love is blind, that love is mad; this is why it says you shouldn't fall into the complexities of love; this is why it says when you are caught in love's entangled web you are lost. The intellect says, "If you stay with me you will be safe. I can think, I can argue, I can discuss for and against, I will be able to help you. But if you go with the heart you will be like a blind man. With the heart there is no thinking, no deliberation, no argument. You will go mad."

There is no greater vision, no more powerful perception than love — but the intellect says that love is blind. Those who have achieved the eye of love have seen all — but the intellect says that love is blind. And from the point of view of the intellect love is definitely blind, because the intellect says to weigh everything, to consider all the arguments for and against before taking any action. And the heart? The heart simply steps into the darkness; the heart takes a jump without thinking about it at all.

The intellect considers the heart to be blind, that is why the intellect has suppressed it. You depend on your intellect, you also do not listen to your heart. You are afraid and so you argue. You say, "Who knows where the heart will lead me?" But Kabir says the seeker who listens to the heart is the only one who is wise, the only one who is a true seeker.

The intellect looks upon love as something one makes, as an act. The intellect considers itself to be very rational, to be very sensible indeed, but what have you ever achieved by thinking, by arguing? Whatsoever has been achieved has been achieved by those who went madly into love. Love will not only annihilate the intellect, love will efface you as well. Love is the fire in which everything is reduced to ashes. Only God will be saved. Only God cannot burn.

People all bound together
As donkey tied to donkey.

People are so tied down by their opinions but being continually *for and against* — just like donkeys that are tied to each other — that they have come to a standstill, they are unable to go anywhere. They simply cannot move any more. Your whole life is like this. You spend your lives tied to things.

Who has inner vision,
He's authentic man.

Kabir says that the man with inner vision will be freed from these ropes, from this bondage. The intellect belongs to the world of thoughts, to the divisions of *for and against,* but the man of inner vision is one who has left all intellectual divisions behind, who has gone deep within himself and reached to his very center.

At present you look at the world through the intellect. But there is another way to look at the world. And it is like this — step down from your brain and into your heart, into the center of life where your soul is. Look at the world from there. Inner vision means looking at the world from this center; intellectual vision is looking from the periphery.

When you start to look at the world with inner vision everything changes — a new manifestation happens. Where yesterday you only saw an object, today you see God. You will see a friend in someone you saw as an enemy yesterday. Where the day before you saw only death, today you will see a doorway to ecstasy. Whatever your intellect told you before yesterday will become meaningless to you now. Now you are looking at life from an absolutely new center.

When the perspective is changed, everything changes. For example — you are enclosed in a dark room with a hole in one wall, and you are looking out at the world through it. You will see something of course, but you will not see the whole view. But based on what your limited range has perceived, you will make decisions about the whole world. And then someone comes and takes you outside; you are taken out of the room into the open sky. You see the moon, the stars, the vast, infinite sky. Now you will be like a man who has given up looking through the intellect and begun to look at the world through his inner vision.

The intellect is just a tiny hole, so whatsoever you see through it will appear very small. It appears very small, not because it is very small but because you are looking at it through a very small hole. When you can set everything aside — all opinions, beliefs and prejudices arrived at through the intellect — and become neutral; when you can stand at the center without the confines of Hindu or Mohammedan, then you will see the infinite sky. You will see the sky in its infinity — the sky where only love is manifest, the sky where only love dances night and day.

Bear in mind that whatever color your glasses are, that is the color you see all around you. Everything looks yellow to the patient suffering from jaundice — his eyes themselves are yellow. And the man who suffers from the intellect sees the whole world in parts, because the intellect itself is divided. The heart is undivided. The heart is whole, total. Inner vision means vision of the heart.

Who has inner vision,
He's authentic man.

Kabir says that a man is only authentic when he possesses inner sight. Before this happens you are a man in name only. You are a man only because you have the form of a man, that is the only qualifying factor; otherwise, there is no difference between you and the animals.

The Sanskrit word for animal, *pashu,* is very interesting. It comes from the word *pash,* meaning one who is tied to something, one who is in bondage. The word is very significant. Pashu does not just mean animal, it also means one who is tied up, one who is in bondage, one who is entangled. The person who achieves inner sight becomes a real man for the first time. Before that he was an animal. Now he is an authentic human being; now his animality, his bondage, is gone. Now such a man is under the open sky.

Now he is no longer a prisoner, now he is liberated.

One who walks alone,
He alone finds truth.

This is a very revolutionary sentence. Kabir is saying that the crowd has never been able to attain to truth. Neither the Hindus as a community nor the Mohammedans as a community have ever attained to truth. Whenever a man attains to truth it is done individually. The crowd has never attained, so do not be part of a crowd. Don't say, "I am a Hindu," because that means you are part of the Hindu community. Has any crowd, any community, any society ever attained? Whenever anyone attains — Buddha, Mahavira, Krishna, Christ, Kabir — he does it on his own. So, walk alone. You are still bereft of truth because you have remained part of a community.

It is difficult for a man to remain alone — the crowd seems to be a great help. But because of the crowd you become involved in thousands of stupid things. You do them just because it is convenient; you think because so many people are doing them they must be right. Millions of people gather in a *Kumbha Mela*, and so you think you should take part because millions of others are doing so. In actual fact there is no relation whatsoever between truth and the crowd. An action is not necessarily right just because it is being done by the crowd, by the community. The reality is quite the opposite — a single man can be right, a crowd can never be right. And the foolish thing is that both you and the rest of the crowd at a Kumbha Mela think there must be some great significance, some tremendous importance in taking a dip in the Ganges.

One Who Walks Alone

You might have heard this particular story. Once a king had a pond dug, and ordered each of his subjects to pour one liter of milk into it so that the pond would eventually be filled with milk. But everyone thought, "If I pour water into the pond at night instead of milk, who will be any the wiser?" So, during the night, all of his subjects poured water into the pond. When the king came to see the pond in the morning he found it filled with water. There was not a trace of milk in it anywhere.

You see, the others think the same as you. Your logic, your way of reasoning is the same as everyone else's. Your calculations are similar; your arithmetic is the same. You are like donkeys tied together.

The crowd acts logically, rationally, but even if the whole world accepts a lie it is still not the truth. Only three hundred years ago the whole crowd believed the sun revolved around the earth. This is not true, but this is what people believed for thousands of years. When Galileo declared that the earth revolved around the sun, no one believed him. He was considered mad, insane. People said, "It is written in all the scriptures that the sun revolves around the earth!"

The word 'sunrise' and 'sunset' are found in all languages, and even now, even after Galileo's discovery, they are still prevalent. Three hundred years have passed since Galileo's death, and science has now established that the sun neither rises nor sets, that the earth revolves and that the sun is stationary — but the words 'sunrise' and 'sunset' are still in use and will probably remain in use forever.

When Galileo was very old he was brought to trial in the court of the pope. The pope said to him, "You must ask for forgiveness, otherwise it is the gallows for you. The Bible cannot be wrong. It is written that the sun rises and that the sun sets. You cannot be wiser than Jesus."

Galileo was a very wise and intelligent man. He said, "Since you order me, I beg your pardon. I will declare that the earth does not revolve around the sun and that the sun revolves around the earth. But my statement will not change the way things are — the sun does not revolve. What difference will anything I say make to the sun? But I shall extricate myself from this difficulty by saying it; I shall be saved from the gallows by saying it. I see no point in opposing you, but I must say this much at least — it is the earth that revolves."

Even if Galileo confirms that the sun revolves around the earth and the whole world believes it, how is that going to alter the truth? The truth is not decided by a majority vote.

One who walks alone,
He alone finds truth.

Whenever anyone has known the truth he has known it by himself, on his own. Why is this? Is it because the crowd as a whole is incapable of rising to that height? It is very difficult even for one among millions to rise to that height. Even in thousands of years it is very difficult to find one person who reaches that height. It will even be difficult, in thousands of years, to find one man reaching that high.

And whenever a man attains to that height, society has done its best to obstruct his path. It has tried all possible ways, because it is an insult to society. Society's ego is affected; society is hurt. That is why we crucified Jesus, gave poison to Socrates, threw stones at Buddha and insulted

Kabir in every conceivable way. We cannot believe it is possible for this weaver Kabir to reach God and for us to be left behind. It is difficult for us to swallow; so we feel it is fine for us to say that he has not reached, to state that he is telling a lie, that his claim is false, that he has gone crazy. But we are not prepared to believe that he has reached God.

Society creates all sorts of obstacles to prevent you from reaching God. Society is an anchor that prevents your ship from moving any further; society is like a dead weight that stops your ship from reaching God.

The very nature of truth is such that it can only be reached in the depths of your silence. You are absolutely alone — there is no space for the other to be there at all. So many of you are sitting here in front of me. All of you meditate; all of you are moving into samadhi. And no sooner do you attain to samadhi than you alone remain, than the crowd disappears. If others sitting near you attain to it, they also become alone. You are not there for them, they are not there for you.

To be in samadhi is to go deeper and deeper into oneself. Being with the crowd means you are standing at the door. As you enter the inner room, the crowd, the market, the highway and all the people disappear, and you remain alone. In that great and hidden solitude your meeting with God takes place. There is no other observer, no other witness. That is why no one can produce a witness to swear that it has happened. If I say I have had a meeting with Him in that deep solitude you may ask, "Who is your witness?" My answer would be, "There is no witness at all. At that point there cannot be any witness. You either believe what I say or you disbelieve it, but no witness to testify to it can be produced."

Your mind will protest; it will tell you not to believe me. Your ego will ask how such a thing can happen. You will say, "I have been left behind and this man has reached? This is not possible! This cannot be!"

If you refuse to believe that Kabir has attained, that Buddha has attained, then the doorway to attainment will be closed to you forever. But if you can accept that Kabir has attained then the door remains open to you. You will say, "If Kabir can attain, then I can attain as well. There is a possibility. When it was possible for Kabir, why should it be impossible for me?"

This is the difference between belief and disbelief. You cannot harm Kabir by your lack of belief, you can only harm yourself. By extolling Kabir you do not add to his greatness — his greatness cannot be heightened — but the quality of the belief, of the faith you have in yourself, is what opens the door of possibility for you.

One who walks alone,
He alone finds truth.

This meeting will only take place when you are alone; this marriage will only take place when you are removed from the crowd; this auspicious moment will only come when you are in absolute solitude. Then the wedding guests have all gone — when the sacrificial fire is being circled there will be no one there to witness it. There will be no priest to recite the Vedic hymns, and so Kabir says, existence itself will sing the hymns of the Vedas. There will be only God or Kabir as a witness. There will be no third party.

Heart absorbed in love
Never again comes back.

When the lover and the beloved meet, there is no returning. The mind becomes so engrossed in love, so much at one with love that the question of turning back does not arise at all. Poets say that the big black bee becomes so engrossed in the lotus that it forgets to fly away when the petals of the lotus begin to close. Such is the case with the lover of God; he does not notice when the petals of existence close in on him from all sides. God surrounds him on all sides, merging him within Himself, and then there is no return.

Wholeness is total vision;
Everything is holy.
Says Kabir: it can't be understood.
This is something unwritten.

At this moment — when you are absolutely alone in total solitude, when you are not on the periphery, when you are standing in your soul, when you are at the center — your total vision unfolds. Then you are total. And in your total vision, totality is visible.

Your vision is complete at present. And you are also incomplete because your desires are not yet entirely fulfilled. If death comes to you and says, "Come with me. Your time is up," you will say, "Please wait a while. Let me finish a few things. I have made a few commitments and they are not yet complete, so let me finish them." But you will never be able to finish them altogether, because in trying to complete them you will have to make many more commitments. They will always remain incomplete. To be complete is not in the nature of sansara, of the world — to remain unfulfilled is its nature.

Here in this world no one is ever able to become

completely satisfied. The only one to become complete is the one who has known this truth — that desires always remain unfulfilled. Even when desires are fulfilled it is never enough. You will only be content when you give up desiring.

As long as you are chasing shadows you will never stop running. You can set out on a pilgrimage trying to ignore the shadow, but the shadow will even follow you there. The man who desires will always meet with dissatisfaction. Desire only begins to fall away from the man who turns his back on it. And such a man will certainly arrive at the experience of totality.

Wholeness is total vision;
Everything is holy.

When desire is totally absent in you, you become total. In that totality you acquire total vision, and in this totality of vision you will experience total ecstasy. All about you, on all sides, you will glimpse God, you will glimpse the one who is total.

Says Kabir: it can't be understood.
This is something unwritten.

"I do not understand that totality," says Kabir. The power of understanding, the one who understands, the intellect, logic — all these have been left behind. Kabir asks, who is there to understand? That is why nothing is understood.

Says Kabir: it can't be understood.
This is something unwritten.

Kabir says he does not understand what is happening now — this falling of the total into the total, this pouring of the total into the total, this marriage of the total with the total. It is as he said in the sutra a few days ago:

Says Kabir: I'm to wed.
And the man's immortal!

Kabir says he does not understand what is happening now, that it is beyond his comprehension, even beyond his imagination.

Says Kabir: it can't be understood.
This is something unwritten.

And this happening is such that it remains unwritten. Kabir says that if he could have read about it, he could have come full prepared. But this kind of thing that has never been written about, never been told, never been explained by anyone before, Kabir says it is so far beyond comprehension that it must remain unwritten.

This is the finality. This is the point beyond which our comprehension is unable to reach. Truth is much greater than your understanding, yet even now you are trying to contain it in your grip — even now you are trying to hold the sky in your fist. This is what Kabir is saying:

Confused, choosing for and against,
The whole world goes astray.

This is why you are confused, why you are disturbed. By being *for and against* you are trying to confine truth in the prison of your own beliefs. You are busy trying to understand truth, but the power of your understanding is so small, how can you attain to truth with it?

Truth is to be lived, not understood. It is possible to be truth, but truth cannot be understood. This is what Kabir means when he speaks of the arising of totality in a man — saying at the same time that the phenomenon always remains beyond comprehension.

Philosophers are busy trying to understand truth while religious people are living it. Be anxious to live in truth, but don't try to understand it. Don't make truth the object of some pointless exercise. No one has ever been able to understand truth; you too will fail. You can live in truth and you can be God, but you cannot know God. You can be one with God, but you cannot establish His existence. You cannot create a science of God but you can live a godly life.

Says Kabir: it can't be understood.
This is something unwritten.

6

WHY WANDER AWAY

Sadhu, who's kidding who?
The formless in forms,
And forms within the formless,
So why wander away?

They say, "He's forever young, immortal,"
But the invisible remains unexpressed;
No family, no character; no color,
Yet permeating every being.

Some say,
"He's in each atom and the whole cosmos."
Others say, "He has no beginning or end."

One says,
"Atomic, cosmic — drop this nonsense!"
Kabir says, "He's Bhagwan!"

Vedas say,
"Beyond forms rests the formless."
With form or not — forget it, blessed woman,
And see in all His home.
Never touched by happiness, sadness;
Darshan day and night.

Covered in light, sleeping on light,
Head resting on light.

Kabir says:
Listen, brother sadhu,
The real master is light throughout.

To call him heavy, I'm much afraid.
To call him light is a lie.
What do I know of Ram?
These eyes have never seen Him.

Life is simple and straightforward. In life nothing whatsoever is complicated. Existence is not a puzzle, but a man's mind is very intricate, and you have made a simple and straightforward thing both complicated and involved. Life is simple and straightforward — and that is the very reason you are unable to attain to life, why you are unable to live life in the right way. If life were arduous the mind would have solved the problem, the mind would have found some way to unravel it.

Existence is just in front of you and you are seeking it somewhere else. Your ego does not enjoy seeking something that is near. It asks, "What fun is there in seeking something close by?" The ego does not like the idea of achieving something which is already achieved; getting that which it does not have, it considers a challenge.

The ego has a habit of turning the simplest of things into the most intricate of problems, and when it has molded things to its own liking, it then takes them as challenges, as things to be achieved. You then become engrossed in solving the very dilemma you have invented yourself. But remember this — if there were any complications in life they would have already been solved. There are no complications in life, and so nothing is ever solved — even though you keep trying, birth after birth.

Preserve this fact in your heart — life is to be lived; it is not a problem to be solved, it is not a mathematical problem. On the contrary, life is a poem to be sung, a dance, a celebration in which you have to participate. Don't stand apart and think about life, don't ponder it. The current of life is a continuous flow. Get into life. Don't stand aloof from it; if you do, your relationship with life, your roots into life will be severed to the same degree.

In these lines Kabir is asking, "To whom should I complain? Who is being deceptive? What is the deceit?" Had this disease been contracted from another the responsibility would be his, but you yourself are the cause of this disease, you yourself are the cause of this deception. The drama of your life is such that you first set up the situation yourself, and then try to unravel it. First you create a problem, a puzzle, and then begin looking for ways to solve it; first you close your eyes and then grope about in the darkness. If someone is sleeping it is easy to awaken him, but if someone is lying awake and pretending to be asleep then how is he to be awakened? And so Kabir asks:

Sadhu, who's kidding who?

Kabir is asking, "What is the deception? Who is the author of this deception? Who should I name? Who should be held responsible for this?" If it were a thief, and he were stealing your property, he could be caught — but you are the thief, and you are the property owner too.

As the quintessence of life, bear this in mind: you will never be able to solve the complexities of your life until you realize that you yourself are the basis and the cause of your own deception. How can you solve it? On the one hand you try to unravel your life, and on the other hand you make it more complicated. And so the whole thing remains virtually as it was in the beginning — there is no progress at all. On the one hand you construct a building, and on the other you knock it down, and so the building is never built, it always remains incomplete. Throughout all your lives you have not made one iota of progress. You are still wandering in the same valley in which you have always wandered.

I have heard that Mulla Nasruddin was once living in a village in the hills. One evening, while he was sitting on his verandah, a car drove up and stopped. The driver asked, "Which is the way to Manali? I have missed the road."

Nasruddin explained the way in great detail; he also drew him a map. The driver thanked him and proceeded on his way. After three hours the driver arrived at Nasruddin's door once again, a very harassed man. "You are a terrible man!" he said, "I followed your map explicitly, and after three hours' driving I am back at the very same place!"

Nasruddin replied, "Yes, I know. Now I shall show you the right way. First of all I wanted to know whether or not you could follow instructions. This was your test. Now I'll show you the right way."

Even after so many births you always find yourself back where you started. Have you progressed as much as an inch since your childhood? It is a possibility you have lost something, but it is a certainty you have gained nothing —

you may even have regressed a few steps. You have not progressed at all. If someone had been pushing you backwards it might be excusable, but no one else is responsible for the condition you are in. And remember, no one but you can reach there either. No one can push you ahead, no one can push you back. No one can mislead you, no one can lead you. The devil does not have the power to mislead you, nor does God have the power to lead you.

Sadhu, who's kidding who?

The beauty of all of this is that you are the only person involved in this drama. You are the actor, you are the director and you are the producer. The drama is your dream, your fantasy. Have you ever thought about who is acting in your dream? No one but you. Who is the director? No one but you. Who is the author of the drama? No one but you. And who is the spectator? No one but you. That is why the enlightened ones have called this world *sansara,* a dream. You are the basis of the dream, you are the root of the dream. You are the basis of the dream, you are the root of the dream, you are the center of the dream. You are the spectator and you are the play.

Sadhu, who's kidding who?

Kabir is asking, "To whom should I complain? To whom can I tell my trouble? To whom can I cry about my sorrows?" You wander here and there asking everyone, "Which is the way out? Where is the key? Where is the door?" You are misleading yourself; you are deceiving yourself. Have you ever asked yourself these questions: "Do I sincerely desire to seek God? Is my search authentic? Is my desire keen? Is my desire sincere?"

Once it happened that a Buddhist monk was on the brink of death. He called all his disciples together and said to them, "I have been explaining to you the way to nirvana, to liberation. I have been telling you about the door to freedom. You have listened to me, but I don't know whether you have understood me or not. You don't seem to move; you don't seem to make any progress whatsoever. You are still where you were when you came to me. In spite of the fact you have been listening to me for years you have not progressed the tiniest bit. Now I am about to leave this body, and so I ask those of you who are really in earnest about achieving liberation to raise your hands."

He had thousands of disciples, and they had all gathered together when they heard his last moments had come. Now they began to look at each other. One disciple stood up, but did not raise his hand. Instead he said, "Please do not misunderstand. I do want to be liberated, but not just now. Yet please show me the way. I am busy with a few problems at present, there is some work as yet incomplete. Let me finish these things first. I shall try to follow the path you have shown me one day. I won't have to worry then, because I will know the way."

You always ask the way. You think it will be helpful to know it now so that you will be able to follow it when some future time comes. But do you really want to reach the goal? Have you ever really desired Him, have you ever yearned for Him with that sincere and powerful longing Sri Aurobindo calls *abhipsa*. He calls it abhipsa and not *akanksha* — even though both words mean desire — to show that it is not ordinary desire, to show that it is a special desire, the desire for God. Akanksha is of the mind; abhipsa is the inner call of life, the call that comes from every cell, from every fiber of the body.

You are like a man who keeps food and drink safely in the refrigerator and eats and drinks whenever he feels hungry or thirsty. But you do not even know what real thirst or real hunger is. Think of a man lost in a desert far away from civilization. The sun is tremendously hot, like fire, and the man is so thirsty he cannot even walk a single, step. He is in great distress, like a fish out of water. Every particle of his body is clamoring for water. At such a moment thirst is not a fancy, as it is when someone feels thirsty at the sight of a Coca-Cola bottle; it is not like it is when someone feels hungry at the smell of some tasty morsel. This man's thirst is not like this; it is not an ordinary thirst he can postpone for a time. This man's thirst is a question of life and death: if the fire in his throat is not quenched within a few moments he is certain to die.

The desire one had at such a critical moment is called abhipsa by Sri Aurobindo. Have you ever longed for God with the intensity of desire that a thirsty man lying in the desert feels? Have you ever yearned for God like that? Have you ever risked your life in search of truth? No? That is why Kabir asks:

Sadhu, who's kidding who?

You do not really long for God.

Now let us look at this question from the other side. If I say to you that I am opening the door to liberation for you right now, are you ready to enter? Will you not say to me, "Please wait a moment; I have to go home for a moment"? If you are ready you will enter immediately without a second's delay. But you will hesitate. You will say, "Many things are still to be done. Many desires are still to be fulfilled." Your mind will argue, it will say, "Liberation is eternal. It is not going to disappear. Let me complete these few things first. They are here this moment, they will not be available again, but liberation will always be there. What is the harm if it waits a little? If I go there tomorrow or the day after, it is all the same. Let me enjoy this sansara, this world of dreams, a little while longer."

The dream of liberation is very sweet and so you say you are not ready to go. You are always asking the way, but you really don't want to make a move — you only want to hear about it. And then you assure yourself that you are a sincere and honest person. "I am not irreligious," you say, "I am longing for truth. But truth is not as easy to obtain as some toy. I shall have to work hard for countless births. Only then will I achieve it." this is how you deceive yourself; this is how you protect yourself. There is no other barrier in your life except you. No one else is barring your way; you yourself are the wall. You have planted your own feet firmly in the ground and are making all kinds of fuss about liberation at the same time.

Your thirst is not the thirst of the desert. It is a false thirst, a deception. If one's thirst is sincere, it is sufficient unto itself; nothing else is to be done. Then your thirst is so strong your whole body is one with it. And then the thirst itself becomes the door. When you call for God like this, he is not even an inch away.

Your thirst is the path. Clamor after God with all your eagerness, with all your sincerity, and the meeting will surely take place.

Sadhu, who's kidding who?

Why Wander Away

But you are great actors. You play this game in such a way that you do not even know you are doing it. You want to have it all — the world as well as truth. You are very crafty. You are sailing in two boats at the same time, so naturally you will never reach anywhere. No one can sail in two boats simultaneously. And remember, these two boats — the boat of religion and the boat of the world — are sailing in opposite directions. You are like the laundryman's donkey; you belong neither to the house nor to the riverbank. It would be better if you were to belong totally to the world than to be like the laundryman's donkey.

If you belong totally to the world, the deception you are practicing will perish one day because you will realize eventually that the world has no substance, that it can never bear fruit. But to avoid such a situation, you live partially in the world and partially in God at one and the same time. This is not the way to experience abhipsa, to experience that keen, inner desire for God. Be aware of your cunning. You have played this game more than enough. How long do you want this game to continue? Come out of it now!

Your mind is behind all this cunningness, behind all this play-acting. The mind has a habit of looking at things in parts, and this creates deception. Whenever you look at things in this way, deception is bound to occur. No matter where you are, always try to look at things in their totality. Your journey will begin from there. Don't look at things in parts. When you see a child being born, know that, along with birth, death is also there. Celebrate the birth of a child and at the same time be sorry; it is also the beginning of death. When an old person dies, weep — but be pleased as well because it is the beginning of a new birth, of a new life.

Why is deception created when you look at things in parts? Deception is created because you consider the part as the whole. That is the deception. You create it yourself. Birth is not a false thing; it is not a deception. Death is not a deception either. But you think of birth as the whole thing and wish to obliterate all trace of death. You wish to forget death completely, and thus the deception is created. Happiness is not a deception, but you look at it as separate from misery, and then there is deception.

You look at the parts and claim each as the whole. If a man is happy and you ask, "How are you?" he will say, "I am very happy." Such a person is living in deception. Misery is already waiting just around the corner. Misery is standing just behind the curtain and yet he says, "I am very happy." He does not know that he will be miserable the next moment. Happiness is not a deception, but now he will tell everyone that happiness is a deception, that it is something false. But the real deception was in his eyes — they saw one half of the thing but did not see the other half.

If you tell someone, "When happiness comes to you, misery is going to follow," he will be displeased with you and ask, "Why do you say such awful things?" If a child is born at someone's house and you say, "Death is being born," you will be considered quite rude and turned out of the house immediately. If an old person is about to die and you begin to dance in celebration, people will say, "What are you doing? Here we are, full of grid, filled with sorrow, and you are dancing! Are you taking revenge onus for something we have done to you in some past life? Why are you celebrating this event?" And if you reply, "This is the beginning of a new life," who is going to listen to you? If a man is in misery and you embrace him joyfully, telling him, "This is the moment to be happy. Your misery will soon be followed by happiness," he will immediately push you away and say, "What a man you are! Here I am, suffering, and you start talking about wisdom and spiritual knowledge! Where is this happiness? My heart is on fire! It is broken; it is in misery!"

When you catch hold of a part and claim it to be the whole, that is deception. You consider the insignificant as the most significant; you take the momentary for the everlasting. When you look at a thing as it is and take it to be something else, that is deception. Then you are the victim of an illusion. This is the essence of illusion, of what the Hindus call *maya*.

Always look at the opposite; always think of the opposite as being just nearby, as being close at hand. Know that death is hidden behind birth. Look at the unhappiness following happiness and look at the happiness following unhappiness, and then you will neither become excited in happiness nor wretched in misery. Then there will neither be smiles in your happiness not tears in your unhappiness. Then you will begin to be beyond both. And to go beyond both is to approach truth. No sooner do you know both simultaneously than you begin to go beyond them. Now you know that neither happiness nor unhappiness, neither birth nor death, neither night nor day will last forever.

Everything comes and everything goes away. But you will last. The witnessing consciousness will last. The witnessing nature will last. The witness will last. All will come and all will go, but experiences do not last. This is why Kabir says:

Nothingness dies, the soundless dies;
Even the infinite dies.

A true lover never dies.
Says Kabir: know this.

All experiences will die. Only the witness will remain.

The formless in forms,
And forms within the formless,
So why wander away?

Kabir says that people are perplexed, confused. Some say that God is without attributes, that he is absolute, and others say He possesses attributes. Some say He has form and others say He is formless. Some say He is the highest happiness; others, that He is the most blissful. And some consider Him so evil that they are unable to accept His existence at all. All religions have their own view, their own opinions about God. All these beliefs are partial, incomplete, and those who entertain such partial beliefs will remain in deception. You may believe that God is blissful, but such a belief is partial — where would evil come from then? If God is all sweetness, then where does the salt in life come from?

The Jews have a very rare book called the *Talmud*. It contains sentences the likes of which are not to be found in any other scriptures in the world. There are sentences like, "God is not nice. God is not your uncle. God is an earthquake." Kabir has also said such things, things like, *The house of love is not your auntie's.*

God is blissful as well as malevolent. The devil is not outside God; he cannot be. God is both. What you call good is in Him, and what you consider as evil is in Him also; both come from Him. Both birth and death are in Him. He is not only the rejoicing at the time of birth, He is also the tears at the time of death. He is darkness as well as light. Looking at things in their totality, and don't worry about what befalls you, because greater calamities will befall you when you see the whole. You will be in great difficulty because all smoothness will vanish from your life. Your intellect will vanish, your capacity for discrimination will disappear and your power of understanding will be uprooted. The ground under your feet will give way and you will tremble. God is both. He is both the earthquake occurs and hundreds of thousands of people perish, that is God too. He is everything — birth and death, night and day. God is all.

The formless in forms,
And forms within the formless...

So don't say He is without form or that He is with form, because the opposites are present in both conditions. God is the ultimate unity of all opposites. All converge in Him; all meet in Him. Nothing is safe from Him. He is the great ocean into which all rivers flow. The sinner and the saint become one in Him.

The distinctions between sin and virtue, between sinner and saint, are our creations. And because of these distinctions we remain in illusion. We worship a saint and hate a sinner: we honor the good and condemn the bad. But God is both. He is as much in the bad man as He is in the good; otherwise how could the bad man live? The bad man exists, and God looks after him.

The formless in forms,
And forms within the formless,
So why wander away?

Kabir says that this is the path, that if you deviate from it, even a bit here or a bit there, you will be lost. To look at the whole is the path. So look at the whole as a whole. Whatever difficulties there may be, whatever impediments there may be no matter how hard it may be for your logic, for your intellect, no matter how much your mind may tremble, you should not worry about anything else at all. You should simply try always to look at the whole.

The intellect always wants to make things smooth and easy. Arithmetic is smooth and easy, that is why our intellects are so very interested in it. Logic is straight and smooth and so the intellect takes a great interest in it as well. Poetry is not so straight, not so smooth, and the intellect is not so interested. Love is a total riddle, and so the intellect never travels that road at all.

God is the ultimate unity of all opposite. "But this cannot be," the intellect argues. "How can anyone believe that night and day are one, that good and bad are one? How is it possible?" "It is impossible," the intellect will say. "It can never be! How can you bring good and evil together? How can you bring night and day together?" It is not necessary to bring them together; they are already united. And here — there is no distinction at all. No one can say when the day is over and the night begins. Each is a part of the same circle.

We think of happiness and unhappiness as quite separate things. But have you ever watched the moment when either happiness or unhappiness begins? Have you ever observed the phenomenon? You will find that all happiness changes into unhappiness. There is no happiness in life that does not turn into unhappiness. And if indeed you could find it, you would have completed a unique research, you would have accomplished something that has never been done before in this world. Nor will you be able to find any unhappiness

Why Wander Away

which does not turn into happiness. You may have to wait a little while for it, but it will surely change.

All things change into their opposites. Youth turns into old age, beauty changes into ugliness. All things change thus. A flower falls and turns into dust, and out of that dust a tree is born. Everything is joined to its opposite. In actual fact nothing like "opposite" exists, but we say one thing is opposite to another just to express it, just to be able to indicate the change.

When you give up the idea of oppositeness, your intellect will stop working and your faith will be born. Your power of discrimination will cease to work and faith will take its place within you. The quality of faith is so powerful that faith can see the opposite of a thing at the same time. It can see both the thing itself and its opposite. The intellect is very weak — it does not have the capacity to see the thing and its opposite at the same time. The intellect sees in parts, and it avoids looking at something that seems beyond reason, at something that appears difficult. The intellect works in a logical way. It is like a gardener who keeps the front garden well-trimmed and tidy. In front of the house the dry leaves and withered flowers are all swept away. There, old age is unseen and death is unknown.

There was once a Zen monk who was an expert gardener, and so the king of that country sent his son to him. About a thousand gardeners worked in the king's garden, and what the prince learned from the Zen monk he conveyed to the gardeners and they followed his instructions. The monk had said to the prince, "I shall come to see your garden in three years. That will be your test. Just keep on working according to my instructions." The instructions were not difficult to follow. There were one thousand gardeners and so the garden grew very well.

After three years, the monk came to examine the prince's work. That day the garden looked superb. It was perfectly clean; not a dry leaf or fallen flower was to be seen on the ground. The king and his courtiers were also present. The monk, after looking all around, seemed disappointed. The prince grew quite nervous. He had followed the monk's every instruction. He had done his best, he thought, so he asked himself what could possibly be causing the monk's obvious displeasure. The monk went around the whole garden, growing progressively sadder and sadder. At last he said to the prince, "This will not do. You will have to study the art for three more years. This garden has been done in a totally wrong way."

The prince said, "Please tell me what mistake I have made. I have followed your instructions to the very letter. I have done nothing whatsoever that goes against your instructions."

The monk replied, "That is the mistake. You have done everything according to my instructions. You have followed them completely. You have done everything so completely there is no room left for God's own work. All there is to be seen all over is human effort. The mistake may appear small, but it is very significant because you have missed the point. I'll correct it."

He ran off and returned with a basketful of dry leaves from a pile of rubbish and threw the leaves on the ground. They were carried here and there by the wind and finally spread themselves all over the garden. Then the monk said, "Now the mistake is corrected. Green leaves alone do not make a garden. Where were all the dry ones?"

To think of youth alone is self-deception; one must think of old age at the same time. The prince had only used his intellect, and the intellect always looks at things from just one side. The prince had preserved the beautiful and removed the ugly.

But there is also ugliness in the garden of life. There are both the intelligent and the dull-witted, the seekers and the nonseekers, the saintly as well as the satanic. All of these exist in the garden of life. And the garden of life is so vast. If there were only seekers living in a society, then it would be like this garden of the prince — green only, just a human creation. God's hand would not be evident there.

If you want to see God's hand, God's creation, you will find it in the jungle, not in a garden. If you want to see God's handiwork, visit the jungle. Things grow there in such mysterious ways you will not be able to understand it. There is neither rhyme nor reason; there is no arithmetical calculation, no logical reasoning. Things grow there by their own life-force; they seek their own way. The beauty of the jungle cannot be found in a garden, because the jungle is the embodiment of the vastness of the omnipresent God. In us, the jungle can create a confidence in the ultimate. Opposites are always there. A garden is a lowly thing, a man-made creation. Everything there is certainly neat and well-groomed, but because of that it is dead.

Life is to be lived in opposites. Life is composed of opposites. And it is beautiful because of them. Whenever you dispense with an opposite your action may appear logical, but truth is lost, religion is lost.

The formless in forms,
And forms within the formless,
So why wander away?

To see formlessness in form and form in formlessness is the straight way, Kabir says. Then you will not miss the path. Then there will never be any need to leave it, because it is the correct path. To remain in the middle of opposites is the right path. And to remain alert while in the middle is the proper way.

If you choose one of the opposites you will be afflicted by intellect, and so both the believer and the nonbeliever remain in confusion. Neither of them is religious — what concern has the religious person with atheism or with theism? For the religious man there are just two alternatives — he is neither this nor that, or he is both at the same time — but he is never one of them.

The religious person cannot be a theist. To be a theist is far too trivial; it means he must say "yes" and ignore "no." How can "yes" help you on its own if you do not have the strength of conviction to say "no"? There is no force whatsoever in the "yes" of a man who cannot say "no" — but there is force in the "yes" of the man who can say "no"!

The person who cannot say "yes" and can only say "no" is also diseased. There is no meaning or substance in his "no" either. But the man who can say both "yes" and "no" simultaneously is able to experience the total truth about life. Unless this happens to you, you will remain in illusion. God expects both things to be in you at the same time. He expects the impossible from you; nothing less will do. This is why only extremely adventurous and daring people set out on the

Why Wander Away

path to God. What greater adventure is there in life than seeing the opposites at the same time?

The theists thought that Kabir was not a theist, and the atheists thought that he was not an atheist; the Hindus thought he was a Mohammedan, and the Mohammedans thought he was a Hindu. Kabir remained in the middle. A religious man will always be a puzzle to others, because sometimes he will say "yes" and sometimes he will say "no."

Kabir was the essence of the Vedas themselves, but at times he would speak out in opposition to them; Kabir was a buddha himself, but at times he would say, *Nothingness dies.* Kabir's words have bee included in the Guru Granth of the Sikhs by the disciples of Nanak, and yet Kabir says, about Aum, *The soundless dies, Even the infinite dies.* Kabir is a jungle. He is like a puzzle; he is difficult to comprehend. Scholars have written volumes on Kabir and they have all tried to trim him, to turn him into a well-groomed garden; they have tried to bring him into line with their thinking. And these scholars are honored in the universities.

I have heard a story. There was once a king who was a great lover of birds. One evening a very strange bird came and sat on his windowsill. The king exclaimed, "What! Can such a bird as this exist?" Such a bird was impossible to find in the king's realm. It was a bird of foreign origin, just passing by on its journey. It was tired and so it sat on the king's windowsill for a rest. The king became worried it might leave, and so he had it caught. He had its wings clipped and reshaped like those of the birds of his country. The bird's beak was quite large and so he also had it cut down to size.

During these operations the bird wept and cried, trying to free itself, trying to get away, but the king would not allow it to go. "No matter what happens," he said, "no matter how difficult it is, this bird must be made into the proper form and the proper shape. This poor bird does not know how birds should be. It seems he has never seen himself in a mirror. What kind of bird can have such wings and such a beak?" So he had the beak and wings clipped and made the strange bird into a model of a perfect bird. Then he said, "Now, dear bird, you can fly away." But it had no strength to fly away. Crying and writhing, it died there on the spot. This is a Sufi story.

The scholars were after Kabir. They wanted to clip his wings, to interpret him according to their own ideas. And that is what they have done. But their Kabir is a dead Kabir; he is well-trimmed, but he is just a shell. There is no life in their Kabir, no substance. Whenever you do a lot of intellectual trimming you lose the substance of the thing you are altering.

You have become lifeless through excessive use of your intellect. You may not have trimmed anyone else with it, but you are certainly doing it to yourself. You have a model, an ideal, and you try to become like that. There cannot be greater stupidity than this. Try to be like yourself. There is no one else like you. You don't have to become like Buddha or Mahavira or Kabir; you have to become yourself. After your death God will not ask you, "Why did you not become like Kabir?" If he were to ask this question at all, He would ask it of Kabir; why should He ask it of you? He will not ask you, "Why did you not become like Mahavira?" Have you any obligation to become like Mahavira? If you trim yourself outwardly; if you become like Mahavira as some Jaina monks do, or like Buddha as some Buddhist monks do, then you will die. These imitators are already dead. Your so-called sadhus and saints are like corpses, and the reason is that they have not tried to become themselves, but have tried to become like someone else.

To be one's own self is a rare phenomenon. Your wings are your wings — there is no formula as to how they should be. The only purpose of wings is to enable you to fly, that is enough. Their shape, their style, their aspect, their color — all these are perfect if they enable you to fly. It is wings that make you free, wings will fly you into the sky. Make your consciousness into your own consciousness. And if you find a dense forest inside, do not be afraid. And do not listen to the advice of your intellect — it will advise you to trim your garden, to keep things neat and tidy. A tidy garden always becomes a prison; a vast jungle is needed for freedom. Freedom is a union of all opposites, a unity of all the opposites.

No one will be able to understand Kabir correctly. A believer in a God of formlessness will say that Kabir keeps on babbling on about God, saying things like *A true lover never dies*. A believer in a God with form will ask what kind of a worshipper Kabir is because he says nothing to contradict the concept of formlessness. No one who tries to understand Kabir intellectually will agree with him, but if you set your intellect aside and then try to understand him, you will certainly find great light in him.

The formless in forms,
And forms within the formless,
So why wander away?

Then Kabir says:

They say "He's forever young, immortal,"
But the invisible remains unexpressed...

Kabir is saying not to be confused by what is written in the scriptures: what is, what exists, cannot be written down, cannot be described. Some scriptures assert that God is formless and others insist that God has form, but don't let these contradictions confuse you.

They say, "He's forever young, immortal..."

Kabir is saying, "Don't be confused; don't be perplexed by what is being said."

But the invisible remains unexpressed...

What God is cannot be said. Why?" All words have been coined by the intellect, and they all share a certain peculiarity — none of them can describe anything completely. That is each word's speciality. If you say that God is favorable you reject the unfavorable. And if you say He is unfavorable, you reject the favorable. Words can only describe things partially, and this is our helplessness. Words can only speak about parts. If you go into a shop and say to the shopkeeper, "Give me this and don't give me this," at the same time, then how will you strike a bargain? Saying yes and no at the same time will not do.

Life functions on incomplete words because what you know as life is itself incomplete. It is man-made; to run it, the currency of words is needed. And it is essential that this currency, these words, be unambiguous, otherwise how could you lead your life? There would be anarchy and confusion. Your words should be quite clear and unambiguous so that whoever hears them can understand you correctly.

Why Wander Away

In life, we have to accept many untruths. When you were born you had no name. Then you were given a name, a label. It is a false label. You are known as Ram, or Krishna, or Rahim, according to the name your family has given you. No one is born with a name; everyone is born nameless. But you cannot remain nameless after your birth. The postman would have to come and ask, "Where is that man who has no name?" If there were only one person without a name there would be no difficulty. He would be know as *Anam,* as nameless. But if everyone were known as Anam, it would be extremely difficult to find the right person.

The police were once in search of a man who has committed a crime and they happened to learn that Mulla Nasruddin knew him well. So a policeman came to Nasruddin and said, "We have heard you know this person very well."

Nasruddin exclaimed, "Very well? I don't even know myself very well!"

The officer retorted, "We have not come here to discuss metaphysical questions. We only want to know if this man is fat or thin."

Nasruddin thought for some time and then replied, "One could say he is both. He is neither fat nor thin. He is in the middle."

The officer said, "Then forget about that. Is he tall or short?"

Nasruddin replied, "Don't put me into a muddle. This man is of medium height."

Then he asked, "Is there anything particular about this

man that might help us distinguish him from others?"

Nasruddin replied, "He is just like any other human being. He has two eyes, a nose, ears. He has all these things. He is nothing special."

The policeman said, "This is becoming very difficult," and began to ask more direct questions. "Has he a mustache?"

Nasruddin said, "Yes, he has. He is a man, why shouldn't he have a mustache?"

"What is the mustache like?"

Nasruddin replied, "How can I tell you? He always keeps trimming it."

This is what would happen. So although it is untrue, a name is required. In the world, in sansara, people go through their entire lives with these untrue labels, with these adopted names. One's name is a convenience; it is not a truth. Although language is needed to move in this world, language does not express truth. The truth cannot be expressed. If you try to do so, not only will you be perplexed but you will confuse others also.

Language is created for communication between people. God is not a person to be communicated with. He is not the object of some communication. There is not going to be any discussion whatsoever between you and truth. Language is not needed there at all, only deep silence is essential. There, all words, all languages, all names and address are left behind. There, only the one you brought with your birth and will carry with you after your death will remain. There, all that has been done between birth and death is simply of no use. That is the difficulty; that is the rub.

Why Wander Away

But the invisible remains unexpressed...

No one can describe truth; no one can express it. No scriptures, no Vedas, no Koran can express it. They have tried. They have given hints, but all efforts have been to no avail. And no effort will ever succeed because language can only express the incomplete. it has only been created for that purpose. It does not aspire to express the whole.

Whenever you try to rise a bit above your ordinary daily experiences, you find it difficult to express things fully in words. The poet experiences this difficulty because what he wishes to say is of the higher strata, of the beyond — yet somehow he manages to say what he wants to. But the enlightened man has a far greater difficulty to face. He wants to describe the ultimate, and so he has to bring it down to a lower level and express it in the ordinary language of the market. And in doing so, everything that is important and substantial is lost. The whole form is changed and something else emerges.

They say, "He's forever young, immortal,"
But the invisible remains unexpressed...

And then he says:

No family, no character; no color...

Kabir says God has no caste, no form, no color, so how can you describe Him? Whether you say He is without form or you say He is with form, both your statements are incomplete. All qualities are His, and yet there is not a single quality in Him.

Let us try to understand this in detail. It is absolutely correct to say that all forms are His, yet He has no form at all.

He cannot be in all forms if He Himself has any particular form. Because He assumes all forms so easily, it is therefore evident He has no form Himself. He is formless and manifest in all forms.

When water is poured into a clay pot it assumes the shape of the pot, and if it is poured into a jug it assumes the shape of the jug. Water does not insist on having its own shape. If water insisted on having its own shape, it would not assume the shape of the jug. But if you make water so cold that it turns into ice, then it assumes a shape. If you were to try to put it into a jug then, the jug would break. The ice will not take the shape of the jug. Water does not insist on having any shape or form. Water is easy; it is not obstinate at all. If water is turned into vapor, then it attains to an almost formless state. Up to a short distance vapor can be seen, but then it becomes invisible.

Water has three forms. One is formless; it spreads into the sky, leaving no trace behind it; it cannot be found no matter how you try. The second form, the middle one, is that of water. It does not insist on having any particular shape but yet has some shape, because it assumes the shape of the container into which it is poured. The last form is that of ice. Ice is obstinate. A fluid thing like water can become as hard as stone!

You also have these three states. You either become obstinate like ice — and this is the condition of great ignorance — or you can be like water. This latter condition is the state of the wise man, of the man who is not yet fully awakened though he has achieved glimpses of consciousness. Now he is no longer obstinate; now he will adopt the form of wherever it is he is placed. And third, we come to the

Why Wander Away

condition of the fully enlightened man, to his condition when he is merged in the supreme consciousness. Now nothing remains to assume shape; now he is like vapor.

People often used to ask Buddha, "Where will you be when you leave this body?" Buddha used to reply, "I cannot go anywhere. I shall be lost, merged into the vastness of consciousness." Meister Eckhart was a very wonderful Christian saint, and someone once asked him too, "When you leave the body, where will you be then?" Eckhart replied, "There is no need to be anywhere." The listener could hardly have understood his answer, because his language was the language one uses to explain the nature of vapor.

Where does vapor go? Now the whole sky is its abode. Water has a certain place it must keep, but water is humble and adaptable and not hard as stone, like ice is. Water adopts the shape of the container into which it is put. And then there is the state of ice, the state of deep ignorance. The state of vapor is the state of supreme knowledge. The state of water is the state of the seeker. He has ceased being like ice and is preparing himself to be like vapor. As a seeker, he is standing in the middle. Can there be any form to God? He is all types of shapes and forms: He is in ice, in water and in vapor. All forms are His, and yet He has no form at all.

Yet permeating every being.

Then Kabir says:

Some say,
"He's in each atom and the whole cosmos."
Others say, "He has no beginning or end."

People say God is in everybody as well as in the universe, but Kabir says God has neither beginning nor end. A body has a beginning and a body also has an end. So has a universe. All are created and all will disappear, but God has neither beginning nor end. This statement does not make clear what we want to say. These hints about Him are not enough. Our minds grow confused: we arrive at the end of our wits. To describe Him, our thoughts are impotent.

Some say,
"He's in each atom and the whole cosmos."
Others say, "He has no beginning or end."

One says,
"Atomic, cosmic — drop this nonsense!"
Kabir says, "He's Bhagwan!"

Set aside the individual, the universe, the shape and the shapelessness, form and formlessness; set all these ideas aside and then say like Kabir, *He has no beginning or end.* If you are able to say something, then it will be about God. Raidas has said, God is not the way you describe Him; He is something like this and something like that.

Kabir says, you will not be able to say that he is with form or that he is without form; that He is the universe or the vastness or any such thing. Kabir says to stop saying anything. Then if you can say something, no matter what it is, it will be God.

In actual fact you will not be able to describe Him at all, you will have to keep complete silence. He is that silence. Only silence can tell you what God is. No words can describe Him, you will be speechless. You will be like the dumb man who tastes the sweet, is pleased, and smiles. He is not able to express the taste, he is only able to smile. You will be like that. But every fiber of your being will be smiling, because now there will be silence and emptiness from your side and wholeness from His. No sooner do you become empty than you are filled. Then God comes to dwell in you; then the guest has entered within. You will not be able to say what has happened, but your whole being will express the happening.

The sweets of a dumb one —
He enjoys ...and smiles.

And then:

Vedas say,
"Beyond forms rests the formless."
With form or not — forget it, blessed woman,
And see in all His home.

Kabir says the state of formlessness is beyond the state of form, that the state of formlessness begins where the state of having form ends. Formlessness begins where form ends.

With form or not — forget it, blessed woman,
And see in all His home.

In the original Hindi sutra, Kabir uses *sohagin* for "blessed woman," for the devotee. It is a very beautiful word. Sohagin is a woman whose husband is living, but Kabir uses this word in a spiritual sense, to indicate one who has achieved God. The opposite of sohagin is *abhagin,* a widow. Spiritually speaking, a widow is one who has not yet attained to Him. Her search is still on. Your life is like that of a widow so long as you have not attained to Him. The life of a widow is like a desert in which no springs of water flow, in which no flowers bloom. But no sooner do you achieve God than you become sohagin, than you share the experience of Kabir:

*Kabir says: clouds of love
Came on me showering;
Soaked the heart,
Greening the inner jungle.*

Generally, the life of a worldly person is like that of a widow. Kabir has chosen a very good symbol. Imagine the condition of a widow. She once had everything, but now all her joy and sparkle have gone. This is why widows do not wear colored clothes; it is symbolic. There are no inner joys, no inner colors any more, so there is no question of showing any color on the outside. Her bangles are broken because the jingling sound of bracelets no longer suits her; all make-up is now finished for her as well. In the old days, a widow even used to burn herself on the funeral pyre of her dead husband.

Really speaking, you are not alive until you achieve God. Your life is like a funeral pyre; you are just like a widow sitting on the funeral pyre. You may keep on doing many things but there will be no music in your life. The music of life will only begin to play when your consciousness joins the dance of the supreme consciousness. Then there is rejoicing:

*Says Kabir: I'm to wed.
And the man's immortal!*

Then your life will be tremendously valuable. It will be just as Kabir says:

*When the bride meets His embrace
The guests all fade away.*

Then, all of a sudden, all your worldly affairs — the shop, the services you perform, your other outside activities — seem pale in comparison, seem to be of no importance whatsoever. But at the present you are caught in the net of these worldly affairs like a fish, and so you forget your self. But no sooner does the lover come to you than all else pales, than all your confusion disappears. Such a condition is called sohagin by Kabir. Kabir calls a *bhakta,* a devotee, a sohagin.

Kabir says, go beyond the Vedas — they are nothing but words, nothing but language, nothing but principles. They are just literature. Who can reduce to writing that which is beyond writing? Go beyond all written things.

With form or not — forget it, blessed woman,
And see in all His home.

Kabir is addressing the devotee, the lover of Ram. He tells the sohagin to forsake both form and formlessness.

As soon as you give them up too, as soon as you give up duality, oppositeness, you will find Him present in every place. Then there is a holy place in every atom; then there is worship in your every breath. Then everything is holy because He is everywhere — in the flowers and in the stones, in happiness and in misery, in birth as well as in death. Then you are no longer a tiny stream. You have met the ocean — you have fallen into the sea. You have become one with Him.

And see in all his home.

The Kabir says:

Never touched by happiness, sadness;
Darshan day and night. Covered in light,
Sleeping on light, head resting on light.

Kabir says: Listen brother sadhu,
The real master is light throughout.

Kabir says that there, neither happiness nor unhappiness

exists, so be careful. When you go in search of religion, honestly speaking you are in search of happiness. Understand that your search is not yet authentic; realize that it has not yet begun. You do not know what you are doing yet. You are creating sansara, worldliness, even in religion.

Anand, bliss, does not mean happiness. It does not mean great happiness either. It means there is neither happiness nor unhappiness, and so there is no antonym, no word opposite in meaning to anand, to bliss. It is a unique word: all words have antonyms, but there is none for bliss. There cannot be — it is symbolic for oneness, for where the two have disappeared. In bliss, there is neither happiness nor unhappiness, neither peace nor restlessness; in bliss, all dualities have gone and only God remains. And when neither happiness nor unhappiness exist for you, there is bliss twenty-four hours every day.

If God is lost to you it is because there is some curtain before your eyes. It may be happiness or it may be unhappiness, but each of them is a curtain. Your eyes become clear when neither is there. Then only God is seen the whole day long. Then you will not go to Mecca or to Kashi or to Kailash. Then for you, in the whole twenty-four hours, there will be no one but Him. Every breath will be His breath.

Covered in light, sleeping on light,
Head resting on light.

What is the condition of the sohagin, of the devotee, at such a moment? That supreme light has become his bed, his blanket, his pillow.

Kabir says: Listen, brother sadhu,
The real master is light throughout.

Such a sohagin becomes a *satguru,* a true master, because his whole life is filled with the vision of God. Now his life is light, nothing but light — now he is totally light itself. But you are in total darkness at present.

Once Mulla Nasruddin was going on a pilgrimage. At a particular station he was arrested by the police. They suspected him of having something prohibited in his bedroll because he seemed to be overly careful of it. Policemen are always of a suspicious nature. If you put your hand into your pocket frequently, a pickpocket will suspect there is something valuable there and will rob you. When there is nothing valuable in a man's pocket, he never puts his hand into it to check.

Because Nasruddin was checking his bedroll frequently, the police asked, "What is in your bedroll?"

The Mulla replied, "Only things that are needed for sleeping. What else would there be in a bedroll?"

A policeman said, "Perhaps, but we have our doubts. Open your bedroll." It was opened. Everything the Mulla needed for sleeping was there, but there were also two bottles of wine. Jokingly, the policeman asked, "Do you use these as a covering or as part of your bed?"

The Mulla replied, "I use them as pillows."

There is a world of darkness where unconsciousness is a pillow, a headrest. And darkness is your covering, your bed. You live, pressed between darkness and unconsciousness.

The condition of a sohagin is the opposite of this — he sees God all around him; he is surrounded by light. He sees God in every atom; he glimpses light in every particle of matter. That is why the enlightened ones have so often asserted that God is light — why the Koran, the Upanishads and the Bible all say that God is light. You will even see His light during the darkest night of the dark of the moon. Darkness no longer exists for you then; it was only there because your eyes were closed. When you awaken there is light all around; then the light of God becomes your bed, your blanket, your pillow.

Kabir says: listen, brother sadhu,
The real master is light throughout.

At such a moment the sohagin becomes the satguru, the real, authentic master. Yesterday he was in search; today he has achieved. Now his whole being — every atom, every breath, every beat of his pulse — is nothing but light.

It is an arduous task for you to see God — you have to prepare a receptacle to receive Him; you must be fit enough to contain Him. It is easy to see a master because he is the middle rung. He is something like you and yet something of him is not like you. If you only look at that which is like you, you will ask, "What is there in him? He is just a human being like me. Why should I bow down to him? Why should I surrender to him? Why? What is so special about him? He is just like me!" But if you set the likeness aside and look for that which is not like you — if you seek this lovingly and sincerely, very soon you will find it. And then a relationship between him and you will be formed. Now you will be able to accept him, because half of him is also like you. Now he can extend his hands to you; now he can help you.

The master is like a halfway camp on the climb to God. You will not be able to proceed on your pilgrimage directly or without help; in the halfway camp you will not only be able to rest, you will also be able to prepare yourself for the further journey. The master is food for the journey; he will prepare you. And then one day you will reach — you too will become light, nothing but light.

The master is a unique phenomenon — he is the greatest wonder in this world. He is just a human being, just an ordinary person, and yet he has something that is not human, that is out of the ordinary; he carries information of the other world. He has seen something special; he has seen some special light. And you can glimpse this light in his eyes.

But everything depends on you, on how you look at him, because his behavior and most of his habits are just like yours. If you can see only this you will be lost in it, and the door to further progress will remain closed to you. And you will be responsible. The trick to seeing the master, to recognizing him, is to eliminate that in him which is also in you and to seek in him that which is not in you. If you can get to that, then seek his help. Then he will be an alchemist to you, and with his help you will begin to transform yourself. It is just like turning milk into curd — you just put a spoonful of curd into the milk. The master is like a spoonful of curd. Until yesterday he was just like you; he was milk too.

Bear the various stages of milk in mind. If you simply allow it to be, it turns sour — and everyone reaches this state at the time of his death unless he becomes curd in time. But for you to become curd it is necessary some curd be put into you; that will change your inner chemistry. With the master's help you will become curd, and then the rest of your journey will be smooth; then you will not need any help.

But for the milk to be turned into curd in the first place the link is needed. That link is the spoonful of curd. A spoonful of curd must be added to you.

The master will also taste a little bitter; he will taste a bit sour as well. He will break you, he will smash you, he will completely transform the chemical processes within you, and you may feel a bit bitter, a little sour too.

If you just keep waiting, you will miss the opportunity — you will become sour milk. And it is very difficult to turn sour milk into curd; this is not the order of the process. Another birth will be needed; new milk will be needed. And then, again, there will be all that waiting for the spoonful of curd. If you become mixed with curd before you turn sour, a transformation will take place in you. The master is like curd.

Kabir says:

Covered in light, sleeping on light,
Head resting on light...

Then:

Kabir says: listen, brother sadhu,
The real master is light throughout.

And the last sutra:

To call him heavy, I'm much afraid.
To call him light is a lie.
What do I know of Ram?
These eyes have never seen Him.

Here, Kabir is saying something very unique. When the whole of one's consciousness is filled with light; when the whole of life is filled with light; when He is evident everywhere, a very strange thing happens — it becomes very difficult to describe what is being seen. It becomes difficult even to say that something is actually being seen, there is not even that much ego left. The observer and the observed have become so united, so at one with each other, that there is no more distance. And without distance the eyes cannot see. That is why Kabir says:

To call him heavy, I'm much afraid.
To call him light is a lie.

You ask me what God is. I am afraid to say He is heavy because you will misunderstand. You will misunderstand because He is also present in the smallest, in the lowliest. And if you hear me say He is heavy you will at once decide that He can be in the Himalayas but not in a grain of sand. You will decide He can be in holy people but not in sinners; because I say He is heavy, in the sky but not in the ground. Kabir says:

To call him heavy, I'm much afraid.

All the enlightened ones are afraid to speak to you, afraid to say anything to you. Before truth was achieved they were not afraid to talk to you, but after the achievement they are afraid to speak about Him to the ignorant. And there is also the fear you will misunderstand what they say. If I say to you that God is lowly I will also be telling you a lie, because He is not lowly; He is not light. God is heavy; He is not insignificant at all. Yet I am also afraid to say He is heavy, because He is hidden in the lowly as well. He is like the Himalayas even in an atom. He is hidden in His total infinity even in the smallest and shallowest breath. There is great difficulty in trying to describe Him. In his totality and wholeness He is even hidden in a sinner.

Why do I know of Ram?
These eyes have never seen Him.

This is the ultimate situation of an enlightened man; this is when he experiences the final helplessness. God is beyond description; God is beyond sight, and although He is present all around, although He is all pervading, no eyes can see Him. All eyes are absorbed into His eyes; all light has merged into the greater light.

Sufi fakirs say that eyes are also part and parcel of light, of the sun. They say eyes exist so they can see the sun, so that one equal can see and know another equal. And the Sufis also say that when God's great light is manifest your eyes are absorbed into it, just as ice is absorbed when it melts and mixes with water. When the eyes are absorbed and the person hidden behind the eyes is also absorbed, this is the point when Kabir says:

What do I know of Ram?
These eyes have never seen Him.

As long as "I" is there, there is no God. And when God becomes manifest there is no "I"; "I" is lost. Along with the passing of the ego, of "I," The eyes also disappear. In the English language there is only one sound for the words "eye" and "I." To distinguish between them they are spelled differently, but it seems as if those who coined these words must have done it intentionally, because both are pronounced alike. They also have a deep relationship. When "I" is lost, the eyes are also lost — and when the eyes are lost, "I" is lost too. That is why we pity the blind so much. We do not pity the deaf or the dumb or the lame as much as we pity the blind. We do not even pity the dead quite as much. The man who has no eyes has nothing — he is deprived of virtually everything.

Eighty percent of your ego is created by your eyes. Your eyes are primarily responsible for the ego, and so when the whole ego disappears the eyes disappear too.

What do I know of Ram?
These eyes have never seen Him.

So, Kabir says, anything I say about Him will be incorrect.

Tale of love, untellable.
Not a bit is ever told.
The sweets of a dumb one —
He enjoys... and smiles.

7

ENTER YOUR TEMPLE

Sadhu, consider this:
Ride in a boat and drown midstream;
Helpless, get across.

Reach the town by some back way;
Get looted on the highway.
By one rope all get tied,
Both the bound and the free.

Enter your temple;
Be bathed from all sides.
Who remains without stays dry.
Chop off the head for eternal joy;
An unchopped head is suffering.

The whole world looks without seeing,
Eyes remaining blind.
Says Kabir: I understand,
Seeing the ways of the world.

To be the opposite to what you are at present is the path. You will attain if you walk in the direction opposite to that in which you are now walking. The Ganges flows towards the ocean, and Gangotri, the source, is left far behind. And as the Ganges proceeds further, the distance from Gangotri will

Enter Your Temple

increase. The path to the ocean is not the way to reach the Gangotri. To reach its source, the Ganges will have to turn back. When the Ganges of your consciousness flows in the opposite direction, flows towards its Gangotri, then you will be able to attain. The one you have missed has been missed at that source. He is not ahead of you; you have left Him somewhere behind. Ponder this deeply. This sutra of Kabir's draws our attention to this fact.

Kabir says that this is the most important piece of knowledge for a *sadhu,* for a seeker, to understand — Him you are seeking has been left behind. He was once part of you, but now you are missing Him. You were once the total celebration of existence; you were once innocence incarnate. You were born a sadhu, a person devoid of sin. Everyone is born a sadhu; *sadhuta,* sinlessness, is your nature. Your state of nonsinlessness has been earned; it has been learned. Through your own cleverness you have become *asadhu,* nonsinless.

In your innocence, when you were born, you were certainly a sadhu. At the time of their births, all children are great sadhus, but by and by they are given the poison of sansara, of the world — education and information impressions and ideas that cut them off from their real nature. A child is cut off from his own center, and the search for it goes on his whole life. But his search is in accordance with tradition, in agreement with the rules of society — and this is the problem. You follow these traditions and move farther and farther away from the ecstasy you are seeking. By following the rules which have caused your downfall, you keep going further and further astray.

Society has become your guru; you have completely

stopped listening to the dictates of your own conscience. Within you, society has created a conscience that is absolutely false. Whenever you think of committing a theft or some other evil act, someone within you tells you not to do it. But this someone, this conscience, is given to you by society; it is not the voice of yourself. Society teaches you what is good and what is bad, and so there are different kinds of consciences in different countries, in different communities. If your conscience were the one given to you by God and it had not been touched by society, its voice would be the same throughout the world, the same down the ages. That voice is eternal perpetual.

If you want to kill someone, your conscience — a gift from society and therefore a deception — will tell you not to kill. But suppose you become a magistrate. That same conscience will not say to you now, "Don't sentence anyone to capital punishment." You will send hundreds to the gallows without any feeling whatsoever. Or say you go to war. Only yesterday the conscience given to you by society said that killing was sinful — even if you killed an ant you used to feel guilty inside — but now, on the battlefield, you will kill others with all your heart and with all your might. And that very conscience society has given to you will tell you that you are doing your duty, that you are doing a great thing, that you are a great hero. People will throng around your funeral pyre to pay their last respects to you, and your name will be immortal, written in the annals of history.

Whether you wanted to murder someone, were a magistrate in the court or a soldier on the battlefield, the voice of your own conscience, of your natural conscience, would be consistent. It would say that you are committing a sin to kill, that it is wrong to destroy because God is the creator of all. It would say, "Who are you to kill, to destroy? If you do so, you are moving away from God." In each and every situation your true conscience, your authentic conscience will pronounce its judgment without any "ifs," without any preconditioning — it will simply say that killing is bad. But your society-given conscience will advise you according to its own convenience or inconvenience. If it is in the interest of society it will even say that killing is a religious act, that it is holy. The real question is not one of killing or of not killing, it is one of convenience or inconvenience to society.

You will never be able to find your own conscience while you remain filled with the one society has given to you. You are using this false conscience in your attempt to seek your real conscience. You are trying to reach religion by the path of morality, but it is morality itself that has bereft you of religion.

These words of Kabir are very revolutionary. One would not believe a saint could utter such words. But remember, only a saint can say such things because a saint is a great revolutionary. He doesn't care about the result; good or bad, he doesn't care what society will think. Try to understand Kabir's words:

Sadhu, consider this:
Ride in a boat and drown midstream;
Helpless, get across.

And then he says:

Reach the town by some back way;
Get looted on the highway.

Kabir says that the man who walks on the main highway gets robbed and that the man who takes the back way, the opposite way, reaches his destination. The sage takes the opposite road, his Ganges has begun to flow towards the Gangotri, towards the source. While society wanders about in the outside world, he turns his back on society and begins to travel within. He does not listen to what society says; he listens to what his own conscience says.

The path of the sage is always the opposite one. That is why we crucify a Jesus; it is not done without reason. And that is why we go on ignoring Kabir, why we try to forget him, why we even doubt his very existence. We poison Socrates and we chop off the hands and feet of Mansoor — none of this is done without a reason. There is a reason. These people are very dangerous to society; they advocate ideas and ways that are opposed to society's established beliefs and traditions.

You have probably heard stories about me, opinions expressed about me. Everywhere they say, "Don't go there. He talks about things that are against established beliefs." They are absolutely right. If you are the slightest bit afraid to walk the opposite path, then stop coming to me.

The highway is the path everyone uses, and if this highway could have led people to the ultimate destination then everyone would have already arrived. A highway is very convenient for walking. It is very broad, it has no obstacles on it, it is very clean and well-swept. All your friends and relatives are walking along it as well, so you are not alone there. I will segregate you from them. You feel comfortable in the crowd. There are so many people walking on the highway you don't even have to walk in an orderly fashion, you are simply pushed along by the jostling of the crowd. Have you ever walked in a crowd? It moves like a tempest. You hardly have to raise your legs, they are practically lifted for you. And if they weren't, you would be crushed to death. The force, the push of the crowd propels you. You don't even have a chance to think; the crowd does not even afford you that.

The crowd gives you your education and your ideas, but it does not give you the power to think. It gives you blindness, not vision. When so many people follow a particular path of action, one would think it must be good — otherwise why are so many people following it? A path that has been trodden for centuries is more trusted than a new one. A new thing is hardly trusted at all, and that is why each religion claims it is very ancient, that it has been there forever, that it was the first, that others followed it.

Why are they all so eager to be ancient? Is religion a kind of wine? Is it because the older something is, the better it is supposed to be? The reason is that something is considered more trustworthy when it can claim to be old. When a shop has been running for years, when it is old, people will say, "Its merchandise must be genuine; they could not have cheated so many people for such a long time!"

This is how a shop acquires a name, a reputation — and then it can even sell rubbish. That is also why all the religions claim to be old.

But bear in mind that God is new every moment. God does not believe in the old. That is why He removes old people and gives birth to children; that is why He casts down the old experienced leaves and brings forth new sprouts, sprouts devoid of experience. Experience makes one deformed; it becomes a burden. Experience creates ego. And it has a bad smell. The freshness of new sprouts is unique. God has trust in them, and that is why He becomes fresh and new every moment.

God may have created the universe in the past, but He has not stopped His work — He is creating it every moment. Creation is an eternal, everlasting and continuing process. It is going on at this very moment. Otherwise how could new leaves come? How could new eggs break open and new birds fly away? How could seeds break apart and new sprouts burst forth? How could a foetus be created? How could new births take place? God creates new things every moment.

God believes in freshness and newness — and your religions believe in oldness. It appears your religions have no relation to God whatsoever. Your own self-confidence increases when you can claim that your religion is very ancient and that hundreds of thousands of people follow it.

People want to be with the crowd because they lack self-confidence. When you are alone you have no self-confidence. When you are walking down a lane at night you begin to hum a song. You hear your own humming and feel that you are not alone; you think there are at least two people, the singer and the listener. Then you feel bolder, then you feel more self-confident. You become as confident as you would if you were surrounded on all sides by a great crowd. And then you think, "If this path were really wrong someone would have found it out by now."

No one has ever reached the truth by walking on the highway. The man who seeks the smooth path of least resistance can never attain to God. The path to God is the

Enter Your Temple

path where one must be prepared to face difficulties. Kabir says that God is only known when one is alone, when one is not accompanied by anyone else. One has to travel there alone, and the meeting takes place in absolute aloneness. There is no one there; not even a witness. Keep this in mind. Remain alert to this fact.

Sadhu, consider this:
Ride in a boat and drown midstream...

Those who rode in the boat were drowned in the current in the middle of the river.

Helpless, get across.

And those, says Kabir, who did not accept the help of the boat were able to cross the river. When those who climbed into the boat did so, their drowning had already begun. They climbed into the boat because they did not know how to swim. But the journey to God is a swimming. And it has to be undertaken on your own. Who can accompany you into your samadhi?

Once a Zen disciple was bidding farewell to his master. The night was dark and he was a little afraid; the road was deserted and he had to pass through a dense forest where there were many wild animals. He looked so nervous his master remarked, "You seem afraid."

The disciple replied, "I am afraid. The night is dark, I am alone, and I have to pass through a thick forest full of wild animals."

The master said, "Wait a moment. I will light a lamp for you." He did so, and handed it to the disciple. As the disciple began to descend the staircase to set out on his way, the master suddenly blew out the lamp. Now the darkness seemed even darker than before.

The disciple had been given a little self-confidence and now it had been snatched away from him. He was startled. He asked, "What have you done? Why did you give me this lamp when all the time you intended to blow it out? What are you trying to tell me? Please explain all this to me."

The master said, "This is the kind of journey where a lamp given to you by another cannot accompany you. It is a journey to be undertaken quite alone. No help is allowed, you must depend on yourself alone. If you are helpless, then remain helpless — but do not grab onto any false hope. Your mind will always persuade you to seek some support, to look for some help."

People come to me and I tell them just to be quiet, just to remain quiet. And then they say, "Give us something to depend on. Shall we repeat a mantra? Can we practice a mantra?" They want a boat, a mantra-boat. They find it difficult just to sit quietly, doing nothing. They want to remain engaged, to keep busy doing something. They do not realize what it is to remain quiet without doing anything at all.

People are afraid to be without any help, to be helpless, so they try to catch hold of anything that is handy. Even a boat in the shape of a mantra will do. It is said that a drowning man clutches at a straw — he tries to make a straw into a log. All your boats are no better than straws. The straw may ease your mind for a while, but you will still be drowned in the middle of the river. How long can you deceive yourself?

The first thing to remember about this journey is that it is an inner journey; no type of support will be of any use

Enter Your Temple

whatsoever. Everything and everyone must remain outside; no friend or relative can be of any help. It is an inner journey and you will have to depend on yourself; you are the only boat.

Awaken your confidence in yourself. It does not matter how dense the forest is or how dark the night is; all you have to do is kindle the lamp within. It will accompany you to the end. Up to what point and for how long can outside lamps be trusted? Won't the lamp the master blew out eventually be blown out anyway by the gusts of wind along the disciple's way? And in the trembling hands of a frightened person, would not the lamp have fallen to the ground and broken in any case? If such a man were to hear even the slightest rustling of leaves he would immediately turn on his heels and run, totally forgetting the lamp. How long can the lamp of the outside world accompany you? Is there really any such thing as help from the outside world?

What Kabir is saying is of very great importance. There is a deep meaning hidden in it, and it is this — the whole of existence helps the man who takes no help from the world outside. God is the support of the man who is help-less. The man who accepts help and support from outside does not need God at all.

Once a Sufi fakir returned from a pilgrimage to Kaaba. All of his disciples gathered together and asked him to tell of his experiences on his pilgrimage. The fakir said, "I have to tell you one thing — God's bounty is the greatest. When I started on this pilgrimage I had only one paisa with me. How can I express His grace, His bounty? There is no end to His greatness. I have completed the pilgrimage and that paisa is still in my pocket. I received food and drink whenever it was needed. All my wants were fulfilled; He filled my every need. There is no end to His grace."

When he heard this, another fakir sitting in the crowd began to laugh loudly. The first fakir asked, "What's the matter? There seems to be some sarcasm in your laughter. Why are you laughing?"

The second fakir replied, "If you had such absolute confidence in Him, then why did you even take one paisa with you?"

To carry even one paisa with you indicates your lack of confidence. What difference does it make whether you take one paisa or ten million rupees with you? You have kept something; you are still depending upon yourself. Whenever you depend upon something in the outside world you are indirectly stating that you have no confidence in God. Otherwise, why should you accept a ride in a boat? Set all help aside. Be help-less. Be willing to drown in the middle of the river, don't even move your hands and feet to help yourself float.

Once a fakir was drowning in a river, and some people on the bank saw what was happening. The river was deep and dangerous, and the people on the bank did not know how to swim. They watched, surprised, as the drowning fakir went under the water and resurfaced time and time again. What surprised them was that there was no struggle, no movement of his hands and feet whatsoever. Even a man who does not know how to swim will flail about and cry out for someone to save him. When the drowning fakir came up for the third time man standing on the bank shouted, "You are killing yourself! Why don't you at least move you hands and feet a

Enter Your Temple

little? Why don't you at least cry out for help?"

The fakir answered, "I have left everything to Him, so the middle of the river is the same to me as the shore. I am willing to drown or to be saved. It is as He wishes. I shall do nothing to get in His way."

Even if this man drowns he will attain to Him. His drowning is a great revolution for him; it will transform him. If he drowns with this confidence in God, the middle of the river is the same as the shore. You cannot drown a man who has surrendered himself — his very surrender transforms the middle of the river into the shore. There is no greater achievement than surrender. There is nothing higher.

And suppose you reach the other bank in a boat? Where have you reached? You will be there and your boat will be there, but that bank will be just the same as this one — it will be no better than this shore. There will be no real difference at all. Your ego will still be there. And it will probably have increased, because you will think, "At least I have reached the other bank by my own effort!" you become more egoistic; you become more worthy to be drowned.

This is why Kabir says that the man who accepts outside help is drowned, while the man who remains helpless crosses the river. From this statement one would think the helpless man reaches the other shore, but whether he reaches it or does not reach it is not the question. The helpless man reaches the other shore the very moment he surrenders himself completely.

Gurdjieff once conducted a small experiment. He gathered some of his disciples together in a solitary place outside the city of Tiflis and said to them, "Whenever I say 'Stop!' you are to stop immediately, then and there, in whatsoever position you find yourself. Even if one of your legs is raised to walk, keep it in that position, do not lower it to the earth. When you hear the word 'Stop', you must stop."

There was an empty canal nearby and three young men were crossing it early one morning. Gurdjieff was sitting in his tent and he suddenly shouted, "Stop!" Immediately the three Young men in the canal froze. At that time the canal was dry, but a few moments later someone opened the floodgates. Those who opened it were unaware that three Young men were standing like statues in the middle of the canal. Gurdjieff did not know it either, he was sitting in his tent. So the three men waited, just standing there. As long as danger is far off, man's mind is able to wait; it just hopes that the danger will go away.

The water kept on rising and was soon up to their necks. When it reached their mouths, one of them jumped out. He said, "There is a limit to everything. Even trust has a limit." But trust has no limit. A trust with a limit is in fact not trust at all, it is a deception. It is a trick of the mind. Real trust is that trust which is limitless.

Can there be any limit to trust, to surrender? If it has a limit, then it is not surrender at all. If you say, "I will only trust up to a certain point" — if you only trust until the water reaches your mouth, it means you have never surrendered. What danger is there if the water reaches your mouth? You are simply playing tricks. You think you are displaying your cleverness, but in actual fact you are only deceiving yourself. When you are faced with danger you know whether your surrender is real or fake. Then your surrender is tested; then the true nature of your surrender is known.

When there is no danger, how can you know whether your surrender is real or not? If your surrender is real then there is no turning back.

One of the men in the canal jumped out, but the second man was a bit more cunning. He waited a little longer in the hope Gurdjieff might shout "Stop!" and tell him to come out of the canal. Even though his lips were under water there was still no danger to his life, but the second the water reached his nose he jumped out. "It is sheer foolishness to wait any longer," he said. "Gurdjieff does not even know what is happening. There is no point in committing suicide."

The third young man just stood there even though his nose and eyes were now under water. Soon even his head was under the water and he was struggling for breath. At that very moment Gurdjieff rushed out of the tent like a whirlwind, caught hold of the young man, and pulled him out of the canal. With great difficulty he was brought back to consciousness. But that very day he reached the other shore. He opened his eyes, bowed down at the feet of Gurdjieff, and said, "I have known what is to be known; I have achieved what is to be achieved."

This, Gurdjieff calls crystallization. He used to say that at such a moment, at the moment when you have risked everything you have and there is nothing left to be saved, a jump takes place — a jump that takes you from the periphery to your center. Then, for the first time, your self, your soul, becomes crystallized, becomes as solid as a rock. And then nobody can shake you.

The first two men missed: they accepted the help of their own powers of reasoning. The third man achieved because he did not grab hold of anything, because he remained help-less, because he was ready to die. And then Gurdjieff rushed to him. It could happen that the master might forget, but God never forgets. When you risk everything, all of existence is ready to save you. If you are trying to save yourself, there is no need to save you at this moment.

There is a wonderful story about Krishna. It happened when he was sitting down to dinner one evening. His wife, Rukmani, had kept his dinner warm for him. He sat down, Rukmani began to fan him, and no sooner was he preparing to taste the first morsel than he suddenly stood up. Rukmani asked, "What is the matter?"

Krishna said, "One of my devotees is in difficulty," and then ran towards the door. But then he suddenly stopped, came back, and sat down to his food once again. Rukmani said, "I can understand your running off to help your devotee in his difficulty; I can understand that it was absolutely essential to postpone your dinner, but I cannot understand why you turned back at the door. Why did you not go to your devotee?"

Krishna explained. "A devotee of mine was walking down the road in a certain town. His love for me is ecstasy, and although people were throwing stones at him he was laughing. Blood was pouring from his head and still he was laughing. Nothing existed within him except my name. And so I had to run to help him."

Rukmani asked, "Then why did you turn back?"

Krishna replied, "No sooner had I reached the door than the whole thing had changed. He had picked up stones to retaliate. Now he is strong enough to protect himself. Now he has forgotten me, he is facing the danger directly. Now it is all in his hands. There is no need for my presence there."

When you take the fight into your own hands, your relationship with God is severed that very moment. As soon as you become clever or active or cunning, your relationship with existence is broken. And, as Kabir says, when a man in his simplicity leaves everything to God, becomes help-less, he cannot be drowned. No matter how hard you may try, you cannot drown such a man. He transforms the drowning — he even transforms that into a way to go beyond. It is impossible to drown him. You cannot kill him, you cannot even cut him into pieces. As soon as you try he will say, "This is ecstasy for me. I have been waiting to be no more; I have been waiting to meet Him." For such a man this is a moment of *paramanand*, of man's greatest bliss. No, it is impossible to harass such a man.

Ride in a boat and drown midstream;
Helpless, get across.

Be support-less, be help-less, and God will be your support. But beware. The mind is very cunning. It will say it is fine to make Him your support — it will say it understands. So then you decide to depend on God; you start to repeat His name, Ram, Ram, making it a mantra, and then you miss again.

Of what value is a God you can make into a support? Such a God is your own creation; it simply means you are depending on yourself. To be help-less means not to worry about making Him your support, and not worry about not making Him your support. Leave everything completely to Him. God knows His job. When you do not try to make Him your support, that is when He becomes it. And not before.

Reach the town by some back way;
Get looted on the highway.

You are being robbed by society. Society can only survive by killing you, by killing your individuality. First it humiliates you; and then it enslaves you. No one can enslave a man of spirit. First society dethrones you, topples you from your center, and then keeps you suspended on the periphery so that you are neither here nor there. And finally, when your life-force is exhausted, you have no idea where you are, what you are or who you are, then and then alone you can be made a slave. Then society can keep you busy with trivialities; then society can be your master.

A society is built by annihilating the individuality of its members. And so you are robbed — you are kept occupied with the kinds of things for which you have not come into this world. Some are kept busy accumulating wealth, some in the race for position, and some in the pursuit of flattery, of false praise. Have you come here for these trifles? Are flattering inscriptions on your gravestone any kind of achievement? What will you take with you when you die? Wealth is useful; it has a purpose, but not one for which it is worth losing one's self. Wealth is a means, it is not the goal. If you amass wealth by forgetting your self, how is that going to help you? You will leave the world empty-handed.

We begin the indoctrination of a child by sending him to a school we have chosen. This is how we begin injecting ego into him. Children hardly make any distinction whatsoever between the first and second grades; they come home jumping and dancing even if they fail in their examinations. Then you explain to them that it is very humiliating to fail, that one must pass an examination; and not only should one pass, one must also stand first so the family's reputation will be enhanced. By and by the innocent child becomes egoistic.

You are aggressive; you are a disease. And you will infect the child with your disease. He will forget his innocence and be preoccupied with this race throughout his life. At first he is pushed by his parents, then by his wife, and lastly by his children. This is your sansara, your world. Someone or other is constantly pushing you to stand on your own feet, but in actual fact your feet have no substance to them at all. This is the highway upon which you are being robbed. Everyone in the world is being robbed like this.

Sannyas is the point from which you begin your journey towards the real riches, towards the authentic wealth. But sannyas is a reverse journey. And all your relatives and those you consider as friends are joined together in robbing you — their happiness depends on robbing you. But this traffic is not one-way, you also rob them; your happiness depends on stealing from them as well. In the final analysis, you come to realize that everyone is being robbed. But by this time your journey is over and you die empty-handed. That is why you die weeping and wailing — you have lost the opportunity that was given to you. You were unable to use it in a profitable way, nothing has been achieved and now everything is lost.

You are so conditioned that, for a while, you will stick to anything that has been propagated over a period of time, no matter what. This is because you are not alert. You may be quite well off in your present house with no need for a bigger one, but if your neighbor begins to build a larger house you will immediately be caught up in his disease. Then you will have to build a bigger house too. It becomes a matter of prestige. In this world who is prestigious? You come from dust and to dust you will return. The one who owns the big house and the one who owns the small house — both will return to dust. There is no distinction between the two; in the face of death, no one is bigger or smaller.

Death makes no distinction between poor and rich, between follower and leader, between fakir and emperor. Death only knows one distinction — the distinction between the ignorant and the wise. But death only takes notice of the wise man; there is no need to notice the ignorant man because he is part of the crowd. When a man like Kabir arrives at its door, death knows that someone important, some VIP has come — that someone filled with nectar has arrived. Death cannot destroy him; death cannot throw him into the dust. Death hides its face from him and runs away. You are trying to hide yourself from death, you are trying to avoid it. Go where you like, death is certain to catch hold of you.

Analyze the workings of your own mind at some point and find out just how it is influenced. Someone buys a new car. Your car is serving you well and you are not sure whether the new model is better or not — generally they are worse — but now you are in difficulty, now you are restless all day and all night. You dream about a new car; you are constantly thinking how you can arrange things to buy a new car. You hanker after luxuries; you cut down on the necessities of life to buy things you don't need. Look around your house carefully and you will find you have purchased many unessential things.

Have you ever gone to an auction? Hearing others bid, you are tempted. You hear someone saying, "One hundred and one," someone else offering, "One hundred and two," and a third person immediately calling, "One hundred and three." Now it is difficult for you to control yourself, and so you shout, "One hundred and four!"

Once Mulla Nasruddin was bidding at an auction. He was very excited and kept on increasing his bid. A parrot was being auctioned and the Mulla finally purchased it for one hundred and one rupees, although it could have been bought for about ten. After making the purchase he asked the auctioneer whether the parrot could speak or not. The man replied, "What do you mean, can the parrot speak? Who do you think was bidding against you?"

When a man is not conscious he does not listen to others; he just keeps on beating his own drum. The ego is your intoxication, and it is because of its intoxication that you are being robbed. You will be robbed in proportion to your egoism and you are as safe from being robbed as you are free of ego. That is why society teaches you to be egoistic; that is the secret society uses to rob you, to exploit you. You can be exploited only when you are full of ego.

Reach the town by some back way;
Get looted on the highway.

What does this *back way* mean? To walk consciously is to *Reach the town by some back way*. People do not know where they are going because they are not alert — they move simply because the crowd is moving. Take every step consciously. Be aware of where you are going, why you are doing something, why you are purchasing these particular things, why you are building a house.

The necessities of life are not many, but desires have no end. A man should be very happy if he can fulfill his needs.

And he can easily do that; his need are not many. He wants food twice a day and a roof under which he can sleep. Man's needs are limited, but his desires are limitless. A roof will not do; a palace is required. And even if it is a big palace, the mind wants a bigger one still. If you look at the things in your house and think about them, you will find that there would have been no inconvenience whatsoever if ninety per cent of them had not been bought. You will see there was no necessity for them at all. And the amazing thing is that you are unable to do that which is essential because of those unnecessary things.

When I suggest to people they practice meditation, they say, "We have no time for it." Yet I see them playing cards. And if you were to ask them, "Why do you play cards?" they would reply, "Just to pass the time." It is difficult to understand man. Those very people who say they have no time are also to be found going to the pictures, to the cinema. And if you ask them why, they will tell you time hangs heavily on them. If you look at these people during their holidays you will find they are very uneasy; they have plenty of leisure time but no idea how to use it. These are the very people who ask without a moment's hesitation, "Where can we find the time for meditation?"

What is the reason for all of this? The reason is that man wants to be with the crowd. Playing cards, going to the cinema, going to a nightclub — all these activities are just to remain with the crowd. These are all highways. But as soon as the question of meditation arises, traveling the *back way* begins. There, one has to walk alone; there, one has to walk with full alertness. So the mind immediately protests, "Where can I find the time for meditation?" It will also argue, "What is the advantage? What will I get out of it?"

Nothing that can be deposited in the bank to increase your balance is obtained through meditation. Meditation neither adds to your bank balance nor lessens it. Are you quite sure anyone is benefited by meditation? Only a few madmen in this world practice meditation. What guarantee is there that these few achieve something? Who knows for certain if they achieve something or not? "They may not be mentally well," you say. "Don't listen to them. Many have been misled by their words. Don't listen to them. Many have been misled by their words. Don't pay any attention to them. Look at the crowd — millions of people spend their whole lives without meditation at all, and they are all wise people." To the mind, the crowd appears wise; to the mind, the majority is right. It is rare one comes across a buddha. A buddha is alone; he has left his palace.

When Gautam Buddha left his place, the charioteer who took him to the outskirts of the city began to weep. He asked Buddha, "Why are you doing this? have you lost your senses? Why are you leaving your palace? I am only your charioteer, only your servant, but I must try to advise you, I cannot help it. Look at what I am saying, think it over. I am old and I have seen life through and through. Men spend their whole lives striving for that which you already have. Where are you going that you can leave all this? Where will you find such a beautiful wife? Where will you find such palaces? Why do you choose to be a beggar? You must be out of your mind."

Buddha replied, "You poor fool, I see nothing but flames in the place you call a palace — everything there is being consumed. I am not leaving in search of some other palace, I am going in search of my self, to find out who I am."

The charioteer was unable to understand this. He began to weep loudly when he saw Buddha begin to cut off his hair and remove his ornaments. Buddha wanted to give them to him as a gift, but he began to argue, "Don't do this thing. No one in our city has such beautiful hair. Please don't cut it off."

Buddha said, "What shall I do with it? Everything is on fire. I will die tomorrow and this beautiful hair will burn; you will put me on the funeral pyre and this hair will burn like grass."

People like Buddha are traveling in the opposite direction. They have taken the *back way,* the unknown, unfrequented path; they are in search of the self. You are also on a journey, but you are seeking something else. Some of you are in search of a beautiful woman, someone else is after a fine palace, and others want wealth or fame. But all of your seeking is worthless. As long as you are not seeking your self, you are being exploited. But no one else is robbing you — it is your mistaken search itself that leads you down the highway where you rob yourself.

Reach the town by some back way;
Get looted on the highway.

By one rope all get tied,
Both the bound and the free.

Kabir is saying a very wonderful and uncommon thing. He says that everyone is tied by the same rope, those who think they are in bondage as well as those who think they are free. All are tied by the same rope. Slaves are undoubtedly slaves, but kings are also in bondage. And the rope is the same.

By one rope all get tied,
Both the bound and the free.

The rope that binds some men is poverty, and in the case of others it is riches. Some may even have precious stones woven into their rope, but it is a rope nevertheless. All are in bondage. Those of you who think you have been defeated in life and those of you who believe you have been victorious are both in bondage. Alexander and Napoleon are in the same bondage as the beggar, because as long as there is attachment, there is bondage. As long as your mind is seeking someone else or something other than your self, you are in the bondage.

There was once a fakir who earned large amounts of money begging by the side of the road. He never asked anyone to give him anything, but passers-by used to throw alms at his feet. People had a great tenderness for him. By and by, his hut overflowed with money. When death was approaching he said, "I wish to give all this money away to some poor man." And, so, many beggars gathered, each claiming to be poorer than the next. The fakir said, "Just wait a little. The poorest of all has not yet arrived."

At that point, the king was passing with his retinue. The fakir called aloud to the kind, "Please wait a moment. Please come here and take all this money away." Then the poor people began to protest loudly, "This is unfair, it is unjust! We did not expect you to act like this! Are you giving all your money to the king?"

The fakir answered, "In this land there is none poorer than he. You are satisfied with what little you have, but even though he possesses much he is still not satisfied. His desire for more is as yet unfulfilled, so it is obvious his poverty is very great indeed. There is no end to his desire, so perhaps this money may help. It may even lessen his thirst a little."

The poor man is poor, but the rich man is also poor. One who is defeated is obviously a defeated man, but if you look at the one who is victorious you will see that he has been defeated too. There is no way to be victorious in this world — to be defeated is the world's only process. Everyone is defeated; everyone remains defeated. The only man who wins is the man who seeks his self.

There is yet another profound meaning to these words of Kabir. Let us try to understand it. Those who think they are worldly men are entangled in *maya*, are entangled by illusion, and your so-called sadhus and sannyasins who claim to be free are also in bondage.

Kabir and other enlightened men stress that when a person becomes liberated he does not claim that he is now liberated. No sooner does a man become liberated than he knows the rope was false. It was not a real rope; it was a rope made of dreams. The bondage was not real, and even the idea of becoming free from it was false. What does it mean, to become liberated from an unreal rope? Your bondage was sheer madness, and your claim that you have become liberated is also madness. The rope was false.

At night you dream you are tied up. When you get up in the morning will you say, "I am liberated now?" You will simply say, "It was a dream; the bondage was unreal." Since you are not in bondage, how can there be any question of liberation? The enlightened man says that both the bondage and the liberation are false, because the rope itself is false.

By one rope all get tied,
Both the bound and the free.

These words of Kabir have a very deep meaning. When

someone claims, "I am liberated," his claim itself indicates that he is still in maya, that he is still living in illusion. It shows that he has not yet known, that he is not yet fully awake.

The Zen master, Rinzai, said there was no doubt that sansara, the world, was false, and that *moksha,* liberation, was also false, was also an imaginary thing. The people who heard Rinzai were very surprised. They asked him, "What are you saying? We can accept that sansara is an illusion, but is moksha also an illusion?"

Rinzai replied, "Sansara is a creation of your mind and so is moksha. When the mind is no more, who is there to think about liberation?"

When the rope is broken, who will be there to think about liberation? People often asked Buddha, "Where will you be when your body perishes? In what stage of liberation will you be then? What form will that liberation have?" Buddha always remained silent in reply. Any answer would have been dangerous, because ordinary men are unable to grasp this phenomenon.

It is as if a sleeping person is dreaming, and in the dream he asks a question about the form of the dream. But when he awakens, where will the dream be? What form will it have then? The fact is that when he is awake there will be no dream at all. Dreams only exist as long as you are sleeping. As soon as you are wide awake, your dreams are broken, your dreams disappear. Then you cannot even find the rope that bound you.

The truly liberated person is one who does not even claim that he is liberated. When he hears you ask he will simply smile. He will say that everything is false, sansara as well as nirvana. There are some famous words of Nagarjuna where he says one has to save oneself from sansara and one has to save oneself from nirvana as well. Otherwise you are entangled in sansara first, and then in nirvana. The rope is the same; there is no difference between the two. First you were filled with ego because of sansara, and now you are filled with ego because of liberation. Now you say, "I am liberated." But as long as "I," as the ego is there, no matter what the cause, you are still asleep; you are not awake. If "you" claim moksha, your ego is still present; if "you" claim, understand that your unawareness continues.

Have you ever had a dream in which you see yourself as awake? You must have had such a dream, many times people have such dreams. When you really awaken in the morning, you realize that you were only awake in the dream — it was a trick to protect your sleep.

You are hungry. You dream that you get up out of your bed and go to the refrigerator. You see all this in your dream — you are awake in your dream. You eat, and you think that everything is real. And then you fall asleep again. Thus it is possible to have a dream within a dream. But then a great difficulty arises. How will you distinguish between the two awakenings, between the one that is real and the one that belongs to the dream? Both look alike. How will you make a distinction between them? There is only one way to do it, and that is, in the state of real awakening, when you are wide awake, not to make any claim that you have awakened.

But the need to make the claim only arises because the awakening is not real — you want to support it by a declaration. You make the claim vehemently — not to convince others, but to convince yourself that it was real. And when others begin to believe it, you will have faith in it too. Your sleep is very deep and very sound. That you are in bondage is for certain, but your so-called liberated people are in bondage as well. They may have gone to a jungle and sat for a long time under a tree, but a new type of ego has entered; now they believe they are beyond sansara, beyond the world. How can anyone be beyond something that does not exist at all? You simply have to rouse yourself from your sleep. You simply have to be alert.

It happened once, when a certain Zen monk arose from his sleep, that one of his disciples entered the room. The monk said, "Before you do anything else, listen to me. I had a dream in the night. Explain its meaning to me."

The disciple said, "Please wait a moment. Let me prepare tea first." He prepared the tea and gave it to the monk.

The monk asked, "Will you explain the meaning now?"

The disciple replied, "Drink your tea quietly. That is my explanation."

Then another disciple entered the room. The monk said to him, "Listen. I had a dream during the night. Will you explain its meaning?"

The disciple said, "Please wait." He went out and returned with a jug of water. "Wash out your mouth," he said. "That is the meaning of the dream."

The monk laughed loudly. He said, "If you had tried to explain the meaning of the dream I would have dismissed you. Is there any need, is there any point in explaining a dream? The dream comes; one's sleep is broken; one takes a cup of tea — the whole matter stops there. There is no discussion — no explanation of these trivial matters is required. What else is there to be done with dreams?"

Both disciples gave correct answers.

This is the sort of question generally asked by Zen monks. Their questions are not like those asked by Hindu gurus — they ask things such as, "What is the meaning of these lines from the Vedas?" This can be answered by any scholar, but when the Zen monk gets up in the morning he will ask a question like the one you just heard, a question that is not written in any of the scriptures.

A lot of investigation is going on these days to define dreams, to explain them. Freud, Jung, Adler and other psychologists have been very busy interpreting dreams. The mind is inquisitive; it wants to know. But the two Zen disciples displayed great awareness. They were very alert. They said, "Why prattle on about it? How will it help us? Why should we bother interpreting something that has no existence at all? A dream is like a line drawn on the surface of water, it cannot be preserved. So what is there to say about it?"

By one rope all get tied,
Both the bound and the free.

And then Kabir says:

Enter your temple; be bathed from all sides.
Who remains without stays dry.

In the art of expressing truths in a topsy-turvy way, Kabir is unparalleled. He expressed them in phrases quite contradictory in meaning. When it is raining it is obvious that someone standing outside will be drenched, and it is also obvious that the man who goes into the house will remain dry. But Kabir says that the man who goes into the house is drenched and that the one who stays outside remains dry. Kabir is speaking of another kind of house, of another kind of rain. He is not speaking of your worldly houses or of the rains you know. His is the story of the inner temple where nectar rains down incessantly. And so, the one who goes within is drenched and the one who remains outside stays dry.

Remaining dry means you are being robbed. The temple was so near you didn't even have to take a step to reach it, it was so near all you had to do was bend your head — but you sat on the bank and remained thirsty, even though the lake was so near. Kabir says, *I laugh when I hear that the fish in the water is thirsty*. The fish was swimming in the water and yet it was thirsty. Kabir is saying this about you, about you fish. But the fishes swimming in the water are not as foolish as you. You are sitting in that place where nectar rains down on all sides, where light pours from all sides, where existence is celebrating on all sides, and you are weeping aloud that you have been robbed. It is your own fault you have been robbed. You are still dry because you did not enter the temple.

Chop off the head for eternal joy;
An unchopped head is suffering.

Kabir says the man who masters his mind achieves that happiness which is everlasting. He achieves *anand,* bliss — not the happiness that is the opposite of unhappiness, but that ecstasy from which there is no fall. And the man who does not master his mind always remains miserable. You are following the dictates of your own mind, so if you are miserable who is responsible for it? To whom should you complain? Who else is deceiving you? If you have remained dry, it is because of you.

Are you trying to achieve happiness by following the dictates of your mind? If you are, you are trying to make the impossible possible. It has never happened; it will never happen. By giving you the hope of happiness, the mind drags you into misery — of this, there is no doubt. Who is foolish enough to go into misery in hope of more misery? The mind gives you hope of heaven and leads you into hell. And you have experienced this so often! Is there anything more to know? Yet you always keep on listening to the mind.

Once Mulla Nasruddin went to a racecourse with four friends. They considered the Mulla to be an intelligent man and so they asked him to decide which horse to back. After a considerable amount of thought and study of the horses' previous records, the Mulla decided to back a horse called Maharajah. His friends gave him the money and he bought the ticket. When he returned he informed his friends that, although it had been decided to back Maharajah, at the betting window he had met a friend who was a great gambler and very experienced in racing. "He advised me to bet on Maharam and not on Maharajah," the Mulla said, "so I have backed Maharam." The horse came last in the race.

His friends told the Mulla not to worry. A second time they selected a horse, and once again the Mulla went to purchase the ticket. When he came back he said he had backed another horse, not the one they had selected, because the same gambler had advised him to do so. "He is a man of great experience," he explained. "There is no limit to your foolishness," his friends said. "We lost the first time because of his advice, and you have followed it again! This tries our patience; it is really beyond endurance!"

"But he argued so convincingly I couldn't help agreeing with him," the Mulla answered.

"He might have been mistaken once, but he cannot always be wrong. Moreover, he is a man of experience. He has no ulterior motive; he has no reason to give us bad advice."

They lost on the second horse too. All the money they had was gone; now they had only a few *annas* between them. They sent the Mulla to buy some nuts; when he came back he had bought roasted chickpeas. The Mulla said, "I met the same man there. He told me the nuts weren't any good. He said to buy these."

You are always running into this man. His name is Mind. Wherever you go he is sure to meet you there. He immediately tells you, "Do this. Do that." If you begin to meditate, even then he will advise you about the method; he will tell you how to do it. Do not heed his advice.

You think because the mind has the experience of so many births behind it, it is good to listen to it. When will you come to your senses? When will you wake up? You have wandered through innumerable lives listening to the dictates of the mind.

You will be able to listen to a master only when you can tell the mind to be quiet, and not before. And you are so cunning, so clever, that you only listen to that master you consider to be right. If you choose your master on the advice of the mind, you will be in the wrong.

The mind's main function is to go the wrong way, to mislead you. This is what it lives on — if you choose the right path, it dies, this is its death. Your mind is your disease. It will not allow you to choose the right medicine. So be a little wary of it. You have followed it quite a long time; now there is no need to give it any more chances. You have given it enough chances.

Chop off the head for eternal joy;
An unchopped head is suffering.

The man who has mastered his mind has reached the source of everlasting happiness, and the man who has not will remain in misery forever. Your mind is your hell. What trick does it use to entangle you? It knows a trick all fishermen use. They put a bit of dough on a hook to entice the fish. The mind uses the same trick. First the mind will tell you, persuade you, that you will be very happy if you acquire a certain thing, and when you try and you get it you find that there is no happiness in it at all. Quite the opposite — you become miserable.

One evening Mulla Nasruddin was sitting on a bench in the park with his wife. Just near them, sitting under some bushes, a young man was talking to a young lady. They seemed very happy, and their conversation seemed quite interesting. The Mulla's wife grew very excited as she overheard them. It seemed as if the young man was about to propose marriage, so she told the Mulla to cough so as to warn the couple they could overhear them.

"Why should I cough?" the Mulla asked. "When I was proposing to you nobody coughed and warned me. I wasn't warned by anybody, why should I warn him? Leave him alone. He will suffer for his own action."

The mind weaves a great net of temptations for you; it

holds dreams of happiness out before you. As far as creating false hopes and making promises are concerned, you will never find a more clever politician than the mind. And no promise is ever fulfilled. Can you point out a single example in your life in which the mind has fulfilled a promise it has made?

There is a limit even to blindness! How long will you continue to have faith in this mind? Set this faith aside. The mind will keep on making promises — it is its habit. Just as an elephant on the highway ignores the dogs that bark at him, you must also ignore this barking mind. Say to your mind, "Go on barking if you enjoy it. Keep exercising your lungs if you want, but it isn't going to disturb me. I am going on my own way." And once you say this with determination, you will find that by and by the mind begins to become quiet.

What is the point of knocking on a door if nobody listens to you? If you want to kill the mind, just gradually stop giving it any cooperation. Your cooperation is its life. It lives on your cooperation; in itself it is powerless. To kill it, nothing else need be done. Just stop giving it your cooperation. It will keep working for a while because of the old momentum, but that will not last long. It has no legs to walk, no heart to throb, no blood to circulate, no hands to work — it has nothing of its own. Now it has you to help it function, but as soon as you stop cooperating with it, the mind is removed and you enter the temple. The temple begins where the mind ends. That is why it is a temple. And at the door of the temple the shower of nectar begins.

Enter your temple; be bathed from all sides.
Who remains without stays dry.

Now Kabir says:

The whole world looks without seeing,
Eyes remaining blind.
Says Kabir: I understand,
Seeing the ways of the world.

Having seen the ways of the world, Kabir says, I have come to know, to understand, that whatever the eyes see should not be taken for the world — it is simply a dream, just make-believe. And whatever the eyes see should not be taken for sight, because the eyes that see the outside world are blind; they see nothing real. When they cannot see you, when they cannot see your self, what can they see? When the one who is nearest is not seen, how can things that are far away be seen? When we cannot see our own quality, how can we see the quality of others? And when we cannot achieve self-knowledge, how can we obtain knowledge of others?

The whole world looks without seeing,
Eyes remaining blind.

Close your eyes. Be without eyes. Stop this race to see. And when you are without eyes and you remain within, your eyes will open in the real sense of the word. And then you will be able to see.

The whole world looks without seeing,
Eyes remaining blind.

Despite the fact that they possess eyes, Kabir says, people remain blind. Only when they close them, he says, do they obtain real sight.

Says Kabir: I understand,
Seeing the ways of the world.

Enter Your Temple

This understanding has come to me, Kabir says, because I have seen the ways of the world. He is not saying this because he has studied the scriptures, he says this from his experience of life and the world. He is describing what he has actually experienced, what he has actually seen. He has seen people being robbed as they walked along the highway, and he has seen those who walk alone in the opposite direction reach their destination. He has seen those who turn their backs on the world reach their destination, he has seen those who stay with the world wandering aimlessly here and there. He has seen those who take a boat, drown; he has seen those who proceed on their journey without anyone's help, arrive.

Kabir has seen that those with eyes are blind — even though people have eyes they are unable to see the real, the only thing worth seeing — and he has seen that those who close their eyes are the ones who see reality. And he has seen that those who stand outside the temple remain dry. And he has seen that those who enter the temple are drenched — he has seen them filled with a new kind of ecstasy. All the dryness of their lives disappeared, and he saw in them the grandeur of a fresh and shining life. Kabir does not say this from the study of some scripture, he is telling us this from his own experience of life.

Keep these sutras carefully in mind. Kabir says that the man who kills his mind reaches the destination, and that the man who depends on the mind is undertaking the journey to hell, the journey from one hell to another and another and another. In the hope of happiness, such a man is dragged from one misery to another. But that hope is just like the dough the fisherman puts on his hooks.

Kabir has seen that both worldly people and sannyasins

alike are in bondage. He has also seen that the same rope binds you all. And what is that rope? That rope is nothing but your sleep, your unconsciousness — nothing but your dreams, nothing but your mind.

8

WHY GO TO OTHERS?

I'm in a muddle.
You resolve it, Bhagwan.
When You are mine,
Why go to others?

Is mind greater than
What's minding mind?
Is Ram greater than
he who knows Ram?

Is Brahma greater than
What he arose from?
Are the Vedas greater than
Their very source?

Says Kabir:
I'm so confused...
is the temple greater than
He who serves God?

An egoist is afraid to accept advice from others, he wants to disentangle himself from his own entanglements. Even to accept the fact that he is entangled, hurts his ego. So an egoist cannot approach a master. And the interesting thing about the whole phenomenon is that all of your entanglements are because of the ego

You try to solve your problems with the help of the ego, and by the very effort of trying to solve them, you become more and more caught up in them. The ego is the cause of entanglement, and so you are certain to become more entangled. The way to unravel your difficulties is not through the ego. You are trying to use as a medicine the very illness that is the cause of the sad plight you call your life, that is responsible for the diseased state your life is in. This medicine simply makes you sicker. you may possibly save yourself from the sickness, but there is no remedy to save you from this particular medicine. There would be no end to the complications in the life of a man who looked upon sickness as medicine.

It is essential to understand one thing first — you must always look within to find the cause of a particular complication.

And at the same time you must move in the opposite direction. You will find the solution there.

The ego is entanglement; surrender is disentanglement. The ego has created the disease; surrender will cure it. That is why all the scriptures, all religious sects and all doctrines have sung the praises of surrender. Surrender means you are unable to disentangle yourself. It means you are becoming more and more entangled and so you finally give up — you finally surrender yourself; you finaly seek guidance from one who has broken away, from one who has moved in the opposite direction.

Unless you set your ego aside you cannot approach a master. But you consult your ego first, and only when it says "yes' do you proceed. This means that your ego is superior to your master, because you only appoint him with the approval of your ego. The master will not be able to help you much.

We have created experts and specialists because of our egos. And these are the kinds of gurus at whose feet you do not have to surrender. At the most, you just pay their fees. That's all you have to do — this kind of guru will not make much difference. You go to such a guru because he becomes your servant, and then he tries to solve your problems and your difficulties without your surrender. Such gurus are multiplying in the world these days, but there is no lessening of people's entanglements whatsoever.

There is an old story you may have heard. It is about five blind men who encounntered an elephant. They were unable to see the elephant so they felt him with their hands. Whatever part of the elephant he felt, each blind man thought that was what the elephant was like. In blindness one cannot conceive the whole, and so these blind men each took one part to be the whole. One of them said the elephant was like a huge basket, another said he was like a pillar, and a third, who happened to grab the tail, said the elephant was like a rope. All five had different opinions.

A teacher in a small school had told this story to her pupils, but had not told them the five men were blind. She had only told them that five men were investigating an elephant. After she had related the story she asked the class to tell her what kind of men they were. It seemed obvious the students would say they were blind, but one child raised his hand and said, "They were specialists."

All specialists are blind. In fact, to be a specialist one has to be blind. To concentrate on a single subject one has to set all else aside. One has to go deeper and deeper into one thing alone, at the expense of all other fields of inquiry.

The advice you receive from a specialist can never solve the difficulties or complexities of your life. His advice may bring you a little satisfaction, it may give you the impression something is being resolved, but the specialist cannot solve anything. You have to disentangle your whole life, not parts of it.

The whole can only be disentangled at the feet of a master. The master is a man whose entire life has been disentangled, but the specialist you expect to solve your difficulties is himself entangled. Western psychologists even investigate one another's mutual problems. They have their own problems, and so one psychologist goes to another for help. They cannot even find the solution to their own problems. Even the greatest amongst them — Freud, Jung, Adler — suffer from their own complications, from their own diseases.

In his memoirs of Freud, Jung has written that if someone raised a point for discussion, and it was something to which Freud was opposed, he would become so angry and so upset that he would often faint with anger and fall off his chair. Freud's anger was such — Jung has written that Freud fainted in front of him three times because of excessive anger. No matter how much Freud may go on advising the whole world how to control anger, his advice will be of no help. It is always easy to advise others — what is cheaper or easier to give than advice — but it is very difficult to follow one's own advice. And advice that has not grown out of one's own experience is of no value at all. And even though he was criticizing Freud, Jung himself was in the same boat. His problems were as complicated. There was never any improvement in them at all.

I have heard of a man who was somewhat eccentric. When he got up one morning he put his hand on his head only to find — so he thought — a rosebush growing there. He was quite crazy; there was no plant there at all. But when he looked into the mirror and thought he saw roses growing out of the top of his head he became very agitated. He ran to a psychologist and asked him to do something about it. He said, "Do you see a rosebush growing on my head?"

The psychologist examined his head in all seriousness and inquired, "What kind of rose is it?"

The man replied, "Why do you ask? Why don't you read the name on the card? There must be one attached to the rose!"

Because of examining insane people over a long period of time, psychologists themselves generlly go mad. I have not heard whether the patients ever become sane or not, but the psychologists themselves definitely do become insane.

Whatever specialists know, they know from books. The master is not a specialist. He does not know anything at all about any particular disease, he only knows the remedy for one illness — and that illness is known as man. It is a total affliction. The master knows the remedy for the sickness named man: the remedy is, the man must dissolve within himself. The master came to know the cure when he became nothing himself, when he lost his self. The knowledge of this remedy is not to be obtained by attending a university or by reading the scriptures or by any such thing; this knowledge is acquired by becoming nothing oneself. And if you want to avail yourself of the advice of such a man, you will have to surrender yourself completely at his feet.

In these lines Kabir is telling us something very rare. The first thing he asks is whom he should approach to solve his problem. He puts his difficulty before the ultimate master, before God Himself. And God is the ultimate master.

The scriptures say the master is God; they say the two are one. When you surrender, the master becomes God. And if you do not surrender, you will not be able to find God anywhere. Those who have known surrender say that no sooner does surrender happen than you not only acquire the outer master but achieve the master within you as well. No sooner has surrender happened than the disciple begins to achieve his own eminence and greatness. But surrender is the key.

I'm in a muddle. You resolve it, Bhagwan.

Kabir is asking God to solve his only problem, his only complication, his only entanglement. And if you want God to solve your problem, then total surrender is essential. Before that, there is no question whatever of approaching Him. Before that even the very existence of God is disputable. You will first raise a doubt; you will first ask, "Where is God?" — but how can you put your problem before God as long as you discuss and dispute His very existence? You can lay your mental confusion before God only when you are fully convinced that He alone exists, that nothing else exists.

And remember this second point as well — for the man who puts his problem before God, the very act of placing it before God solves it. God does not solve your problem; there is no need to solve it. Through the very act of putting it

Why Go To Others?

before Him through your surrender, through your acceptance, the entanglement is disentangled.

Up to this point there was no acceptance on your side. Up to this point you had kept your problem hidden, you had looked on it as a valuable diamond and had kept it tied up in a knot in your handkerchief. You were afraid to show it — you only showed what was not really there. Your attitude was, "I know everything. How can anything be a problem for me? there is no question. I have all the answers."

As soon as you open your heart to God, the very act of opening itself becomes the solution. God does not give you any answers. He is not an individual who will give you answers to your questions. The answer is hidden in putting the question in the right way.

If you can understand this sutra in depth you will be able to comprehend this phenomenon. When you understand the question rightly, the answer is there. The man who has understood the question rightly, who has understood it in its totality, is at ease. Such a man is at peace. The answer is not to be found anywhere else — the answer is there, hidden in the question. And He whom you are seeking is not somewhere else either, He is seated within you.

These words of Kabir — *I'm in a muddle. You resolve it, Bhagwan* — are endearing. He is speaking to existence as if it is standing before him. Only a devotee can speak like this; only a devotee can use such a direct approach to solve his entanglement. For Kabir, God is not an imaginary person — for Kabir, He is the very existence itself. Now you can speak to Him too; now you can talk to Him as well.

People thought of Kabir as mad. "Which God is he talking

to?" they would ask. "We do not see that God," they would say. And a psychologist would say Kabir suffered from a kind of neurosis. "It may be a religious neurosis, but it is certainly a neurosis," he would say. "Where is this God? Where is this *Bhagwan?* Who is it you are talking to?" he would ask.

Kabir is sitting in his cottage, saying, *I'm in a muddle. You resolve it, Bhagwan.* And if there is a problem in your life, where else will you take it? You have only to discolse it to existence — if a problem arises within you, then ask existence. Ask the existence out of which everything has come, out of which we have come, out of which your problem has come. Ask the existence into which we will all be absorbed. Is it not possible that your knot, your problem, will be absorbed into existence along with you? Can you see any way out for your tiny problem when we will all be lost like drops of water into this vastness? Will not the disease be cured when the patient himself is lost?

Then why do you beg from house to hose? Why should you consult anyone else? Why should you not simply bare yourselves, simply surrender yourselves before that totality? This is the essence of prayer. And Kabir's love of prayer is very profound.

Let us try to understand this a bit more deeply. There are two ways to reach the destination. One way is that of meditation; the other, that of prayer. The path of meditation is for the pursuers of knowledge; the path of prayer is for the lovers, for the devotees.

On the path of meditation there is a danger that the ego, the "I," may not vanish, because the idea that "I am meditating" remians. In meditation there is no one else but "I"; ther is neither God, nor anyone else. In meditation you are alone. Unless you remain tremendously alert in meditation, the ego, the "I," will thwart you. No matter what heights you reach in meditation, the stone of the ego will remain heavy on your chest and you will be unable to fly. So at the final moment the meditator has to give up the ego. This is his emptiness. This is what Buddha calls the void, when the ego vanishes completely.

To attain to meditation is not enough — after that you will have to give up the ego. The ego will be purified, but it will still be there. That is the final veil. It is very fine, you can see through it. The veil will be transparent, but you will also have to remove it or it will simply remain there like a glass wall. You will be able to see what is beyond it, but you will be unable to meet Him, you will be unable to become one with God.

On the path of prayer, one has to give up the ego at the outset, at the initial stage. The devotee sets aside first what the yogi, the meditator, the sage, give up at the end.

Prayer means surrender. Prayer means to absorb oneself, to lose oneself at the feet of another. If you are able to pray, in the real sense of the word, there is no need for meditation.

I lay stress on meditation because I know you are not able to pray. My emphasis on meditation will begin to diminish when I see you are becoming strong enough to pray. I stress meditation because meditation can be practiced in spite of the ego, but prayer cannot. And this century is an age of great ego. Never before in history has there been such an egoistic age. The stumbling block of this centry is that every individual is filled with ego. Everyone has become a peak unto himself; everyone considers himself complete, without defect. "Why and for what should I surrender?" you ask.

To surrender has become very arduous; your spine has become paralyzed. This is why I talk so much about meditation. But I am really preparing you to enable you to pray. As you are able to go deeper and deeper into meditation I will begin to talk about prayer. There is a purpose in my beginning to speak about the saints to you. It is because I want to take you gradually from meditation into prayer. There is nothing else like prayer. That is why Kabir says:

Nothingness dies, the soundless dies;
Even the infinite dies.
A true lover never dies.
Says Kabir: know this.

Kabir says that meditation will die, but that prayer will not die; he says that knowledge will die, but that love will not die. Only one thing is immortal — love. And you must also achieve love through meditation. But if you are ready there is no need to undertake such a long journey, you can also take a direct jump.

Kabir just asks God. This is prayer. This is the beauty of prayer, the inner meaning of prayer. Kabir speaks as if God, the beloved, were in front of him. In the eyes of the so-called worldly-wise he is undoubtedly mad, but these so-called wise people will never be able to understand the heart of a devotee. For a devotee, the real question is not what he says; the real question, the final and deciding factor, is what he becomes.

Kabir lays his difficulty before God. Kabir says he is sad,

Why Go To Others?

that he has a problem, an entanglement, and he asks to whom he should go for advice, to whom he should go to find the solution. He has no answer, he says, and so he asks God.

Try to understand this a little more deeply. Whenever you are in search of something, you will first of all use your head. You will think, "I shall find out for myself. I shall solve the problem myself and then I won't have to reveal it to anybody." That in itself is the cause of your problem.

And what is your problem? Your problem is that you yourself are trying to solve your own problem. You are like a man trying to pull himlself up by his shoe-laces; you are like someone trying to pick up one spoon with another.

During the sunny days of winter, have you ever seen a dog that has been sitting and basking in the sun suddenly trying to catch hold of the tail lying by his side? He pounces upon his own tail. But is it possible to catch one's own tail by making a rush at it? As soon as the dog rushes at his tail, his tail rushes away. And then the dog rests for a while. He begins to wonder what the difficulty is. "It is so near," he says. "It is such a small distance. I have caught things before that were much further away than this." And then he begins to pursue his tail with renewed and greater vigor. If the determination to catch his own tail seizes hold of a dog he will go mad.

Philosophers are caught up in such a trap. And this is why they have all gone mad. Philosophy is the effort to catch one's own tail. But it can never be caught. So in spite of your efforts, in spite of jumping at it, in spite of running about hither and thither, in spite of trying various tricks, nothing is solved. When you jump, your tail jumps right along with you. Your entanglement is part and parcel of you yourself. It is your tail, it is joined to you.

How can you solve your problem? What you are trying to resolve is concealed, like the dog's tail, in the very attempt at a solution. Even in the solution you come up with, the problem does not disappear. The problem remains.

So, man tries to solve his own problem first. It is the first sign of his ego. And when he finds it is impossible for him to solve his own difficulty, then he goes in search of an expert. Finding an expert means finding some other person.

Understand the distinction carefully. You are not in search of a master. The master is one who has now become God's representative, but the expert is just like you. There is no need to have any respect for him, no need to touch his feet, no need to surrender to him.

You approach an expert when you become helpless yourself. But going to an expert is like going to yourself — he is just like you. The difference is completely superficial. The expert has only studied a particular subject a little more than you have. And you pay him a fee for his advice. You are simply asking advice from a person like yourself.

This kind of advice will not solve your difficulty at all. This is also an ego trip. By doing it you will be afforded a little solace. The expert will simply suppress your entanglement for a while. He will give you long explanations; he will create a network of theories that will engross you for a time and make you think your difficulty has been resolved. But, after a bit, the problem will stand before you once again, in new colors, in a new form, in a new shape. And it will pursue you throughout your life.

As soon as you go to a man in whom you can see God the solution to your problem begins. Really, the solution has already been achieved. And when you see God pervading all of existence, then you can talk directly to Him. This is what happens to the devotee in the end. And it is in such a moment that Kabir says, *I'm in a muddle. You resolve it, Bhagwan.* Then there is no need for any intermediary between you and existence, not even a master. And the beauty of it all is that your problem is solved as soon as you reveal it to existence. The problem only existed because you had tied it up into a neat bundle and kept it hidden away, because you were living in unconsciousness, in perplexity. Before God, keep yourself open. This is the real significance of prayer — keeping your heart completely open to Him, surrendering to Him totally.

When you are praying it is unseemly to make a display of your spiritual knowledge or to recite the scriptures. That is why the prayers of children bear more fruit. And when a saint prays, his prayer is as good as that of a child.

Once a young boy went into his bedroom, jumped straight into bed, and covered himself with his blanket. His mother reminded him that he had not said his prayers. The child replied, "Is it right to awaken God from His sleep on such a cold night? And so late?"

From such a child, God needs no prayer composed of words. His concern that the night was so cold and that it was too late to disturb God's sleep is prayer itself. Feeling like this is enough; there is no need to say anything.

And the word 'God' is merely an excuse, a help in expressing our feelings to the totality. In fact, the whole of existence is God. All is divine. And when you are filled with this feeling of divinity, you become united with the whole of existence. The solution to your problem is in that union.

Your real problem is that you are uprooted. And because you are uprooted you are thirsty. Your roots are unable to absorb water, that is why you feel so afflicted. Even when you have everything you have wished for, you still have the feeling you are missing something, the feeling that you want something. If your roots are not deep beneath the soil you will not be able to absorb water even if the rain is falling. And so you are certain to remain thirsty.

To be united with existence is prayer. Prayer is this particular state of feeling.

There is a very fine anecdote about a famous Hebrew mystic named Baal Shem. He was a peculiar kind of devotee — in his prayers he generaly quarreled with God. Only lovers can quarrel. If something he didn't like happened, he used to make a lot of fuss. His prayers were worth hearing because they were direct conversations with God.

Baal Shem thought the world was getting worse and worse every day, so he complained to God, "Why don't You come down to earth as You promised? You said You would come when things really got bad. Why are You delaying?" The story tells us that God was greatly harassed by him in this way, and quite often too.

One of Baal Shem's disciples used to make a note of whatever he said. He was writing Baal Shem's biography, and he also used to jot down these chats with God.

The story goes on to say Baal Shem once bothered God so much He sent His messenger to earth, telling him to brainwash Baal Shem and his disciple so they would forget everything.

Baal Shem was that much of a nuisance. The divine

messenger carried out his instructions to the letter. When Baal Shem arose from his prayers, he had forgotten everything. He could not even remember his own name. He did not remember that the world was full of problems and that he wanted God to come and remedy them immediately. He could neither remember who he was nor where he was. But when he looked at his disciple he had a vague recollection, as if in a dream, that he was a mystic and that this man was his disciple. He asked the disciple to tell him what he could remember of the past. The disciple was unable to tell him anything, he had been brainwashed totally. He replied, "I do not even remember who I am either."

Baal Shem said, "I have given you many lessons in the past. Try to remember a sutra from any one of them and repeat it quickly. Time is passing and we may find ourselves in some difficulty."

The disciple replied, "I remember nothing but the Hebrew alphabet — *aleph, beth, gimmel, deleth*..."

Baal Shem said, "Be quick. Speak the letters aloud." The disciple began to recite the alphabet, and Baal Shem followed suit. This one clue brought their memories back. And then Baal Shem began to take God to task. "Why did You play this trick on me?" he asked.

It is said that Baal Shem finished his prayer by repeating the alphabet and thus regained his lost memory. There is nothing of substance in the letters *aleph, beth, gimmel,* or *deleth,* but he repeated them with such attentiveness that he regained his original self. And then he shouted to God, "It is absolutely essential the Messiah come down to earth now!"

God recalled His messenger and told him he had not done

his job very well. The messenger replied, "It is dangerous to work on this man. No matter how hard one tries, his prayer cannot be snatched away from him. We can take everything from him except his prayer. His prayer has no relationship whatsoever with his brain — his prayer comes from his totality. His intellect, his words, can be snatched away from him, but his love cannot, his prayer cannot. There, even you are helpless."

That is why Kabir says:

Nothingness dies, the soundless dies;
Even the infinite dies.
A true lover never dies.
Says Kabir: know this.

Even if God wants to kill your prayer He cannot do so. Here, He too his helpless. Love is the ultimate.

How sweet and beautiful are these words of Kabir:

I'm in a muddle. You resolve it, Bhagwan.
When You are mine, why go to others?

What is the problem? It is very deep; it is the final, ultimate problem, and so Kabir asks:

When You are mine, why go to others?

"Why should I be concerned with other people?" he is saying to God. "I ask You directly. When You, the solution to my problem, are there in front of me, why should I go to others?"

Is mind greater than what's minding mind?

Now Kabir is asking which is greater, the mind or the witness.

Why Go To Others?

The he asks:

Is Ram greater than he who knows Ram?

And then:

Is Brahma greater than what he arose from?

Is Brahma greater, Kabir is asking, or is He who is the creator of Brahma greater? Is the existence that is the root of all supreme power greater?

Are the Vedas greater than their very source?

And then Kabir asks God whether the Vedas are greater than that ultimate consciousness out of which they have been born.

Says Kabir: I'm so confused...
Is the temple greater than he who serves God?

Now we shall try to understand each sentence; we shall try to grasp the nature of the problem, to understand why it is there.

This problem is the final problem; I know it is not just your personal problem. When all other problems are solved, this remains as the fianl problem as the last beyond this there is no question at all.

The beauty of this sutra is that it is complete in itself. No answer is received from God. Kabir already has the answer, that is why the sutra is complete. No discussion arises over the answer. No sooner is the question raised than it is solved. And you can also see that the answer was hidden in the question. It was only a matter of putting the question; the solution was already there.

I'm in a muddle. You resolve it, Bhagwan.
When You are mine, why go to others?

Ponder over this a bit. You cannot be free from others, free from the crowd, so long as God is not yours too. You are not strong enough on your own, and so you feel you are in need of the crowd. The crowd is very great and you are sorely tempted to become part of it. This is because your soul is anxious to be linked with existence.

But you know nothing at all about existence. And so you create your own tiny existences. You say, "I am a Hindu," and by doing so you cease to be alone. Then two hundred million people are with you. For you, Hinduism has now become a miniature existence. Your ego feels expanded — now you no longer feel trivial. You have created an imaginary existence.

But, after all, it is imaginary, a false thing. A crowd has no authentic existence of its own, only individuals exist. There are two kinds of existence — the existence of the individual and the existence of the totality, of the infinite. Everything that lies between these two is simply talk, nothing but imagination.

So if you think of yourself as a Hindu, you become linked with two hundred million others. You have created a big circle for yourself. But no matter how great it is, it has its limits; it can be measured. And so it is small. Even though it is small, it brings you some satisfaction. Otherwise, you yourself seem so small, just encircled by the skin of the body. And this displeases you. This is why people join mass movements.

If you become a communist, then you can become even bigger than a Hindu. Half the world is communist today. One and a half billion people are communists. And so you connect yourself with a very large assembly. Now you are not small at all. You will die, but communism will remain. You

Why Go To Others?

feel you have achieved a kind of immortality, but it is a false immortality. You will die, but the country will endure, the nation will remain. The Hindus may die and the communists may also die, but Hinduism and communism will remain.

The truth of the matter is, whether you live with a small crowd or with a larger one there is no life, no reality in any of them. They are illusions. The individual has his own existence, that is for certain, but the crowd has none. A crowd simply means that many people have come together and are standing in a group. But even in a crowd each individual is a separate entity. Although it appears as a crowd, it is a deception. Where will you go to find society? If you set out in search of it, will you ever be able to find it? Wherever you go you will only find individuals. The individual is a reality; society is merely a word.

You are sitting here, each individual is a reality, but where is the reality in your sitting in a crowd? Where is the substance in it? If you leave this place one by one, will a crowd remain behind? I would not be able to see any crowd here then. The crowd would have disappeared as well. Will any quality of being a Hindu remain if you separate each Hindu from the group? No quality will remain whatsoever. "Quality of being a Hindu" is only a phrase, only words. Nation, society, race — all are just words.

The thirst to be existence itself is great; it is deep-rooted in the mind of man. The thirst is real, but you are trying to quench it with imaginary water. It is not wrong, there is nothing wrong in having this thirst. That thirst is telling you that you will remain thirsty until you become God.

Man is a reality as an individual. God is a reality as an

infinite totality. And everything in between is imaginary. No matter how great your idea of manhood is, where will you find it? Wherever you go you will find man, you will find the individual, but where will you find "manhood"? And yet one feels that it exists. But where is it? If each and every individual were to die, manhood would not remain. It is merely a combination of words, it is not real at all. And man is miserable because of these dreams.

You hear phrases like "Hinduism is in danger" or "Islam is in danger." Islam does not exist at all; how can it be in danger? A Moslem can be in danger as an individual — but will Islam be in danger? It is not a living thing, how can it die? Islam is an empty word. Perhaps that is why it has lasted. Something that is living will die, but a word can go on living for centuries. A word has no life in it. It is life-less; it is a dead thing. Try to understand this correctly.

A devotee becomes free of the crowd. Kabir asks why he should go to others when God is his. He asks why he should have anything to do with other people, with the crowd, with society?

When the individual awakens within you only two shores remain — existence and you, God and the devotee. And the river that flows between these two is prayer. As long as you think of the crowd as real and follow it, you will be living in delusion, in deception. You are not able to live alone, you are not that strong. Alone, you feel insecure. And so man clings to the crowd to his last breath.

I have heard that Mulla Nasruddin once drank too much wine and fell down in the street. It was midnight, and it was very cold. A policeman approached him and asked, "What are you doing here? What has happened to you?"

The Mulla thought he was dying, so he said, "My death is approaching. Please bring a brahmin to me."

The policeman asked, "Why a brahmin? What is your name?"

"Mulla Nasruddin," he replied.

The policeman said, "What do you want with a brahmin? I'll call a Mohammedan priest."

The mulla said, "No. I want to convert to Hinduism before I die."

The policeman was a bit surprised and asked, "Why? You have lived as a Moslem all your life, why do you want to change at the time of your death?"

The mulla replied, "I do not want a single Moslem to die. It would be much better if a Hindu were to die instead."

Man holds fast to the crowd even with his dying breath, and so it is preferable to decrease the Hindus by one so there should not be fewer Moslems. The crowd gives you a sense of security. You are surrounded by the crowd in life as well as in death, but the devotee has to be alone. The devotee will have to leave the highway and proceed in the opposite direction.

Reach the town by some back way;
Get looted on the highway.

Those who choose the by-ways reach their destination. Such people are ready to make their journey quite on their own.

The real prayer will arise out of your heart only when you are prepared to be alone, because only then will you be able to see God. Kabir says, these kind of people have one foot on this shore and one foot on that shore, and that the bridge between the two shores is prayer. And prayer moves deeper and deeper until finally this shore disappears and that shore disappears and prayer alone remains; until neither the devotee nor God remains, until only devotion remains — until only its fragrance remains. Now both the devotee and God are lost.

Kabir's question is about the mind — about this mind which is a web of thoughts, causing all this trouble; about this mind which gives rise to problems and anxieties, dreaming all sorts of foolish dreams; about this mind which is the home of desires: about this mind which is the total expanse of this dejected and uneasy world. Kabir asks if this mind is great, or if the witness that hides behind and observes it is greater.

When anger comes, it is the mind. If you become alert and look within you will see the smoke of anger rising. Then you have become the witness. If you consider the mind as you, then you are a *sansari,* a worldly man. But if you have started to see yourself as a little outside the mind, even the tiniest bit, then you are a *sannyasi.* And when you have realized that you are completely outside the mind, then you become God.

Kabir asks if this mind is great, or if he who knows the mind is greater. And bear in mind that the one who knows, even the one who knows the mind, is you. And so you will never know your self, because when you know your self, the knower himself is you. Whatever is known is not you. And so the soul will always keep on receding, moving backward. Whatever can be known by you will become detached, separate, different — it will stand apart from you. So how will you know your self? To know one's self means this much only — that you have realized you are the supreme element which can never be known. That is self-realization.

You have already known all that can be known. But all these things are of the outer world; they are not of the inner world. And you have ignored that which is, that which is to be known. When you try to know that, you will begin to move deeper and deeper within.

The one who knows what is happening is you. Continue to go within, deeper and deeper, until there is nothing left to know, until only the knower is left. That is meditation, where no one but the knower is left.

If the knower is a man of intellect alone, then he will be in meditation, but if the knower is a man of the heart he will be in love. If the knower is dry like a desert, then he has one step further yet to take; the cloud of love has not yet showered on him. This is the cloud Kabir describes:

*Kabir says: clouds of love
Came on me showering;*

*Soaked the heart,
Greening the inner jungle.*

Your jungle has not yet become green. You have almost reached your destination, but the seed has not broken apart yet, the seed has not blossomed yet. You have just been freed from your rubbish.

It is just like a person making a new garden. At first he removes the rubbish, cleans the whole area, pulls out the weeds, and thus prepares the soil for the seeds. But as yet there is no garden.

Meditation is the preparation; love is the fruit. That is why Buddha says not to consider your knowledge as complete as long as the stream of compassion does not flow from it. Buddha uses the word *karuna,* compassion, for love. If knowledge is not mixed with love, if it remains dry, it is like preparing the soil but not planting seeds in it. So there will not be any flowers. And if there are not to be any flowers then what was the point of preparing the soil? Then all your labor has been in vain — flowers must blossom in a garden.

Bear in mind that love is the ultimate. Meditation is just the preparation, it is just the path. Love is the goal, the destination. So understand this — the meditation from which love does not flow still has ego concealed in it. That is why you are dry. The ego is without feelings, it is like a stone. And so we say that a heart without love is a heart of stone. You cannot get any juice from it, it is dead. Life only flowers out of love.

Whatsoever you know is just your mind. What else have you known up to now? Even the worldly things you know are hardly your own experiences. You only know things through the mind, you only know them mentally.

You see a tree in front of you, but you have not really seen it. You see its shadow in the mirror of your mind; that is what you see. When you touch a tree you think you are touching it, but you are mistaken — your hand touches it. And there is a great distance between your hand and your mind. Your hand touches it and tells your mind about it. You only know the mind — you are always following the mind.

This is why the enlightened ones say there is no difference between the world and dreams. The world and dreams alike

Why Go To Others?

both happen in the mind, they are both creations of the mind. And there is even no proof that the world outside exists. How can there be any proof? You only know the world through the mind. And no one who has removed the mind has ever known the world. So what guarantee is there that the tree is outside? You can also see a tree at night in your dreams, and you even think it is as real as the one you see during the day.

When the enlightened ones say that the world is like a dream, it means that both are known through the mind. It is difficult to decide about the reality of things. Their reality is doubtful. It is possible you are seeing a dream now, that I am not here. How can you definitely say whether you are hearing my voice in a dream or in a waking state? What test do you have to decide the truth, to decide whether you are hearing me while awake or in a dream? How do you know that I am present here? Whatsoever you find out will be found out through the mind — the mind will always be there.

You have seen the world, but you have only had a glimpse in a mirror. You have never seen beyond the mirror, so how can you be certain about what you have seen? Therefore the enlightened ones say the world is an expansion of the mind, an extension of the mind. That is what it is. Whatsoever you know is only a reflection created in the mind. The mind is nothing but the sum total of all those reflections. Know this well: the mind is sansara, the mind is the world, the mind is illusion.

I have told you one Zen story many times. Once two Buddhist monks were standing at the door of a temple, hotly discussing why the flag at the top of the temple was fluttering in the air.

One monk said, "The wind is making it flutter." The other monk insisted, "The flag itself is fluttering, and that makes the wind blow." The discussion was heated; it was a difficult point to decide.

The master came out of the temple and said, "Both of you are silly. Neither the wind nor the flag is fluttering. It is your mind oscillating; it is your mind swinging back and forth."

The master means to say that both happenings, the blowing of the wind and the fluttering of the flag, are known through your mind.

You can be certain of one thing only, and it is this — the mind swings to and fro. Other things are not definite either; nothing definite can be said about anything.

The sansara, this world about which nothing can be definitely asserted, this world we cannot pinpoint as real or unreal, is called maya. The word 'maya' is wonderful.

Truth is that which is — that about which we can be absolutely certain, that about which there can be no doubt whatsoever, and the only thing like this there is, is your existence as the witness. About the witness there can be no doubt. "I am' is the only thing about which there is no doubt at all. Even if you wish to doubt it, the presence of the "I" is necessary. Otherwise, who will raise the doubt? Whatever does not exist is false, exactly opposite to truth.

About the existence of truth no thought is possible; about the nonexistence of truth no thought is possible either. These are the two situations, and maya is between the two. Maya is that which appears to exist but in fact does not. Maya is a phenomenon about which you can neither assert nor deny. It is doubtful.

Why Go To Others?

And why the doubt? The doubt exists because we have not known it directly — no one has. And those who come to the state of no-mind say that, along with the mind, the world also disappears. All agree on this point. All the enlightened ones agree on this single point, that no sooner does one attain to true knowledge than sansara, the world, is no more. No mind; no sansara. And what is left they call God. Those that do not know call it sansara.

God is the form of existence seen when the mind is not, when the mind is not interfering. Then on one side there is the soul and on the other side there is pure existence. Maya is existence seen through the mind; truth is existence seen by the witness. That is God.

Kabir is asking:

Is mind greater than what's minding mind?

What is the need for a reply? The reply is hidden in the question. If you unravel the puzzle first, then the whole thing becomes so clear. The one who sees is greater; whatever is seen is smaller. The one who sees is consciousness; what is seen is matter.

Is Ram greater than he who knows Ram?

And then Kabir raises a difficult question. If a man is unaware that his mind is not as great as the knower of his mind, then this question will crop up.

Is Ram greater than he who knows Ram?

If God is also known, Kabir is asking, then is the knower of God greater than God? If God is also known, then the knower is certainly greater, then the witness is certainly greater. Some enlightened men put self-knowledge above

God; they consider it greater than God. Mahavira did, for example. Mahavira said the soul was supreme.

And so, in the final analysis, only the knower remains. God is also known, so He too cannot be greater than the knower. It is a very subtle thing to understand that everything vanishes at the moment one attains the highest knowing, at the moment one achieves the ultimate knowledge. Sansara vanishes, and the creator of sansara also disappears. Existence disappears too, and only consciousness, only pure consciousness — the seer, the witness, the soul or whatsoever name you want to call it — remains. The knower is certainly greater; consciousness is undoubtedly greater.

At the final moment, consciousness becomes God. When the devotee reaches this final stage he becomes God, he himself becomes *Bhagwan*. Now everything is smaller. Whatsoever is known — all experience — becomes small, and the experiencer is the greater. All perceptions, all things seen become insignificant, and once and for all the seer, the witness, is ultimate.

Is Brahma greater than what he arose from?

Kabir asks if Brahma who created the universe is great, or if the great existence in which Brahma himself was born is greater.

Ultimately, the original source is greater. And that original source is hidden within you. Kabir is indicating this fact, that no one is greater than you. And how small and insignificant you consider yourself to be! You are the ultimate, the finality. Nothing is beyond you or above you. Yet how small you thing you are!

And it is because you think of yourself as so small that the

Why Go To Others?

ego is born in you. The ego is born in you because you do not want to believe you are so small. And so you claim you are big. All such assertions are false. And yet the inquiry that underlies these claims is very significant, very meaningful indeed. Indirectly you are asking, "How is it I am willing to be so small?" The innermost consciousness within you is unwilling to be small and so you make false claims. You have no idea of what truth is and so at times you say, "See how much wealth I have! See how learned I am! Look, I have renounced this! Look, I have renounced that!" But you do not realize what you are saying. All this egoistic talk is false. You are in fact greater than God; you are greater than *Bhagwan*. You are the ultimate.

This feeling that you will not be at ease until you have become the ultimate, until you attain to the highest state, pervades every particle of your being. You hanker after significant positions, but ultimately find them all to be useless. Whenever you attain to a particular position, you immediately find it to be insignificant.

There was a very famous American president named Coolidge. He once fought for election and won; he became president. He was very popular, and unlike most politicians he was a man of saintly character. He was also a man of very few words. It was difficult to make him talk; he liked to be quiet, to remain silent as much as possible.

A lady once invited Mr. Coolidge to dinner and made a bet she would extract at least four words from him. She went on talking for a long time but Coolidge remained silent. Finally, she pressed him to say something. He answered, "I don't know." He only uttered three words. She could not even get four whole words out of him!

Another time Coolidge was strolling up and down in front of the White House. A stranger to Washington stopped him and asked who lived in that huge house. He answered, "No one lives here. People just come and go. It isn't a house, it's a tavern." It was only afterwards the stranger realized that the man himself lived in the White House; that he had spoken to the president of America himself. Coolidge was that kind of man.

When his first term as president was over, his friends and followers requested he stand for election once again. They said success was assured. Coolidge replied, "No further now." Why? His words were wonderful. He said, "There can be no further promotion. I have been president once. Now there is no post higher. What is the point? Now I know that this position, this status, brings no contentment either."

No matter what you obtain, it will not satisfy you. You will not be satisfied until you attain to the ultimate. There is no contentment until you achieve God. God is your original source; God is your nature.

Kabir asks if Ram is greater or the one who knows Ram, if Brahma is greater or the one out of whom Brahma was born, and now he asks:

Are the Vedas greater than their very source?

Kabir asks if the highly-praised Vedas are greater than the *rishis,* than the consciousness which created them.

The Vedas are only the utterances of the enlightened, so is the utterance greater, or is the consciousness by which it was uttered greater? What benefit will there be in knowing the Vedas? Try to attain to that state out of which the Vedas were created.

Why Go To Others?

The Vedas descended upon the *rishis*. And the Koran descended upon Mohammed. So is the Koran greater, or is the consciousness of Mohammed, the consciousness out of which the Koran was born, greater? The Vedas are merely words, and that wordless witness from whence they came is the greater.

The questions of Kabir are so clear and so unambiguous that no answers to them are needed.

Says Kabir: I'm so confused...
Is the temple greater than he who serves God?

There are reasons for this question. Kabir spent his life in Kashi, never going to bathe in the Ganges, and when the time of his death drew nigh, he asked his followers to take him to Maghar, a small village near Kashi.

It is said that whosoever dies in Maghar will be reborn as a donkey, and that whosoever dies in Kashi will go to heaven, will become liberated even if he is the greatest sinner in the world. So Kashi is a sort of cremation ground, and people journey there when death is approaching. Old men and women congregate there, waiting for death, so that they can go straight to heaven. But it is said that he who dies in Maghar, even if he is a holy man, becomes a donkey after death, while from Kashi, it is said, there is no other possibility but liberation.

So when Kabir asked his followers to take him to Maghar they said, "You have gone mad! You have spent all your life in Kashi, and now, at the time of your death, you are thinking of going to Maghar? At the end of their lives people from Maghar run to Kashi!"

What Kabir said in reply is very significant. "If I die in

Kashi and go to heaven," he said, "I will know nothing about God's grace. Where will there be any room for His grace if I die in Kashi? To reach heaven just because I died in Kashi is not at all palatable or agreeable to me." He said, "If I die in Maghar and go to heaven, then and only then will it be because of his grace. To enjoy the bliss of God's grace it is necessary to go to Maghar. And so I shall die in Maghar!"

Says Kabir: I'm so confused...
Is the temple greater than he who serves God?

Why is a holy place considered holy? A place is considered holy because some devotee of God must have lived there at some point. There doesn't seem to be any other reason for it. A devotee attains to God in a certain spot and so the site becomes a holy place. It is easy for another person to reach God from there because the place is charged with the vibrations of the devotee who attained.

Buddha achieved the ultimate knowledge under the bodhi tree, so the tree became holy. Buddha didn't become enlightened because of the tree, but the tree became holy because of Buddha's enlightenment. And so Bodhgaya became a place of pilgrimage. Under that tree one man was absorbed into the highest consciousness, and this happening is so great its effect remains for eternity. The impression can never be effaced. The effect on the place is immortal; the effect of an individual giving up his mortal life and attaining to the immortal one is eternal.

At some time in the past divine nectar poured down on Buddha on this spot; he was drenched in the downpour of the infinite, and the place will always be fragrant with the sweet smell of that nectar. This piece of earth has known an extraordinary event. This small plot of land has witnessed a small crack in the sansara, and through it an individual has gone beyond. And so it has become a holy place. The place where the devotee of God walks becomes a place of pilgrimage.

The *pundits*, the scholars of Kashi, condemned Kabir as a sinner. They never liked him; they could never tolerate him. They were incapable of digesting Kabir. To digest Kabir great courage is required, and the pundits, the learned men, are not so bold. Kashi is the home of pundits. From time immemorial, Kashi has abounded the pundits. And if the pundits of the world have ruined anything, it is Kashi. If a place becomes holy because of an enlightened one, then what happens because of an enlightened one, then what happens because of pundits has happened to Kashi. Refuse has collected there.

The pundits used to harass Kabir. They used to say, "You have not studied the Vedas, you do not know Sanskrit, and yet you are bold enough to talk about the supreme wisdom, the supreme knowledge! And you do so without knowing the Vedas!"

So Kabir asks:

Are the Vedas greater than their very source?

The pundits also used to say to Kabir, "You are living in a holy place like Kashi, so go and bathe in the Ganges. She will make you holy." So Kabir asks:

Is the temple greater than he who serves God?

The question is rhetorical: the answer is already there. Wherever the devotee of God walks, that place becomes a place of pilgrimage. Nobody reaches God because he resides in Kashi; Kashi has become a place of pilgrimage because someone residing in it has attained to God.

All the Hindu places of pilgrimage are situated on the banks of rivers, because the Hindu technique of meditating on the flow of a river is a very deep and meaningful experiment in meditation. If a seeker continues to meditate on the continuous flow of a river for a long time, his mind will also flow away.

To understand this phenomenon, it is worth reading *siddhartha* by Hermann Hesse. Hesse understood the deep significance of this Hindu technique to an extent no Hindu could ever do. Sitting on the bank of a river, witnessing its changing moods, working as a boatman on it, Siddhartha, the hero of Hesse's book, achieves liberation.

With the seasons, the river changes its form, its appearance. When it is in flood, its fury, its youth and its turbulence are something to see. When the dry summer days come it loses its force and assumes a rather sorrowful appearance. Pits form and pools gather at various places; all its splendor, pride and mischief are gone. It is now a skeleton. It is as if the river were old, as if it were not on its deathbed.

Siddhartha watches all these changing moods of the river. He spends hours sitting on the bank, and by and by, slowly, slowly, he recognizes the changing moods of his own mind in those of the river. Youth, old age, misery, happiness — he watches them all pass away. The river of the mind is always flowing; the witness, steady and hidden, simply observes. This is the Hindu meditation technique.

This is also the reason the Hindus created their holy places

Why Go To Others?

on the banks of rivers. Innumerable people have achieved liberation there, it has been happening since time immemorial. But a holy place is a holy place only because of them — they did not achieve liberation because of the holy place. Nobody become liberated just by going to Kashi. The place where you achieve liberation will become a Kashi.

The Jainas have made all their places of pilgrimage on hills and on mountains. Their technique is not linked with rivers at all, their technique is linked with mountains.

Try to understand this. The Hindus created holy places on the banks of rivers because the nature of the mind is ever-changing. It is just like the flow of a river. The river is flowing, and the unchangeable, ever-steady witness is simply standing there, observing. The Jainas created their places of pilgrimage on mountains, exactly opposite to the Hindus. The mountain is a symbol of steadfastness; the mountain stands there, unchanged, solid. The Hindu technique is to transcend the mind, while that of the Jainas is to remain in that steadfastness. If you remain steady you will automatically transcend the river; if you transcend the river you will automatically become steady. These are the two banks. You can transcend from either of them.

Mount Girnar and the Shikharji mountains are holy places because down the ages countless people have achieved liberation from there. Twenty-three Jaina *tirthankaras* achieved liberation on the hills of Shikharji. Mahavira is the only exception. So the atmosphere of the place is filled with the vibrations of these great masters. Every particle of the place reminds one of their presence. When you visit that place you feel as if you are falling into that flow. It becomes easy to do so. Your journey becomes rather easy from there. This is the only significance of a holy place. But the devotee of God is certainly greater than any holy place.

Kabir says no one is greater than you, but you will only achieve that greatness when you surrender totally. In this *sadhana,* in this journey, the paradox is that no one is greater than you — even Ram is not greater than the one who knows Ram — but you will only attain to this greatness when you become the smallest of the small. You will become a deep chasm, a deep abyss. When you surrender, when you become smaller than a particle of dust, you become as great as God.

To be humble, to surrender, to give up the ego is to achieve the highest possible greatness. If you remain egoistic, you remain insignificant. The ego is mean, inconsequential. If you hold on to it, you will be no more substantial than a grain of sand. It is absolutely essential to be free of it; the ego is the only impediment to your greatness. You are insignificant only because of it. When it is no more, no one is higher than you. Then you are the sovereign sound of existence, then you are the supreme music. And this is the answer to all your problems.

The whole problem exists simply because you have been unable to come to know what you really are. And your innermost desire is to know that, to be that. This means you have been trying to achieve greatness with the help of something utterly insignificant. You are like a certain king of Egypt the Sufis tell about.

The king loved a certain fakir very much, and the fakir used to go to the palace whenever he was sent for. Many times the king said to the fakir, "I wish to come to your cottage," but the fakir always said, "No. There is nothing worthy of you there. Whenever you want me I shall come to you."

This reply aroused the king's curiosity. It instilled a desire in him to visit the fakir's cottage, and so one day he went there without warning. The fakir's wife was at home, but the fakir was working in the fields. The wife said, "Please sit down here. I will just fetch him." But the king kept pacing up and down in front of the cottage.

The wife thought, "He is pacing up and down because there is nothing to sit on," so she brought an old torn carpet from the hut and spread it upon the ground. She then requested the king to sit on it, saying she would go and fetch the fakir. The king said, "Yes, go and fetch him," but did not sit on the carpet. He simply continued to pace up and down. The woman was a bit surprised, but went to get her husband anyway.

On the way back she said to him, "The king seems to be a very strange person indeed. I asked him to sit down several times. At first I thought he wouldn't sit down because there was no rug, so I spread the carpet out but he still wouldn't sit on it."

The fakir replied, "You made a mistake. We don't have a place fit for him. That is why I never invited him here. If we press him to sit down on that old torn carpet, he will become impatient to leave rather than sit on it for any length of time. You should not have asked him to sit down." When they arrived at the cottage the fakir began to talk to the king, walking up and down with him at the same time.

When he noticed this the king was somewhat surprised —

the fakir's wife had asked him to sit down several times and the fakir did not invite him to sit down even once. So when the time came for him to depart, the king inquired, "Why did you not ask me to sit down, not even once, when your wife asked me so many times?"

The fakir said, "My wife is a simple woman. She knows nothing about court etiquette. We don't have a place suitable for you. You are used to sitting on a royal throne. You would have been very uneasy on an old torn carpet. It would have been very difficult for you."

Although this is a Sufi story, it is also about you. You will always be uneasy as long as you remain less than God. And your ego is no better than that old torn carpet. Your ego is dirty all over. Your ego is false. Its claims have no meaning; they are undisciplined and wanton. You know this too, but your problem is that you are unable to see the royal throne.

How long can you go on pacing up and down? So you become willing to sit down on the old torn carpet and then you try to persuade your mind that it is not an old rug but a royal throne. If you do not persuade your mind thus, imagine how long you will have to go on pacing up and down! So you make the false assumption that the old torn carpet is a royal throne.

If someone notices it and ask what you are sitting on, you will exclaim, "What are you saying? Are you blind? This is a royal throne!" The whole world sees you are sitting on an old torn carpet, only you are unable to see it. And the one who points this out to you becomes your enemy, you think he is trying to snatch your throne away from you.

Your ego's claim, your claim that you are God, is bogus.

There is no need whatsoever to make such a claim — that is what you already are. The problem is the old torn carpet. You keep on claiming it is a throne. And if I were to place a throne before you, you would protest. "What is the point of this?" you would ask. "I am already sitting on a throne," you would insist.

From birth to birth, through countless lives, you have convinced yourself that the old torn carpet is a royal throne, that there is no seat higher. That is why you experience great difficulty when an awakened master, a *satguru,* asks you to give up your ego. He says to you, "Look, I am giving you a throne," but you are incapable of seeing the throne he is offering. You can only see your old torn carpet. You feel at least you have something to hold on to as long as the carpet is in your hands, but when you listen to the master you feel the carpet slipping from your grip. And you do not know whether the throne he is offering you is truly a royal throne or not.

You will only be able to see that the throne is really you when you are able to set your ego aside. Then your dream about the old torn carpet, about sansara, about the world, will end. And then you will begin to experience the existence of God.

9

RELAX IN JOY

Lord of death turns into Ram.
Misery gone, I relax in joy.

Foe reversed becomes a friend;
Fiends are seen as gentle men.
Now, for me, all is blessed.
Knowing Bhagwan, silence descends.

A million problems in the body
Turn into joyful, simple samadhi.
A recognizing deep within my heart:
Disease no more affects me.

Mind now becomes the eternal.
I know now: I was living dead.
Says Kabir: I'm simply joyous.
I'm not afraid, nor frightening others.

There is an ancient anecdote about Valmiki. He was not a learned man and he forgot the particular name for God his guru had given him as a *mantra*. He had given him "Ram," but the reverse of Rama — *Mara* — became fixed in his mind. 'Mara' means death. It is said that he repeated this mantra for quite a long time and ultimately achieved liberation. If the words "Mara, Mara, Mara" are repeated continuously, the sound of "Rama, Rama, Rama" will begin to emerge of its own accord.

Whether this really happened or not is unimportant, but the story is very symbolic and very beautiful. You are also repeating "Mara, Mara," but it does not turn into "Rama, Rama." Everyone is afraid of death and keeps repeating "Mara, Mara" within.

Kabir says a man dies a hundred times a day, and whenever any fear whatsoever catches hold of him the sound of "Mara, Mara" does not become like that of Valmiki — you have not repeated it with as much sincerity, rapidity and continuity as Valmiki did. The point of this story is that if anyone continues to remember death correctly, that remembering of death will itself become the remembrance of God.

When someone remembers death correctly his attachment to life is broken. Such a person will see death hidden in every moment of life. The attachment to life, the infatuation for life, of someone who has known death rightly will be killed naturally, will naturally disappear. Such a person will soon come to know the nectar hidden behind death, will soon come to know that death is one side of the coin and God is the other. On one side there is death; on the other, nectar.

Those who have known death have also known nectar. This is the substance, the inner meaning of the story that prevails about Valmiki — that while repeating "Mara, Mara" he achieved Ram, he achieved nectar.

You also remember "Mara, Mara," but there is no density in your remembering. You do it slowly and at great intervals.

You say "Mara" once, and then repeat it again after a long time, so they are not linked together. The sound of "Rama" will only be created if they are linked together rapidly. Then the remembering of death will itself become the remembering of Rama, of God. This is the first thing to be remembered before we move into the sutras of Kabir.

The second thing to remember is that no matter what you have in this life, nothing is useless. It is possible you may have been unable to arrange things in your life properly, and so no harmony is produced from them; it is possible you may not have been able to time things properly, that you may not know the art of beautifying your life; it is possible your life may be upside down, but if you master the art of tuning it properly you will find that nothing you have is meaningless. Everything is useful. Not even the smallest thing in life is useless — it cannot be. How can anything be useless? It is all the gift of the great existence from which life is created, of the great existence which has given life to us as a gift.

It is possible your understanding of life may be incomplete, that it may be faulty, but speaking truthfully, nothing in life is useless. There should simply be proper planning and arrangement, proper harmony. As you are, there is much disorder, much noise in you. But if a musical expert were able to catch hold of all these noisy sounds he would use them to produce harmonious music, to create a sweet and pleasing song. Through them, he would pour out his heart.

You have everything already, except this art of arranging things correctly. Were you to know this art your anger would be transformed into compassion, but you are ignorant of this art and so compassion itself is turned into anger. If you know this art your hatred is transformed into love; if you do not

Relax In Joy

know this art all your love will sour into the poison of hatred. You can turn a friend into an enemy or an enemy into a friend in the same way. It all depends on whether you know the art or not. If you don't know the art of life, "ours" becomes "others"; if you do know it then "others" becomes "ours."

No one else is ever responsible for anything that is wrong in your life. The fault lies somewhere in your arrangement of things. So don't slander life, you will gain nothing by it. When you slander life you are severing the limbs of your body, and they have been very useful in life. When you realize it later on, you will be sorry to see that you have made yourself crippled. Nothing is worth throwing away. If any limbs, if any part of life is giving you trouble, understand that you have arranged it badly. Put it in its proper place and the trouble, and uneasiness, will disappear.

You are restless and uneasy, and the whole reason is because you have your ears where your eyes should be, your hands where your eyes should be and your legs where your head should be. You are standing on your head. This is the cause of your uneasiness.

Giving proper and correct form to your life is the real task, the real *sadhana*. When you feel that something is giving you trouble, is making you uncomfortable, is pinching you, don't begin to condemn it, begin to think deeply about it and find out if you have made some mistake, find out if you have been keeping it in the wrong place.

With these things in mind let us now enter these sutras of Kabir.

Lord of death turns into Ram.
Misery gone, I relax in you.

Foe reversed becomes a friend;
Friends are seen as gentle men.
Now, for me, all is blessed.
Knowing Bhagwan, silence descends.

A million problems in the body
Turn into joyful, simple samadhi.
A recognizing deep within my heart:
Disease no more affects me.

Kabir says that which he considered as death, that person he considered as the messenger of death, has proven to be God Himself. He says he has known that death itself is nectar, but that he made a mistake seeing death in this way. Death is nowhere to be seen. There is no death except in ignorance. Nobody had ever died; nobody can ever die. Death has no existence. It cannot have. Whatever is will remain forever.

How can that which is be destroyed? To be destroyed means that existence becomes nonexistence, that whatever existed became nonexistent, yet scientists say we cannot even destroy a particle of sand. No matter how hard we try, even if we blast a sand particle apart with an atomic bomb, it will not be destroyed. It will be broken into pieces, but it will not be destroyed. There is no device to destroy it — there is none to create it.

To destroy means that what was there now becomes nonexistent; to create means that what is now there has been caused by us. What we call creating is only rearranging things, and what we call destroying is only a scattering here and there.

For example, we construct a building. Everything was

already there. The bricks, the stones, the water, the earth — they were already there. We simply arrange them, and the building is built. And now we pull it down. Then everything will still be there — bricks, stones, earth. The union among them is all that is broken.

Nothing is destroyed and nothing is created — only unions and scatterings take place. Union is life and scattering is death. As soon as you realize this you will see God standing behind death.

You remain afraid of death because you think it will obliterate you completely. There is no possibility whatsoever of your being obliterated. Death has visited you many times and you are still not canceled out. You have remained untouched. There is not even a mark of death to be found on you. Death has played all its tricks on you, has tried to blot you out, but you have remained invincible. And still you are afraid of it. It only appears as death, as obliteration, because of your ignorance. You have not looked at it in full consciousness.

A few moments before death a man becomes unconscious, and so you do not remember your past deaths. The only person who remembers his past death is the man who dies in consciousness. Remembering happens when one is aware; it cannot happen in unconsciousness. If a man sees death in awareness, then the lord of death turns into Ram, then Mara becomes Rama, then death becomes God. That was what happened to Valmiki.

As Valmiki was repeating "Mara, Mara," he all of a sudden became enlightened. The mantra reversed, and the continuous sound of "Rama" was heard. The letters in

"Rama" and "Mara" are the same, only their positions change. In "Mara," "Ma" is first and "Ra" is next; in "Rama," "Ra" is first and "Ma" is second. This is the only difference. But there is a great difference between "Mara" and "Rama," between death and God. God is ultimate existence; death is fear and darkness.

But enlightenment only happens when you are able to face death in awareness. So don't run away from death — wherever you go it is sure to follow you. There is no escape from it. Stop and look at death bravely.

Raman Maharshi has told how he achieved enlightenment. When he was seventeen years old, all of a sudden one day he felt that death was approaching. He had been wanting to know death, and so he lay down on the ground. When it is coming what else can be done? No one is ever saved from it. If death is certain, then die bravely, then meet it in awareness.

His hands and feet grew cold, his body became numb and he saw death approaching. The body lost its vitality and became almost lifeless, and yet he watched it approaching. At that moment the transformation took place. The body was dead, but he was alive. He sat up. He realized that death had happened to the body, but that there was no death for him. The fear disappeared that day; that day his search was over. That day the word "Mara" reversed, that day it became "Rama." Then there was nothing left to know.

And so the technique of Raman Maharshi is very easy. He says only this much — learn to die. And when you have learned this you will find, at the time of your death, that there is something within you which does not die. Your consciousness does not die. The body will be lying there, absolutely lifeless, but you will be fully alert, totally alive within. You have never been this alive, this alert, because up to now you have been one with the body; up to now its whole load has been on you. But now the body lies there dead, and there is no burden at all. Now you are free to fly in the sky.

If you practice how to die for a few days — lying down for a time every day and allowing the body to be as if dead — you will attain to meditation. You only have to remember one thing — that the body is now dead, that it is now just a corpse. It is not to be shaken or disturbed at all — a corpse does not move. Suppose an ant bites you. Then what will you do? You are lying there dead, and the ant is biting you. You should only observe it.

If you can lie down as if you are dead, if you can lie there absolutely motionless for some time each day, suddenly one day the happening will take place — the relationship between you and the body will be shattered, the consciousness and the body will separate from each other. Remaining apart, aloof, you will see your body alongside. An infinite distance happens then. And there is no way to bridge it. In this moment "Mara" is reversed, and the sound of "Rama" is heard. Now there is no death. Now you have known death and it has disappeared forever. The person who tries to run away from death without knowing it only becomes more and more afraid of it. You are trying to run away from it, and because of this you are in great difficulty. You are great escapists. Whenever you see danger you always run away. Yet you do not realize that your fear increases by running away, it does not decrease.

How can you run away from your shadow? Where will you run? If you run faster and faster you will see that your shadow runs just as fast. Your shadow is just behind you so you will say you are not running fast enough. You will run faster, and then your shadow will run even faster. Your mind will even tell you to risk your life to save yourself. But no matter how hard you try, you will always find your shadow next to you. It is your own shadow, it can never be avoided.

If you don't want your shadow to pursue you, then don't run. Just stand there and look at it. You will laugh when you look at it, because it is not there. Something's shadow appears as soon as that something obstructs light, and, in the same way, any obstruction to knowledge is death.

Death is your shadow. Death is not there; it only seems to be solid because you are running away from it. You want to save yourself from it and so it pursues you. But if you stand still, it will also stand still. Look at it attentively; it will be no more. There is no need to destroy it, no need to take a sword in your hand and cut its throat. Nothing has to be done to it. You have only to know its real nature, to know that the shadow is merely a shadow.

No sooner do you realize untruth as untruth, than it is no longer there. As soon as you recognize illusion as illusion, it ceases to exist; as soon as you recognize maya as maya, where can it exist? There is no need to know truth, you only need to know what falsehood is. When you know something as untruth it topples immediately. What remains is truth.

Don't try to seek truth directly, just try to know what untruth is. Don't try to know the meaning of life directly, try to know only what death is. Where are you going to look for God? Just know what death is. The shadow that looks like death is also God. Just look at the shadow attentively, and with its help you will reach Him whose shadow you see. At present you are trying to save yourself from the shadow, and so you are unable to attain to Him whose shadow it is you are seeing.

The shadow is the ladder. That is why Kabir asks, "When shall I disappear? When shall I see that total bliss?" When you look at the shadow with great attentiveness you will cease to be and only God will remain. As long as you are afraid of the shadow you cannot be authentic. How can you be authentic when you are afraid of untruth?

The thing that is afraid of the shadow is your ego. Understand this, and the meaning will be clear. The ego is afraid of death. And its fear is quite natural, because it will surely die. You have become one with the ego; you have identified yourself with it — and so you are afraid. It may not be easy for you to understand that the ego is going to die, but your fear is completely beyond comprehension. You are worried and anxious without any real cause.

As soon as you stand still the shadow and your ego will both disappear. These two are linked together. And in that moment of light and wisdom the messenger of death proves to be Rama. Then the whole meaning of life changes. Seen from this angle life is perfect bliss, the ultimate of existence. It all depends on how you look at it. Suppose someone has a glass half full of water. If you look at the unfilled part you will say it is half empty; if you look at the filled part you will say it is half full.

When you look at life from the angle of death you are looking at the unfilled part. Your emphasis is on the unfilled part, on the shadow. And so all your experiences will negate life. You could also have looked at life from the angle of fullness. Why do you choose to look at it from the angle of death? Why don't you look at it from the angle of life? Why do you look at it from the negative angle? This is the very deep-rooted habit of your mind. To look at the absence of something is the nature of the mind.

You do not see what you have — you only see what you don't have. The mind lives in that which is absent and so it always remains in misery and in anxiety. How can anyone live in joy if he is always thinking about things that are not? The road to joy is to live in the things with which we are full.

There once was a Jewish mystic called Jhusia. He was so poor none was poorer. One day the king was out riding on his horse and he passed a certain road, a road where Jhusia could always be found sitting under a nearby tree. If it were cold he would just sit there, trembling. He didn't have enough clothes, nor did he have wood with which to make a fire. He lived on whatever food was given him. The king had always noticed him praying in the morning, and so one day the king stopped to listen to his prayer.

Jhusia used to say, "O God, you are so very kind. You look after all my needs and fulfill them." The king could not endure this. He waited until the prayer was over and then he said, "Jhusia, you should be ashamed, telling such a lie. A seeker should not lie. What you are saying to God in your prayer is completely untrue. It is cold and you have no wood for your fire; you haven't enough clothes to wear and your body is trembling with the cold. You get your bread with great difficulty and you don't have a roof to shelter you — you are living under a tree. Your poverty is so great and yet you say to God, 'O God, you are so very kind. You look after all my needs and fulfill them.'"

Relax In Joy

Jhusia began to laugh and said, "Poverty is my needs." For such a man death will be reversed, Mara will become Rama.

This sentence of Jhusia's, "Poverty is my need," is really wonderful. There are certain things that only flower in poverty. If you are able to see this, if you are able to understand this, you will know the meaning of "Poverty is my need." There are certain things that die in prosperity, and if you are able to understand this you will see that richness is not a necessity. There are also certain things that flower in richness, in prosperity, and if you are able to see this, then richness is a necessity. It all depends on how you look at things. Jhusia said, "Poverty is my need." He said, "I need it now and so He has made me poor and kept me poor."

What angle do you look at life from? Why do you immediately begin to look at it from the angle of the shadow? You are alive now, but you do not see life; the fear of death has engulfed you. But that fear is not there at the present moment, is it? In fact, it never exists.

You are unable to see life, and it is standing just at your door. The sun has just risen but you don't see it; you are trembling in fear for the night that will come in the future. But for you the night has come now! Now what need is there for night to come? You have already brought it. In the bright morning, the night has already come. There is darkness at high noon.

And just as you have turned the bright sun into darkness, you can also create the opposite state. One who looks at things with a positive attitude, and not with a negative one, sees his own sun rising even in the dead of night. His sun never sets, it cannot. It all depends on how you look at things.

Always remember to look at things with a positive attitude, to look at things from the angle of what truly is. Slowly, slowly, climbing each step of the ladder you will reach the final step — Ram, the ultimate. But if you look at things from a negative viewpoint you will slowly and surely descend into the valley of darkness, into the valley of nonexistence, into the valley of death. It all depends on you.

The ladder stands between darkness and light. It is one and the same ladder. Have you ever noticed a ladder? It has two parts. One part is composed of small fixed bars or steps. These are the steps of positivity, the steps one uses to climb towards reality. The other part is that of voidness, of nothingness. This is negativity. And if you put your foot on this part, on the negative part, you will fall down into deep darkness. That is death. That is the shadow, that is darkness. But if you step on the rungs of is-ness, you will attain to *sat-chitanand*, to the highest and most perfect bliss. Kabir says:

Death — the whole world fears.
Death — my heart overjoys.

How do you look at things? How do you live? What is your way of life? Is it negative? Are you a nonbeliever? A believer? An atheist? A theist?

I call a man a theist, a believer, when his outlook is positive, and a man whose outlook is negative, I call him an atheist, a nonbeliever. To be a believer has no relation at all to believing in the existence of God, and to hold such a belief is completely unnecessary. To see what is, to know what really exists, is the way of the theist, of the believer; to see what does not really exist is the way of an atheist, of a nonbeliever. And if you form the habit of seeing what really does not exist, you yourself will cease to be. And that is death. By forming the habit of seeing what is, you will become the highest existence. And that is God.

Lord of death turns into Ram.
Misery gone, I relax in joy.

"My unhappiness is gone," Kabir says, "and now I am at rest, now I am happy." When there is a lot of running about, a lot of running here and there, man is unhappy. Happiness is being at complete rest. You run here and there in search of happiness, but your arithmetic is wrong, your calculations are faulty. You think you will find happiness by running hither and thither, but in the end all this running only makes you miserable. The final result of all this running about is unhappiness. The more you run, the more miserable you will be. Happiness is that moment of rest when there is no more running, when you are just at rest, when you are simply there where you are, when you do not move even an inch. And then, in that moment of rest, there is happiness, there is nothing but happiness. Meditate over this.

The extent to which you run is the extent to which you are deprived of happiness. And the more you keep on running, the more and more unhappy you become. Happiness is to be found by stopping. And stopping is meditation, prayer, worship. Stopping means having no idea or thought of the future whatsoever. As long as you remain attached to the future your running will continue.

The present moment is everything, so why run? Where will you reach by running? There is no place to run, no time in which to run. Existence is celebrating this very moment and you are cut off from it. You are so unfortunate. And you are unfortunate because you are running. If you expect happiness to come to you tomorrow you will receive nothing but misery. Why don't you take your happiness today? — it is already there. Please just stop for a while. You are missing happiness because of your running, and because of your running you have no free time, no leisure to enjoy it.

All the enlightened ones have said that desire is the root cause of misery and that contentment is the foundation of happiness. Contentment means rest, contentment means that whatsoever you have is enough, more than enough. Where is your ability to enjoy what you already have? Think about it a moment. Do you even have the capacity to enjoy that which you already possess? You are unable to contain all that is given to you already, and yet you are running after more and more.

There are two types of people in the world. The first type is the kind who enlarge their vessels, because what is given to them is so much more than the vessel can contain. The vessels of these seekers are not large enough to contain all, and so they try to enlarge their vessels, they try to expand themselves.

The second type does not even care enough to see whether there is a vessel or not. This type simply keeps running about in search of happiness. But even if they succeed in this search what will they find? They will find they do not even have a vessel. In their search for happiness they shrink more and more; their vessel becomes smaller and smaller. As you keep on running, your vessel gets smaller and smaller, your vessel goes on shrinking. Only when you stop, only when you cease running does your vessel become great. At the moment of stillness, of no-movement, your self becomes like the sky.

You have been given much more than necessary — the lake holds much more than you can drink. There is always more celebrating than you can enjoy, and it will be so even until infinity. Make your vessel larger and larger. Don't worry about how to get happiness, just be concerned about how to become big enough to contain all that is.

Each of these two types of people moves in quite independent ways. One changes himself, transforms himself; the other goes on changing circumstances. From a smaller house to a larger one, from lack of money to lots of it, from poverty to affluence, from failure to success — the second man goes on seeking and seeking, goes on trying to change circumstances.

The first man changes himself — he looks to his own vessel. He sees that it is not upside down but that it is open to the sky; he sees that it is not so weak it won't be able to hold anything; he sees that it is not broken anywhere, that it has no hole from which the nectar can leak, from which the nectar can drain out. All a seeker's concern relates to his self; that of a man of the world, to worldly affairs.

Whenever your mind becomes very restless and you feel you want to change a particular situation or circumstance, always wait for a while. If you follow the advice of the mind at that particular moment it will mislead you. Just cleanse yourself as much as possible, and the moment your vessel is ready to hold the divine nectar, that is surely the moment you will receive it. There is not a moment's delay; the only requirement is that you be worthy of it. God is ready the very moment you become ready. He has been ready forever. He has only been awaiting your readiness.

Misery gone, I relax in joy.

And the Kabir says:

Foe reversed becomes a friend...

The whole world changes when you change. If you can transform Mara into Rama, if you can reverse death and begin to see God, then how is it possible for anyone in the world to be your enemy? You only see someone who threatens to kill you or someone you fear will kill you as an enemy because you are full of fear. Your fear creates the enemy. And so a person who is very afraid will have many enemies. The number of your enemies depends on the intensity of your fear. So if you have no fear you will have no enemies. Someone may consider himself as your enemy, but to you he will not be an enemy.

Kabir had enemies, but they were only enemies from their points of view. Those who were afraid of Kabir looked on him as an enemy, but for Kabir, he had no enemies at all. The learned men, the pundits of Kashi, were very afraid of Kabir because he cut away the roots of falsehood and hypocrisy. He spoke of things that seemed to be against the tenets of the scriptures; he used to tell people that the temples and mosques were without significance.

"What is a Hindu?" he would ask. "What is a Moslem?" It was all hocus-pocus, he said. He spoke about things that appeared to be in opposition to the religious sects, in opposition to the society, the civilization, the culture; he said things that seemed against accepted beliefs. He said:

Reach the town by some back way;
Get looted on the highway.

Relax In Joy

He said:

*One who walks alone,
He alone finds truth.*

He said some wonderful things to the people, but the pundits were afraid of him.

Many people became his enemies, but only on their sides. Kabir knew no enemies. Even if someone had cut his throat he still would not have seen him as an enemy. Kabir knew that the cutting could not happen to "him," that what could be cut was not "him." He knew the assassin would be exerting himself uselessly, and as far as Kabir was concerned, such a man would simply be committing a sin without any purpose. Kabir had no cause to worry. Such a man would simply be committing a pointless sin, unnecessarily creating a web of complications. Kabir would have pitied such a man.

Kabir could not have any enemies, because there can only be an enemy as long as there is fear. A fearless consciousness knows no enemies. And when one has no enemies, everyone is a friend. Your friends are not true friends; your friendship is a political device. Your friends are friends because of some self-interest, because of some selfishness. When you die they will not accompany you; when you are in misery they will be nowhere to be found.

Mulla Nasruddin once told his wife that fifty percent of his friends had abandoned him because he was on the verge of bankruptcy.

His wife asked, "And haven't the other fifty percent gone too?"

The mulla replied, "They do not know about it yet. Only

those who know have left."

Your friends stay with you in your prosperity; they only remain with you while they can bleed you. When they find there are no more dinner parties, that you have become penniless, that you are completely sucked dry, they will throw you out just like a stick of sugarcane from which all the sweetness has been sucked. What is the meaning in such friendships?

A Sufi fakir always prayed to God saying, "O Lord, I shall settle things with my enemies myself, but please save me from my friends." Friends are also secret enemies. But Kabir is not using the word in this sense when he says the whole world has become his friend.

As soon as your fear leaves you the whole world becomes your friend. As soon as you cease to fear death the whole world becomes friendly, and until this happens there is no such person as a real friend. Until then it is all just a case of more or less. Until then some people are more enemies and some are lesser enemies, some are close enemies and some are distant enemies, some are enemies from your own people and other enemies are strangers — but all are enemies because they all seem to be destroying your life.

You do not know that life is a perpetual stream that can never be exhausted. "I" cannot be exhausted no matter how much you may try to disturb it. Even if you give away your all, you will remain as full as you were before. The Upanishads say that if you take the whole away from the whole, the whole will remain, that it will not make the slightest difference at all. On the contrary, you will become fresher and fresher. Your stream will receive fresh water. New sources will keep opening to you and you will never be empty.

As soon as water is drawn from a well the place from which it was drawn is immediately filled up with water. The well is linked with the boundless ocean; the small streams are linked with hidden springs. In the same way, you are linked with the infinite, with the whole. Who can rob you? Who can destroy you? If the well is afraid, if the well is frightened and says, "I will not allow anyone to draw water from me" — a timid person is always afraid of sharing, of giving, and becomes miserly — then the well will perish. It will become dirty, it will begin to stink, and by and by the source will dry up. Sources that remain unused dry up.

Your poverty, your helplessness, is all because of your fear. You are closed to the sources of fresh water, and as the level goes on decreasing you become apprehensive, you worry about getting a fresh supply. And so a vicious circle is created.

You could have become a clean well, one that could have given and yet not been exhausted, one that could have been continuously replenished with fresh water to the same degree it has been giving it away. Then another kind of circle begins, because now you know that no matter how much you give away, it goes on increasing.

Kabir says to draw it out, to distribute it with both your hands. Even if you had a thousand hands it would not decrease. You are unbounded; you are limitless. You are not what you appear to be. From above the well may look small, but it is linked with the ocean. Its mouth may be small, but its soul is vast. In the body you may look small, but this is only the mouth of the well; deep within you are limitless.

And bear in mind that he who does not give will take.

Taking is sin; giving is holy, sacred. This never occurs, but if a well were to take water from other wells do you know what would happen? Water seeks its own level, and if a particular well began to take water from others, then the sources from which it was obtaining its water would themselves begin to take water back from the well. The level of water always remains the same.

The level of consciousness, of the essence of life, always remains the same as well. Whether you give or you don't give makes no difference; the level of consciousness within you always remains constant. Your divinity neither increases or decreases in the least. You are worrying unnecessarily. Even if you give the limit, the level remains the same — but then you will become more delighted, more blissful. What causes more joy than giving? Only those who have given have known joy. If you do not give, you will remain miserable, worried, guilty. And the beauty of the whole phenomenon is that the water maintains its level whether the well gives or the well takes away. There will be no difference whatsoever in your being, but there will be a great difference in your experience. If you give you will feel happy and in bloom; if you take you will feel miserable.

Foe reversed becomes a friend;
Fiends are seen as gentle men.

Kabir is speaking about those who worship the goddess Shakti, the goddess of power. Their way of life creates fear in the hearts of others. The devotee of Shakti lives on the cremation ground, and his way of life is terrible. The cremation ground is his home and he decorates his body with the ashes of corpses. A skull is his drinking bowl. People are always afraid of these devotees of Shakti.

Foe reversed becomes a friend;
Fiends are seen as gentle men.

The devotee's drinking bowl, the skull, reminds you of your own skull and so you become nervous. You think, "This will happen to me too," and that is why the devotee of Shakti drinks water from a skull. He does not do this to create fear in others; he does not do this to be harmful to anyone. Making friends with death is his technique, his sadhana, and so he lives in the cremation ground, he lives in a place that is supposed to be the realm of ghosts and evil spirits. He is acquainting himself with death; he is diminishing the distance between life and death. He creates fear in our hearts because his appearance is unpleasant. Yet Kabir says:

Foe reversed becomes a friend;
Fiends are seen as gentle men.

Kabir says he is happy to see them. "When I have made friends with death itself," he says, "why should I be afraid of these devotees? As soon as I knew death I attained to Rama, so I shall also find Him in the company of these devotees."

When death is no longer death for you the whole style of life changes. At present your fear of death is the basis for your whole way of life. When the foundation is changed, the whole structure changes.

Now, for me, all is blessed.
Knowing Bhagwan, silence descends.

Now there is no death, so how can anything be unfavorable or inauspicious? Behind whatsoever is looked upon as unfavorable, death is hidden somewhere. The shadow of death is what is seen, and it is that which is looked upon as evil.

When a dead body is being carried along the road a mother will tell her son to stay in the house and keep the door shut. No one considers the sight of a dead body lucky or auspicious. If you are out of your house in the early morning and you happen to see a dead body lying beside the road you will consider the whole day as inauspicious. You will think, "I will meet with failure today." But why? What is wrong with a dead body? Those who are alive are seen committing sins but no dead body has ever been found doing so.

Mulla Nasruddin decided to go to a hill-station for a while. But he wanted to take his dog with him, and so he wrote to the manager of the hotel asking whether he would be allowed to keep his dog with him in the hotel.

The manager replied, "In my experience running this hotel for the last thirty years, I have never found a dog drinking wine, hiding wine bottles, nor damaging the bedding by smoking. Moreover," he added, "I have never caught a dog with stolen towels, weights, spoons and such in his suitcase. In thirty years I have never called the police because of a dog. We have no complaints against dogs. And if your dog is willing to bring you with him, you are welcome too."

Has a dead body ever wronged anyone? Has a dead body ever been found stealing or murdering or committing adultery? But still, if you happen to see a corpse lying on the road, you rush back home, you consider it a bad omen. Evil acts are only performed by the living. Dead bodies are in the ultimate state — how can any wrong or evil emanate from them? No, all these ideas are because a dead body reminds you of your own death. And so when you encounter a corpse you immediately rush back home and life seems dull and uninteresting to you. When you see a dead body you have a small taste of what death is. And then you begin to tremble, then you begin to think inside, "This is going to happen to me too." The taste of success disappears; your zest for life disappears.

With great expectations you are on your way to open your shop, and then you see a dead body on the road and all your interest in doing business evaporates, all that madness to do business cools down. "What am I going to get out of this shop?" you begin to think. "The shop will remain after my death," you say, "and these people who are carting this corpse away will also carry me off tomorrow." Such are your thoughts; such are the thoughts that begin in you when you see a dead body. You are reminded of the facts of life, and so you consider the dead body to be an evil omen.

But there is nothing wrong in a dead body. Buddha became aware when he saw a corpse — and you are looking upon a dead body as inauspicious? It only looks like this to you because your world is shaky. If you realize that this is the ultimate state of each and every one, then your rosy dreams and all your hopes and desires will begin to vanish; then your house of cards will tumble and your paper boat will sink. A dead body destroys all your dreams.

But if you are a man with a bit of sense you will find it is tremendously worthwhile to go deeply into the meaning of death. It would be very helpful if you were to visit a cremation ground and sit there for a while. That which will not happen by your going to a temple will happen if you go to a cremation ground. It is essential to imprint the realization of death upon yourself, and it should go so deep that the repetition of "Mara, Mara" begins in you — so deep that your breath is filled with the sound. And then all of a sudden, "Mara, Mara" will change to "Rama, Rama." You will not even be aware of exactly when it happens. Valmiki achieved Ram by repeating "Mara, Mara."

Don't run away from death; don't repeat the name of Ram out of fear. Fear has no connection whatsoever with God. Only when you call on Him with joy and happiness is your call meaningful. But this moment of joy only comes when you are not afraid of death, when death ceases to be death for you.

How can someone who is afraid of death be happy and joyful? How can the fragrance of life's flowers emanate from such a person? Only the stinking smell of the corpse will exude from such a man. And how then can your prayers to Ram be offered up with fragrance? Prayers and mantras filled with stink, with this odor, will not reach to Him.

Now for me, all is blessed.
Knowing Bhagwan, silence descends.

Understand this properly. You desire peace and rest, but you want them without knowing God. But this can never happen because the root cause of your restlessness is that you do not know God. People come to me and they say, "We are not so anxious to know God but we do want mental peace." Their desire seems logical to them. They say, "We are not in search of God. It is just that our mind is restless and we want it to be at peace."

When I hear them speak like this I am in great difficulty. For such people there is no remedy, there is no way out. They have already closed the door before anything can be done. Up to now no one has become restful and peaceful without knowing God. It is just not possible. To know God means to

Relax In Joy

attain to one's own inner music. That is peace; that is rest. To know God means to be God, to be totally contented. That is peace; and before that there cannot be any. Only when you see God in death will you be able to be peaceful, will you be able to be at rest.

Your restlessness and your uneasiness are quite natural. You are not blind — you see death approaching. You are not deaf — you can hear death's footsteps. You know that you too will one day be no more, and so you tremble. That is your restlessness.

So no matter what steps you take to protect yourself, all your efforts will finally prove to be unsuccessful. You put up a large building and then you see someone with a bigger one dying; you earn a lot of money and then you see a richer man dying; you achieve prestige and a great name and then you see a more famous man returning to dust. And so you know that all your efforts are pointless. You can try as hard as you can to persuade your mind otherwise, but you will never succeed. And that is why you are worried and uneasy.

All the consolations you resort to are false. The older and older you grow, the more you begin to be aware of this, the more you begin to think about what can be done. You hanker after peace. But you are worrying about peace without worrying about God! How is that possible? You have been doing this very same thing through countless births.

If you think the search for peace is not the same as the search for truth then you are mistaken, then you are laboring under a delusion. The search for truth is most certainly the search for peace. Peace comes as the shadow of truth — peace is a consequence, a result. No one can find peace or happiness directly.

When you become deeply engrossed in something, all of a sudden you will hear a sort of music ringing within you. This is the music of peace. At times when you are listening to good music this absorption can happen. You forget yourself for a moment; for a moment the past and future disappear and you are drowned in the sweet sound of music. Live in the present and you will experience that moment of peace all about you. At times such a moment comes in love, at times in the beauty of nature. These are the moments you experience peace.

But then your restlessness increases, because the second that moment goes you become even more uneasy. You have tasted it once, but the taste has not lasted for long. That is what Kabir is indicating:

Lord of death turns into Ram.

This man-created music, this love between two people, is bound to be momentary. Only the love that happens between man and God can be everlasting. Only the music that happens between God and man can be eternal. That is why Kabir says:

Lord of death turns into Ram.
Misery gone, I relax in joy.

The man who knows God knows everything. Then there is nothing left to know — he has heard the ultimate music. And this music is not the kind of music that will pass away. This music is not created by someone, it is hidden in existence, it is the way of existence. And then permanent peace comes.

Now Kabir says:

A million problems in the body
Turn into joyful, simple samadhi.

What was causing anger has now become compassion. Kabir says the energy that was creating mischief and disturbances has now reversed its course, it has now become an effortless samadhi, an effortless meditation. What was causing anger has now become compassion; what was causing ignorance has now become wisdom; what was creating darkness is now bright light. You only have to reverse your position. As you are now you are upside down. If you take the reverse position now, you will be straightened out. As you are now you are in *shirshasana;* you are standing on your head. You have to stand on your feet.

A recognizing deep within my heart:
Disease no more affects me.

How can any disease spread in a person who has known this himself? The body can be sick or unwell, but the self does not become sick. The body will die, but the self does not die — the consciousness remains untouched.

Mind now becomes the eternal.
I know now: I was living dead.

Kabir says that the mind from which it is so difficult to become free is now reversed and becomes the everlasting God. There is no need to be free from the mind, but it must be put into well-planned order. As long as the mind is active it is still there, but when it stops talking, when it ceases its activity, when it becomes silent, then it is the *atma,* the soul.

The ocean becomes a wave, and when the wave passes

away it becomes the ocean again. is there any difference between the ocean and the wave? The only difference is that the wave is agitated and uneasy, but it most certainly is part and parcel of the ocean. It has simply been caught up in the air currents; it has simply struck up a temporary friendship with the wind. But in the end it will be quiet; in the end it will be lost in the ocean.

The mind is a wave. It has just become a little disturbed by the currents of the world — it has just made a few wrong friends; it has foolishly become identified with the periphery. But then, in the end, everything becomes quiet. And then the mind is no more — then there is everlasting peace. You may call it the everlasting itself.

Mind now becomes the eternal.
I know now: I was living dead.

When one knows this, one knows death while one is alive. This is the whole art, this is the whole secret. The whole art of religion is to know the secret of death, to die while alive.

Everyone dies. As Kabir says:

Dying, dying, all go on dying.
None die a proper death.

People die in a wrong way. They die without living; they die without knowing Him. People are given the chance to live correctly, but the opportunity becomes lost in their unconsciousness and they simply pass away.

Kabir says he died a wise death, a death that was correct and proper. And what is that death? That death is to die before death happens. One day the body will perish, and you will die that day too because by then the opportunity will

Relax In Joy

have slipped through your hands. The body is right here at present and you are still breathing — so die right now. This is an experiment for a sporting man — to die while living.

Die every day. Set aside one hour for death every day. To live for twenty-three hours each day is quite enough. For one hour a day just go deeply into death. Let the body lie there as if it were dead and just go on observing it, just be a witness. No matter what happens, do not be a doer. You will be very surprised.

On the first day you will experience great difficulty — something will always seem to be happening somewhere in the body. Your leg will feel cold or there will be a pain in your stomach or an ant will be crawling on some part of you. But if you look for the ant you will be surprised to find that there is no ant at all, you have simply imagined it. These are the tricks of the mind.

The mind will create a thousand and one excuses; it will urge you to get up and go about your affairs. So for one hour every day, die. By and by you will come to know all the tricks of the mind, and when it presses you to be busy you will say, "I am already dead. What can I do now?" If an ant crawls on you, then let it crawl. What can you do when you are really dead? Then you won't be able to do anything at all. The meaning of dying while alive is to let that which will happen after death happen to you.

After several days of continuous practice this technique will become strong and stronger. You will simply be able to lie there like a corpse, and by and by you will notice that your breathing is becoming slower and slower. As you practice more and more, your breathing will become weaker and weaker. And then a moment will come when your breathing has suddenly stopped and your body is lying there like a corpse. And in that moment you will know, for the first time, that you are separate from the body. At that moment death disappears and Ram becomes visible; at that moment you experience what nectar is. Then you will keep on living but you will behave like a corpse towards the world. You will get up in the morning, you will take your walk, you will do everything there is to do, but all the while you will remain conscious that this body is going to die, that it is really already dead.

Your present condition is such that you do not have a correct idea of what the body is and of what you are. The body is mortal; you are immortal. But in your mind there is great confusion. Mortality and immortality are all mixed up together and you are unable to distinguish between them. The whole substance of one's sadhana, of one's journey to self-realization, is this and this alone — that you are able to separate mortality and immortality, that you come to know what the body is and what you are. Then you will not live the way others live. Kabir says you will be alive within, but on the outside you will be like a corpse.

Says Kabir: I'm simply joyous.
I'm not afraid, nor frightening others.

Kabir says that he has now achieved the true *samadhi*, that he is now dead although he is alive. Now, he says, he threatens no one and no one threatens him.

Why do you threaten others? You threaten others because you are afraid of them. In actual fact this is just a trick to protect yourself from fear. You try to threaten others before

Relax In Joy

they have a chance to threaten you. One makes threats and the other is afraid.

We create fear in others; we browbeat them. This is not only a trick for self-protection, it is also the way of a coward. The coward knows that if he does not threaten the other first, the other will threaten him. When someone threatens you, know well that he himself is afraid of you. So there is no need to fear him; in fact he deserves to be pitied.

The man who is unafraid threatens no one. He is nobody's master; he is nobody's slave. He is beyond both. He lives in a novel way — while he is alive he is like a corpse. He does everything that is worth doing, but now he is no longer the doer. Now he becomes an actor, acting on the stage of life. Nothing pleases him or displeases him. Now there are two levels to this man's life. On the outer level, worldly actions continue; on the inner level, he remains a witness. Although he does everything there is to do in the outside world, it is all a play to him — there is no seriousness in any of it. He is like Ram in the Ramleela pageant.

When Ram sees his beloved Sita being carried away, he weeps aloud, he sheds tears. He wanders all over the jungle crying all the while, "Where is Sita? Where is my Sita?" Within, there is no weeping; within, he remains a witness. When the curtain falls he will go home and rest, and in his dreams no Sita will trouble him. This is a play, a *leela*.

The original Ram was like this, and Ramleela is not really a drama because the real Ram was just like the hero of the pageant we watch today. Ram was also playing; it was all leela for him. Sita being carried away, his weeping — it was all acting. That is why we call it Ramleela. It is just a play.

Nothing penetrates the inner; everything remains on the outside. This *sansara,* this outer play, only touches such a man outwardly, it does not penetrate within. This is what it means to be like a corpse while alive. If a thorn pricks such a man he will experience pain, but the pain will remain outer, he will not be affected within. No trace of happiness or of unhappiness will now reach the inner; no wave will rise within. Everything will be peaceful and silent within.

The inner will become the abode of the everlasting. All the changes will keep on happening in the outer world but there will be total silence within, a dead silence, a void, a sky. Birds fly in the sky but leave no trace behind — after they pass, the sky is as blank as ever. Planets will be created and destroyed, but nothing of their history will ever be recorded in the sky. Wars will be waged and peace treaties will be signed, but there will not be the slightest disturbance in the sky. To be like the sky within is the meaning of dying while alive. Then you will live in the inner sky alone, and whatever happens in the outer world will be like a dream.

This does not mean that you will run away, that you will abandon the outer. Kabir did not run away. What need is there to run away? When you become free within — dead while alive — where will you run? You will simply stay where you are. Kabir kept on weaving lengths of cloth and selling them. He had a family, a wife and a child, and everything stayed as it was.

So Kabir says he is neither afraid of anyone nor is he a threat to anyone. Now there is fearlessness within. Now death has disappeared, and now Ram is within. Try to maintain this tone, this attitude within yourself.

There is infinite pleasure to be found in maintaining this attitude, but you will find it very arduous in the beginning because your identification with the body is so very, very old. To sever any kind of relationship is always very difficult — marriage is easy but divorce is very difficult. And many births have gone by since your marriage with the body, so to divorce it will be very difficult. That divorce is sannyas. That divorce is not from your wife or children, that divorce is from your own body. This is not renouncing something, it is the separation within yourself, of the fields of death and immortality.

Everything that happens is a dream, and the one before whom all these things take place is the truth. As you play more and more with the inner witness you will be able to understand Kabir's words better and better. Kabir's songs are not to be taken literally, they are not meant for that.

Not of written words
But of experiencing.

Truth is not a matter of recorded words, it is something to be experienced. If you experience truth you will also understand it, you are strong enough for that. You only have to make a small effort to remember your own capability, your own strength, your own kingdom. You are the master, you are the emperor, but you have forgotten and so you stand there like a beggar. As soon as you remember, your begging will disappear. The empire has never been lost, it has always been yours. It is just that you have been lost in dreams for a while, and this dreaming has become your life.

Awaken from this dream and you conquer death while you are still alive. You will be dead although you will be alive.

I know now: I was living dead.

When you are dead but alive you will know this too. In the long series of your births you have died many times. This time, die while you are alive. Then there will be no death for you. Then you will not have to come again. The man who dies while alive has no birth or death.

10

COME WHAT MAY, ALLOW

Stop wavering, mad mind!
Come what may, allow it!
The sati is ready for the fire of death.

Dance in ecstasy, beyond all doubts.
Drop greed, attachment, fancies.
Do the brave fear death?
Does the sati cling to her body?

Society, scripture, family prestige —
The hangman's noose at the neck.
Move on the path and return midway —
Ha! Ha! Everyone laughs.

This whole world's so nasty.
Only he who prays is true.
Says Kabir: never abandon the name.
Fall down! Stand up! Fly high!

Certain things must be understood before we try to grasp what Kabir is saying. First, the mind is never sick nor is it ever healthy: the mind itself *is* sickness. It is never quiet and so it is meaningless to say that it is restless: Restlessness is the mind. The mind can never become mad because only one who is not mad can become a lunatic: the mind itself is madness.

The mind will always remain unsteady, because unsteadiness is its nature. If a wave does not move, it will cease to be a wave. It is called a wave because it is moving, because it remains in motion. What would a silent wave be? The existence of the wave is in its motion, in its restlessness.

Never hope for your mind to be quiet; it does not know how to be at peace. As long as the mind is there, there is certain to be restlessness. When the mind is no more, what remains is peace. The absence of mind is peace — to be in no-mind is peace.

The mind will always be shaky, will always remain indecisive. If you wait for a decision by the mind — if you think, "I shall do this when the mind decides" — you will never be able to do anything. To remain in indecision is the way of the mind. It will always remain divided, broken into parts. Some parts will be for something and other parts will be against it. Within the mind there is always a civil war, there is always an internal conflict, there is always a duel going on.

What is this duality? It is important to understand its roots.

In you there are three things, three factors. One is your body. Your body is a fact; it has a material existence. And then there is the flow of consciousness within you. That is your atma, your soul. That is also a fact. Between these two is the mind. The mind is not a fact; it is a false thing.

It is a little bit body and a little bit soul — it is a situation created between the two. It cannot be total, it is always divided, always with one side or the other. And so it remains partly with the body and partly with the soul. It is created by the union of these two, and so it can never be totally with the body.

Come What May, Allow

The desire to be a saint, to be a holy person, is hidden in everyone; it is even hidden in the mind of the greatest sinner. Whenever you are going to do something terrible — even though you may have been doing it for lives — the mind will caution you not to. It will say, "Don't do this. It is bad." If the mind were only body, then nothing would be bad. At the body's level nothing is good or bad; neither holy act nor sin can exist. In the case of the enlightened man both disappear, and for the ignorant man neither exists. For the ignorant man, there is no possibility of the existence of good or bad, and the enlightened man has reached a place where both of these are left far behind.

When you are at prayer or at worship the mind will ask, "Why are you wasting your time?" When you are going to steal something, when you are going to commit a theft, the mind will ask, "Why are you committing a sin?" When you are preparing to give something away in charity the mind will ask, "Why are you throwing your money away unnecessarily?" Then you are in a great fix trying to figure out what the mind wants.

The mind is like a bridge joining the two banks — the bank of the body and the bank of the soul. Half of the mind is on either side, and so there will always be a problem. If you follow the mind you will always be unsteady. Whatsoever you do, bad or good, the mind will repent it. Then you will fall into great difficulty and confusion; then you will be at a loss to know what to do.

When you are in good spirits you lean to one side, and when those good spirits have left you, you lean to the other. In between the two you are torn to pieces, just as a rock is reduced to dust between the stones of a gristmill.

Kabir has said:

*Between two millstones
None remain unbroken.*

These two stones are within you, and you are that gristmill.

Kabir says:

*Seeing the wheel turning,
Kabir broke into tears.*

If you become a little alert you will be able to see this gristmill working within you; you will be able to see yourself going round and round. The mind joins the two millstones.

Because of the mind you think, "I am the body," and because of the mind you also think, "I am the soul." When the mind disappears, these mistaken notions that you are the body and that you are the soul disappear. They evaporate because the person who made these claims is no more. Only you, the soul, remains. Only your original nature remains; the claimant is gone. What will there be to say then? To whom will the soul speak when the body is not? That which is opposite to the body we call the soul. That is where the highest delight arises.

So the first thing to be understood is that the mind can never be whole, can never be total. The mind will always reman divided. And if you decide you need the mind's approval before doing something you will never be able to do anything. You will never commit a sinful act or a holy deed, a religious act or an irreligious one, an act of sansara or an act of sannyas. You will not be able to do anything at all. The mind will always remain indecisive, perplexed.

During the second world war a very famous philosopher

was recruited for military service because there was a shortage of soldiers. Enlistment was compulsory, and so he was recruited against his will. He was a great philosopher. He had spent his life thinking and thinking, he had never put anything into practice, he had simply thought and thought.

This world of thoughts is quite a different world, it is quite distinct. Philosophy is a kind of exercise that pleases the mind greatly, because you never do anything so there is never any question of repentance. If you simply think of sin, no harm is done because no one is hurt, and if you think about some act of merit there is no problem either, because no one is benefited. You simply sit and think. Something only happens when there is action involved; nothing happens just by thinking. Philosophers think a lot. They waste their lives thinking, and do absolutely nothing. You will not find them among the sinners, or among good people either. They just stand on the side of the road. They do not walk, they think. And they make no decisions.

This particular recruit was a very famous philosopher. The general under whose command he had been put also knew of him — he had read the philosopher's books. The general thought, "What can this man do? Before he has to shoot he will think about it a thousand times. And the enemy won't wait for him."

His training began. The first time the order "Left turn" was given everyone turned accordingly, but the philosopher stood where he was. He was asked, "What are you doing?" He answered, "I can't do anything without thinking it over first. When I hear 'Left turn' I ask myself, 'Why? What is the reason? What harm is there if I don't turn left? What is the advantage if I do?'"

If all soldiers were to ask such questions you can imagine what would happen, but because he was a very famous philosopher and because he could see no other way out, the general decided to give him a very small and unimportant job. He sent him to work in the kitchen.

On the very first day the philosopher was given a dish of peas and told to separate them, to put the big peas on one side and the small peas on the other. After an hour the general went to check on his work. He found the philosopher sitting in front of the dish with his eyes closed. The peas were untouched. He was thinking. The general asked, "What are you doing?"

"A great problem has arisen," he said. "If I put the big peas on one side and the small ones on the other, then where shall I put the medium-sized ones? It is not right to start anything until the whole thing has been settled."

The mind is a great philosopher — it is unable to decide anything. Philosophers have never been able to decide anything.

Look at it in this way — knowledge that is associated with the body is science, knowledge that is associated with the mind is philosophy, and knowledge that is associated with consciousness is religion. Science has certainly accomplished some very substantial things; it has been able to do much in fact. Religion has also done a lot. Philosophy is associated with the mind. Philosophers simply go on thinking, they simply go on finding arguments for and against. And there is no end to it. The chain is endless. That is why, even after thousands of years of thinking, philosophy has not yet reached a decision. Not one single decision has been made.

Come What May, Allow

There have been questions, thousands and thousands of questions, but not one single solution.

Do not bother about pleasing the mind — you will be wasting your life. Just set the mind aside. If you can do that, then your life will be meaningful. if you understand the mind correctly you will see that it is only a process, only a series of thoughts. No action is born out of the mind, it just thinks a lot. At times you mistakenly believe the mind has arrived at a particular decision. You go to a temple, for example, and you vow never to tell a lie from that moment on. And hiding in its dark corner the mind laughs at your vow, at your decision, because it is a decision made by half a mind, by a partial mind, and you have not consulted the other half. Then you go to the market or sit in your shop and begin your business. You enter the world of business and then that hidden part of your mind will induce to lie.

Your vow is a challenge to the mind. You did not consult it before you made your resolution and your mind will not be still until it breaks it. You have taken many vows, and many times you have broken them. The only reason you keep doing this is that you take your vow after listening to the mind. The real vow is born when you give up the mind.

There are two kinds of vows. One is the kind you take following the dictates of the mind. You hear a sadhu or a saint and you like what he has to say. But who likes it? It is liked by the mind. The half of the mind near the soul is delighted to hear such talk, is enchanted by these words; it will become enraptured by them and will take a vow. This vow is taken, but you have not yet consulted the other half of the mind. Now the other half will take revenge. It will never pardon you, it will immediately start some game to make you break your vow.

Even in small matters, challenges play a great part in life. When a person decides not to smoke, for example, this becomes a challenge to the mind. If today you decide to fast, then the half portion of the mind that belongs to the body will decide to break your vow. For the whole day it will make you think of food, it will make you dream about food. It will try to entice you in a thousand and one ways. And the opposite of this is also true. If you follow the dictates of the body, then the other half of the mind will create trouble for you.

The man who follows the mind is like a traveler who is trying to sail in two boats, and each boat is going in a different direction. Such a person will always be in a quandary — he will always remain suspended in the middle. He will have no place to stand; he will be neither of the earth nor of the sky.

There is another type of vow which I call *mahavrata*, the great vow. This is not taken by the mind. This vow is taken after the full realization that the mind is afflicted by duality, that the mind is duality, that the mind is conflict. In taking such a vow the mind is set aside. It is not that the mind makes a vow it will not speak the truth. When you have realized what the mind is, the feeling that arises in your consciousness is not this sort of vow. The feeling comes because you have realized what falsehood is and what the mind is, and now your understanding, your realization itself becomes the greatest vow.

The man who has understood what smoking is does not have to throw his cigarette away; the cigarette falls from his hand by itself. And the man who has realized what wine is watches the bottle slipping from his hand. When you quit

Come What May, Allow

something it is the mind that is giving it up; if it goes away by itself it is mahavrata, the great vow. But if it is you that is putting something aside, you will surely pick it up again.

Mulla Nasruddin once went to address a meeting. It generally happens that speakers say one thing but act differently. You may be surprised at this, but it is what usually happens. It is not their fault, and you are mistaken if you think they are deceiving you on purpose. On such an occasion it is that part of the mind nearer the soul that begins to function.

Addressing a gathering, who will speak out in favor of sin? It is only talk, no doing is involved, so one can speak of high ideals and of great deeds. It is only discussion. Nothing is at stake, there is nothing to lose. So at the time he is speaking, a speaker will talk about nonavarice and not about greed, about nonviolence and not about violence, about truth and not about falsehood. When he is speaking, the speaker becomes a pious man, a sadhu — when he is speaking.

The Mulla also spoke about great and wise things — about truth, nonviolence, about honesty. The audience was surprised. And the Mulla's son, who was also there, was surprised as well. The Mulla explained that anyone could achieve liberation by climbing the steps of truth — by being honest, by practicing nonviolence, celibacy and non-possessiveness. "This ladder is right in front of you," he said. "You just have to begin to climb." I was present the next morning when the Mulla's son said to him, "I had a dream last night, and I saw the ladder you spoke about yesterday."

Seeing that his talk had greatly impressed his son, the Mulla was eager to hear more. "Go on," he said. "What happened next?"

His son replied, "The ladder rose high towards heaven — its top was lost, far away in the sky. At the base of the ladder there was a notice board with sticks of chalk, one foot long, kept near it. The instructions on the board said that whoever climbed the ladder was to take a stick of chalk with him and make a mark on each step for each one of his sins."

The Mulla was becoming more and more excited. He said, "Go on. What next?"

The son continued, "I took a stick of chalk, made my first mark, and began to climb. After climbing a little I heard the sounds of someone climbing down."

The Mulla asked, "Who was it?"

The son said, "I wondered that too, so I raised my eyes and saw that it was you climbing down."

The Mulla said, "Me? Climbing down? What are you talking about? Why should I climb down?"

The boy said, "I asked you the same question and you replied, 'I am going back down to get more chalk.'"

Actions are full of sins, while talk is only about great deeds. You keep on sinning and at the same time go on taking vows that you will perform acts of great merit. And so both parts of the mind are satisfied. The part of the mind near the body is satisfied with sin and the other is satisfied with the scriptures. You sail in both boats and seem very pleased with yourself. But you never reach anywhere, you cannot. No one has ever reached anywhere this way. Even if you choose one boat the difficulty remains the same — both boats belong to the mind.

Kabir says that those who sit in a boat, in either boat, drown. The voyage across the ocean of life is such that those who accept the help of a boat are the ones who sink. One has to swim oneself — there is no need for any boat at all. Both the boats are of the mind; their names are sin and holiness.

And so you remain divided, in duality. I see that the man sitting in the shop is divided; I see that the man sitting in the ashram is divided as well. The man in the shop thinks about holy acts because he is committing sins, and the man in the ashram performs holy acts and thinks of sinful things. There is no difference in their perplexity; both are in difficulty. So you have to give up the mind completely. The mind is madness. And to give it up means to understand it. When you understand the nature of the mind it will be easy to let it go.

Now let us try to understand these words of Kabir:

Stop wavering, mad mind!

The mind is mad. This is not poetry; what Kabir has to say are direct truths of life. Madness is another name for the mind. There is no need for anybody to explain this to you; you are very well acquainted with your mind. If you have even the slightest ability to see through it, to see through the workings of your mind, you will realize that it is mad.

The mind is always asking you to do something over again, something you have already done so many times before. And every time you see that by doing it nothing is achieved. What else can madness be?

Many times you have tried to extract oil from sand, but it does not work. You know that sand is sand, that oil cannot be extracted from it, and yet you do the same thing over and over again. If this is not madness, what is?

You have indulged in the pleasures of the flesh countless times, innumerable times, and yet you have achieved nothing. You still do not know what real joy is, you still do not know what ecstasy is. You simply remain thirsty and miserable, weeping and repenting what you have done. And in spite of this experience, the mind induces you to repeat things over and over again. If this is not madness, then what else is it?

To be mad is to keep repeating something that has already been seen as useless, as worthless. To be mad is not to do something even though there may be a little substance in it, not to go near something that has a glimpse of some substance in it.

People come to me and they say, "We practiced meditation for a few days and then gave it up." I ask them how they found those few days. They say, "We experienced great joy and peace." This seems very surprising, giving up meditation in spite of the fact they experienced peace while doing it. They say, "It was the mind that made us stop."

Do you give up those things that make you unhappy and miserable? You have been angry many times. Have you ever experienced any joy from your anger? Has it brought you joy even once? Whenever you have been angry you have experienced unhappiness — but the mind does not give anger up. Whenever you meditate or pray, or go to a temple and sit in silence, you feel happy — yet your mind asks you to give it up. And you take its advice!

You do things from which nothing but misery results because the mind says, "Make another attempt. This time you might succeed. It may have borne no fruit up to now but you might get some in the future, so keep on. Who can definitely say you won't get it just because you haven;t obtained it up to now? So keep on seeking. Keep on making an effort."

And so your mind pushes you on a fruitless journey. What else can madness be?

Some time just sit quietly and examine your mind. See what is going on there. Will you be able to differentiate between your mind and that of a madman? The mind is a mad thing. There are simply differences of degree. Some minds may be eighty percent mad, some may be ninety percent mad and others may be ninety nine — just ready to boil. Some people are one hundred percent mad and others have gone beyond one hundred. These people are kept in lunatic asylums.

A priest once went to an asylum to give a talk. He spoke on his subject in great detail, but he used simple terms because he was speaking to madmen. He explained things from all points of view.

One of the inmates kept staring at the priest and was obviously listening to him with rapt attention. The priest was very impressed; no one had ever listened to him so intently. The man was so engrossed it appeared as if he were not even taking a breath. When the meeting was over the priest noticed the man going to the superintendent and whispering something in his ear. He thought the man must have said something about his talk, so as soon as he had a chance he asked the superintendent what the man had said to him. "Was the speaking about my talk?" the priest inquired.

After a little hesitation the superintendent replied, "Yes, it was about your talk."

The priest became quite uneasy. "What did he say?" he asked. At first the superintendent was unwilling to answer, but the priest pressed him and so he said, "He came to me and began to whisper in my ear, 'See what the world is like! This man is outside, while we are shut up in here. A great injustice is being done!'"

There is not much difference between those who are out and those who are in. There is only a wall between them. You can be sent in at any time; you are standing very near the wall and the door is always open. For the people on the inside the door is closed, but for those who go in from the outside it is open. The guard at the door is not there to stop people coming in from outside, he is there to stop those who are inside from going out. A welcome awaits you there, and sooner or later you will go inside. It is a wonder you have not already done so. You know this very well too, and so you exercise great control, hiding yourself, not exposing yourself. Sometimes in a weak and unconscious moment you are exposed, and then you know that you too have been acting like a madman.

Sometimes your anger exposes you, and after a while you beg forgiveness. You say, "I was mad then. How could I have done such a thing?" But it happened! You say you are incapable of doing such a thing, so how did it happen? You did it. The anger was yours. No other spirit entered you; no ghost or spirit compelled you to do it.

What is the difference between you when you are angry and you when you are not? There is only this much difference — in an unconscious moment of anger whatsoever is going on within you comes out. Ordinarily you are careful about your behavior; ordinarily you keep yourself in control. When you are thinking about whether to do something or not, hundreds of thoughts are going on within you — and you only bring one of those hundreds of thoughts to the surface. No one is ever free from madness until he becomes free from the clutches of the mind.

The beauty of it all is that the mind disappears as soon as your hesitation, your doubts and your restlessness go. As long as the mind is still there hesitation will not go, but when hesitation goes, the mind also goes. The wave goes to sleep; it is lost in the ocean.

Kabir says you are linked to the world as long as the mind is still there, but that when the mind becomes quiet it ceases to exist. Then only the abode of the everlasting exists. This is the key to being linked to God.

Stop wavering, mad mind!
Come what may, allow it!
The sati is ready for the fire of death.

The symbol used here is worth understanding. Before the British came to India there was a custom whereby the widow, the *sati*, would willingly burn herself on the funeral pyre along with her dead husband. Later, in ninety-nine cases out of hundred, there was compulsion involved and so it was finally banned by the government. But there was a time when there was no compulsion. Such women were called satis.

When the custom of sati started it was born out of great love, out of very deep relationships. Such a thing has not happened anywhere else in the world. It happened only in India, because only India has known the highest peaks of love. India has known the feeling of oneness, the feeling of unity between lovers. Based on the heights of this unity, the custom of sati was born.

If love has become so deep that it becomes another word for life, then there is no other choice but for the beloved to join her lover in death. When the husband dies, the wife's life also ends — if there is deep love between them. Then there is no meaning in continuing to live. Mornings will come but now there will be no beauty in them. Nights will continue to come and the stars will go on shining, but from now on there will be no stars for the poor widow. Now everything is dark for her; now her light has gone. When the lamp of love is extinguished there is no more meaning in life. The wife would climb the pyre willingly, carrying a pot of vermilion in her hand.

The sati is ready for the fire of death.

The pyre would be lit and the flames would be rising, and the wife would go to become a sati. Vermilion is a symbol of good luck. It was used because the pyre ceased to be a pyre for the wife whose husband had passed away; the pyre became her good fortune.

Now the sati is not going to meet death, she is going to meet her husband. Her lover is standing on the other side of the flames, the pyre is the door to heaven. This is not death, for her this is the door to life. And so the sati, with the vermilion, with the symbol of good luck in her hand, climbs the pyre.

Come what may, allow it!
The sati is ready for the fire of death.

Kabir says that whatever happens he is ready, because now there is no question of going back. He is standing there like a sati with a pot of vermilion in his hand — if he has to pass

Come What May, Allow

through the flames he is ready. If God is standing on the other side, Kabir is willing to pass through death; Kabir is prepared to meet death.

Come what may, allow it!

He asks his mind to drop all hesitation, all indecision. He says he is going away now; he says this is the last moment. He is willing to pass through death because he is determined to know what life is. And so he tells his mind to set aside all its mad talk, "Now it is more than enough," he says. "I have listened to you long enough."

Kabir does not try to quieten the mind, he simply tells the mind it is worrying unnecessarily. He has already begun his walk; he has the pot of vermilion in his hand and his next step will be onto the pyre itself. He is ready to die; his beloved is calling from the other side, "What are you hesitating for, you fool?" But no reply comes from the mind. "Now I am absolutely ready," he says. "Now I am not going to listen to you anymore." When this moment comes, the mind gives up. Not before that.

As long as there is the slightest hope the mind will try to seduce you, to trap you. It will try various tricks; it will try to persuade you in a hundred and one ways. It will put forth many arguments trying to dissuade you from your course; it will create all sorts of enticements, all sorts of attractions and dreams to ensnare you. It is only possible to be free from the mind when your resolve is total, when your determination is absolute and you can say to it, "Whatsoever you say will make no difference."

Stop wavering, mad mind!

Now the listener has gone. His journey has already begun;

there is no question now of turning back. And when the mind is convinced you are not going to return to it, it will become quiet.

People come to me and they say that they want to take sannyas, but their minds are unsteady. In various ways their minds persuade them against sannyas. The mind tells them they have children, wives, social obligations; it says if they walk about in orange clothes people will laugh. As yet there is no question of dying, as yet there is no question of embracing the flames of the funeral pyre, but you are so timid you are even afraid to wear clothes that are the color of flames.

The Hindus have chosen orange clothes, ochre clothes, from the color of flame. Orange is the color of fire. If you want to enter the fire, the color is useful as a first step. But if your mind will not even allow you to wear clothes the color of fire, how will it ever allow you to enter fire itself? These clothes are also the color of vermilion, the color of luck; they will help you to achieve the highest and greatest good fortune. This is the beginning, the preparation for your death, but if you listen to the mind it will never allow you this opportunity. The mind will not help you in any way.

There are two kinds of situations — following the mind or opposing it. If you listen to the mind you are following it, but if you oppose it you are still related to it. Then the other half is opposing. But Kabir is not obstinate, he does not say to the mind, "I will fight against you." His words are worth understanding. He speaks to the mind as an elderly person would talk to a weeping child. He says, "Now be quiet. There is no reason whatsoever to complain. It is up to you if you continue to cry. If weeping and crying brings you pleasure, then go ahead. It does not concern me at all."

Kabir is neither for the mind nor against it. Just as a snake casts off its skin, Kabir steps out of the mind and leaves it aside. The mind will simply lie there, just like the snake skin.

When we call the mind mad it means we are neither in favor of it nor in opposition to it. Suppose a madman standing by the side of the road was abusing you. You would not become angry with him or displeased with him, you would simply go on your way — the whole affair would be finished. Would you quarrel with him? He is not abusing you consciously. There is no intent in his abuse; there is no purpose behind it.

It once happened that Akbar was taking part in a procession on a particular celebration day. A man standing by the side of the road began to insult him. Akbar had him arrested and kept him in jail for the night.

In the morning the man was brought before him. Akbar asked, "Why did you insult me?"

The man seemed surprised. He said, "I insulted you? That's not true. I was drunk. I am not responsible for the one who insulted you. You can punish me for drinking liquor if you want, but you cannot punish me for drinking liquor if you want, but you cannot punish me for using abusive language. Liquor spoke those insults." Akbar thought this over for a while and then pardoned the man.

His courtiers asked why he had given the matter so much thought.

He replied, "It was worth thinking about. When he did not insult me consciously, how can he be responsible?"

There had been no intention of insulting Akbar, and so there was really no complaint at all. The matter was over. Had it been done consciously, there would have been a crime. The abuse is the same. If it is done consciously it is meaningful; if it is done in unconsciousness there is no meaning in it whatsoever.

Kabir tells his mad mind it can go on chattering if it enjoys it, but he is going to go his own way. "The wedding procession is ready, the bridegroom's horse is ready, and I am going," Kabir says. "Whatever may happen now," he tells the mind, "let it happen. Don't try to dissuade me, don't talk nonsense. There is no time now for discussing the pros and cons. Now whatsoever may happen and howsoever it may happen, let it happen."

Kabir is not concerned. Now the sati has taken the pot of vermilion in her hand; now there is no question of turning back.

Dance in ecstasy, beyond all doubts.
Drop greed, attachment, fancies.
Do the brave fear death?
Does the sati cling to her body?

Drop all doubts and dance. Be elated and dance. Set greed, infatuation and illusions aside.

Do the brave fear death?

The mind tries to persuade you that you are on the way to meet your death, that you will encounter nothing but death. The mind says there is no God; the mind says there is no liberation. It says this is all hot air, nothing but empty words spoken by cunning people.

Come What May, Allow

Charvaka said the Vedas were the creation of crafty men, and that all talk of God and liberation was simply a trick perpetuated by clever and satanic people. Charvaka said that if you want to drink the best ghee then do so, even if you have to borrow money from others. No one returns after death, he said. He said there is no need to repay anyone, that there should be no concern about repaying, that there is no such thing as a holy act or a sinful one. He said these are all devices, all cunning tricks to ensnare one.

In modern times Marx advocates the same thing. He said religion was an opiate, a device to exploit the poor. This is the same thing Charvaka said three thousand years ago. But the minds of all such men echo the words of Charvaka within. The mind is always communist, always nonbelieving.

Kabir says now is the time for him to dance. He tells himself not to hesitate, not to lose purpose; he says this moment is not to be wasted in sadness, not to be lost in thinking and more thinking. He sees the moment of his dissolution coming nearer and nearer and he is so filled with delight that he dances. Why? The meeting with the beloved will only take place when Kabir is no more: Kabir knows he will only achieve Him if he loses himself. "Then I shall know my soul," Kabir says. "My soul will be born out of the ashes of my ego when it is reduced to dust on the funeral pyre."

The mind has three tricks to ensnare you. One trick is to create greed in you for something. The mind will say, "It was within your reach, it was almost in your hands, so where are you going now? Because you are going away your whole effort will be wasted. You should have worked just one more day, you should just have waited a little bit more and then you would have been successful."

Or the mind may snare you in the net of infatuation. "Whom are you leaving? Are you leaving your own people? Are you going away all alone?" it will ask. "You have your dear ones, your friends, your relatives, society; do you intend to take the opposite path, do you intend to leave all these people behind? Taking an unknown path is definitely a mistake."

Kabir says:

Reach the town by some back way;
Get looted on the highway.

The mind will tell you to walk on the main road. It will say there will be thieves and highwaymen on the other road and that you will be robbed. It will tell you there is always a crowd on the main road, and that being with the crowd is a way of protecting yourself. It will tell you that people will stare at you if you are alone.

Who are you listening to? The mind will crate either greed or infatuations or attachments or new illusions to ensnare you. The mind is the creator of dreams; there is no craftsman more clever or cunning than the mind.

The mind will always ask you to try once more. A gambler is in the same predicament as you are. If he wins or loses, he is in difficulty. When he is winning, the mind will say, "Play one more hand. You have been lucky so far; you have a lakh of rupees in your pocket. Stake it all now and double it!" The winning man becomes intoxicated. And to the loser the mind says, "This time you lost — but don't worry, try again. It is a shame to go home like this. Who knows, your defeat may turn into success." So in either condition, in success or in defeat, the gambler is trapped. The mind is the creator of illusions.

Do the brave fear death?

When you do not listen to the mind it has one last trick up its sleeve. It will threaten you with death. All the saints say the path to God is only for the man who is prepared to cut off his head and put it aside; they say the path to God is like the naked edge of a sword. Jesus says you will be saved if you sacrifice yourself, and he says if you try to save yourself you will be lost.

No one has ever tasted divine nectar without dying. Yet the mind will say, "Why do you listen to such useless talk? These men are agents of death; they are trying to persuade you to die. I am your friend. I am in favor of life. Your gurus are your enemies."

And you like the advice the mind gives. You agree with what it has to say. It says to live fully while there is life; it asks why you are in a hurry to die. It says that death is sure to come at its appointed time; it asks what need is there to die before that time comes. Kabir says that only he who dies while alive attains the divine nectar.

Do the brave fear death?
Does the sati cling to her body?

Kabir asks his foolish mind, "Is a brave man ever afraid of death?" He asks it, "Are you trying to threaten me with the fear of death?"

Death is a challenge; it is not something to be afraid of. If you accept this challenge as a play, you will experience the greatest joy of life.

Does the sati cling to her body?

The sati does not decorate her body. She knows the body is just an earthen vessel, but the mind tries to persuade her to look after the vessel, to save it. Kabir asks, "Should I risk everything for this trivial thing when my lover is there, beyond the flames?"

When a sati determines to follow her husband into death, her mind will certainly try to persuade her not to. "What are you doing?" it will ask. "You are still young," it will say. "One lover has died, but have all the others died too? Let this fresh wound heal, and then find another lover, find another husband. Why are you in such a hurry to die? Wait for a while; you will enjoy life again. You have such a beautiful body and now you are going to burn it? That body you adorned so often, that body you looked at in the mirror so often, that body men were mad after — you are going to throw that body into the fire?"

Does the sati cling to her body?

The real sati does not fall into the traps of the mind; she turns a deaf ear to its persuasions. You beware too. Kabir's mind has said all of this to him and your mind will tell the same thing to you. Before they become enlightened, before they become *siddhas,* the minds of all seekers say the same thing. All seekers pass through this stage. This is the nature of the mind.

Society, scripture, family prestige —
The hangman's noose at the neck.
Move on the path and return midway —
Ha! Ha! Everyone laughs.

People, society, the Vedas, the scriptures, tradition, family prestige — all these are like nooses around one's throat. The mind will use them to keep reminding you that what you are doing is against the social structure. People come to me and they say they would like to be initiated into sannyas, but that they are afraid of society. What is this society? Where is this so-called society? It is nothing but a crowd of timid people just like you; it is nothing but people standing on each other's shoulders because of their fear. People who are full of fear themselves create fear in others.

The crowd is never happy when a man attains to his self, because such a man abandons the traditional path of the crowd. Such a man seeks out a small footpath, finds his own way. He has confidence in his own two legs, and slowly, slowly, his dependence on others becomes less and less. If he depends on anyone at all it is on God, and not on other people. The crowd is just a collection of ignorant people. Of what use are such people to him?

Kabir says the crowd is a noose. Kabir, Buddha, Mahavira — they all saw society as a kind of noose. As long as you consider society as your life, as the all in all, then it is a noose. You are a slave because of society. The people around you, the Vedas, the scriptures, tradition — these are the impediments that stand in your way. People will say what you are doing is against the scriptures. They will tell you it is written in the scriptures that one should only enter into sannyas in old age, when death is approaching, and they will be shocked that you are becoming a sannyasi in your youth. This is against the scriptures, they will say.

One very old man came to see me. He must have been eighty years old. His son had taken sannyas. The son was not young; he must have been nearly fifty, but the old man was very sad. He said to me, "You give sannyas to such young children?"

Was the son a small child? He had brought his son with him. The son was at least fifty years old. The old man said, "This is against the Vedas. There it is clearly written that sannyas is the last stage. The first stage is *brahmacharya,* the second is *grihastha* and the third is *vanprastha.* Sannyas is the last."

I said to him, "Let us not speak about your son... What is your intention? Has your last stage come yet? If you take sannyas, I will persuade your son not to."

He said, "I shall think about it. I will come again. Let me think it over." Even at eighty he finds an excuse to think about it. And when the son takes sannyas he says, "Not now, do it at the last stage." He himself is in the final stage. What he is saying to his son is simply this — "Don't take sannyas at all." The business of the "final stage" is just an excuse.

Does sannyas have anything to do with age? How can age be a condition for awakening? How can age be an obstruction to awakening? If you cannot be awakened while you are young it will be very difficult when you are old. To awaken requires energy. When you are old you will be weak, you will have no energy left, but that is when you go to surrender yourself to God. The flower should be offered when it is fresh, when it is full of energy, when it is overflowing with fragrance. You want to surrender when there is nothing worth surrendering. But that will be a false surrender. And who are you going to deceive?

Move on the path and return midway —
Ha! Ha! Everyone laughs.

Come What May, Allow

Be "everyone" Kabir does not mean society, he means existence. If someone turns back when he is about to attain to samadhi, Kabir says, the whole of existence will laugh at him, but if someone jumps into samadhi, the whole of existence will be delighted. Then existence will be filled with ecstasy; then it will dance.

This whole world's so nasty.
Only he who prays is true.

This whole sansara, this whole world, is unholy because it is born out of the mind. The mind is conflict and unholiness. Only those men are holy, Kabir says, in whose hearts the word Ram is heard, on whose tongues the name of God lives. They are the only holy people, Kabir says.

Says Kabir: never abandon the name.
Fall down! Stand up! Fly high!

Kabir says never to forsake the name of God. You may fall, he says, but don't be downcast, just stand up again and again. Don't let His name go for a moment; just hold fast to His name and don't worry at all. You may fall down, you may make mistakes, but if you hold fast to His name the attainment will surely come; you will reach certainly. Don't be afraid to fall.

Fall down! Stand up! Fly high!

The man who is afraid to fall stops walking; he stays seated because of his fear. Do not be afraid to make mistakes. Bear only one thing in mind — do not make the same mistakes again. Do not fall into the same old traps again and again; this is a sign of an unconscious person. You may fall, but do it in a new way. And then get up again. Whenever you fall and get up again, just let one thing be there constantly — the remembering of His name. The sound of His name should reverberate within you night and day, in darkness and in light. The thread should never slip from your hand.

Don't miss the boat that carries His name, and don't worry if it rises or falls in the waves. Through this process of falling and getting up again, you will reach to that peak where God is. Remember only one thing — God's name should never be forgotten.

Nothingness dies, the soundless dies;
Even the infinite dies.
A true lover never dies.
Says Kabir: know this.

The experience of the highest happiness, of *shunya*, nothingness, will die. The inexpressible sound of Aum also will die. And the experience of the boundless, of the infinite, will die as well. Only one thing — the love for God — does not die.

This whole world's so nasty.
Only he who prays is true.
Says Kabir: never abandon the name.
Fall down! Stand up! Fly high!

Hold fast to one thing only, to the remembering of God's name. That is the only refuge, the only support. Be conscious of Him every moment and then even if you fall often don't worry. Just don't let that thread slip out of your hand. With the help of that tiny thread you will be able to stand up again.

It once happened that a certain emperor became displeased with his chief minister and sentenced him to life imprisonment. He was shut up in a high tower, in a minaret on the outskirts of the city. Escape from it was an impossibility. If he were to try to escape he would fall and die — the minaret was about five hundred feet high, and there was a strict watch around it.

His wife was anxious. What to do? How to free him? The sentence was for life, and the chief minister was a young man, he had a long time yet to live. So his wife went to a fakir and asked to be shown a way out. The fakir said, "We know only one way, and you can use it too. All you have to do is hold a thread to him. We know one thread, the thread of remembering God, and you can see that we are out of the prison of the world. This is such a small prison, just hold a thread to him, just extend him a thread."

The minister's wife was puzzled, "I do not follow you," she said. "Please don't speak in riddles."

The fakir said to her, "Catch hold of a worm that is sensitive to smell and put some honey on its nose. Following the smell of honey, the worm will begin to climb. As it goes higher and higher the smell will also go higher and higher; the smell will always be in front of the worm's nose. Just tie a thin thread to the worm's nose. Just tie a thin thread to the worm's tail." The woman did as she had been told, and the worm began to climb upwards, trailing the thin thread along behind it.

All this time the minister had been thinking about escape, he was very anxious to get away. He kept hoping that someone, his wife or his friends, would find a way out, would find a way for him to escape. He was alert to any opportunity.

That morning he noticed a worm climbing the tower wall and also saw that a thread was following it. At once he knew a means of rescue had been found. He grabbed the thread and began to pull. A thin rope was tied to the end of the thread, and he caught hold of the rope and continued pulling. A thick strong rope was tied to the end of the thin one and so, with the help of the thick rope, he climbed down and ran away.

Later he asked his wife who had shown her the trick. The wife explained that a fakir had shown it to her. Her husband said, "With the help of that thread I am now out of prison. But that was just a tiny prison; now I am out of a greater prison too." He said to his wife, "I am not coming home! Take me to that fakir who freed me from prison. What point is there in going home now? Now I must escape from this prison of the world completely. And that fakir knows the secret."

This is the great secret:

This whole world's so nasty.
Only he who prays is true.
Says Kabir: never abandon the name.
Fall down! Stand up! Fly high!

ABOUT OSHO

Osho defies categorization, reflecting everything from the individual quest for meaning to the most urgent social and political issues facing society today. His books are not written but are transcribed from recordings of extemporaneous talks given over a period of thirty-five years. Osho has been described by the *Sunday Times* in London as one of the "1000 Makers of the 20th Century" and by *Sunday Mid-Day* in India as one of the ten people – along with Gandhi, Nehru and Buddha – who have changed the destiny of India.

Osho has a stated aim of helping to create the conditions for the birth of a new kind of human being, characterized as "Zorba the Buddha" – one whose feet are firmly on the ground, yet whose hands can touch the stars. Running like a thread through all aspects of Osho is a vision that encompasses both the timeless wisdom of the East and the highest potential of Western science and technology.

He is synonymous with a revolutionary contribution to the science of inner transformation and an approach to meditation which specifically addresses the accelerated pace of contemporary life. The unique Osho Active Meditations™ are designed to allow the release of accumulated stress in the body and mind so that it is easier to be still and experience the thought-free state of meditation.

OSHO INTERNATIONAL MEDITATION RESORT

Osho International Meditation Resort has been created so that people can have a direct experience of a new way of living – with more alertness, relaxation, and humor. It is located about 100 miles southeast of Mumbai in Pune, India, on 40 acres in the tree-lined residential area of Koregaon Park. The resort offers a variety of programs to the thousands of people who visit each year from more than 100 countries. Accommodation for visitors is available on-campus in the new Osho Guesthouse.

The Multiversity programs at the meditation resort take place in a pyramid complex next to the famous Zen garden park, Osho Teerth. The programs are designed to provide the transformation tools that give people access to a new lifestyle – one of relaxed awareness – which is an approach they can take with them into their everyday lives. Self-discovery classes, sessions, courses and meditative processes are offered throughout the year. For exercising the body and keeping fit, there is a beautiful outdoor facility where one can experiment with a Zen approach to sports and recreation.

In the main meditation auditorium the daily schedule from 6:00 A.M. up to 11:00 P.M. includes both active and passive meditation methods. Following the daily evening meeting meditation, the nightlife in this multicultural resort is alive with outdoor eating areas that fill with friends and often with dancing.

The resort has its own supply of safe, filtered drinking water and the food served is made with organically grown produce from the resort's own farm.

An online tour of the meditation resort, as well as travel and program information, can be found at: www.osho.com

This is a comprehensive website in different languages with an online magazine, audio and video webcasting, an Audiobook Club, the complete English and Hindi archive of Osho talks and a complete catalog of all Osho publications including books, audio and video. Includes information about the active meditation techniques developed by Osho, most with streaming video demonstrations.

The daily meditation schedule includes:

Osho Dynamic Meditation™: A technique designed to release tensions and repressed emotions, opening the way to a new vitality and an experience of profound silence.

Osho Kundalini Meditation™: A technique of shaking free one's dormant energies, and through spontaneous dance and silent sitting, allowing these energies to be redirected inward.

Osho Nadabrahma Meditation™: A method of harmonizing one's energy flow, based on an ancient Tibetan humming technique.

Osho Nataraj Meditation™: A method involving the inner alchemy of dancing so totally that the dancer disappears and only the dance remains.

Vipassana Meditation: A technique originating with Gautam Buddha and now updated for the 21st Century, for dissolving mental chatter through the awareness of breath.

No Dimensions Meditation™: A powerful method for centering one's energy, based on a Sufi technique.

Osho Gourishankar Meditation™: A one-hour nighttime meditation, which includes a breathing technique, gazing softly at a light and gentle body movements.

BOOKS BY OSHO IN ENGLISH LANGUAGE

Early Discourses and Writings

A Cup of Tea
Dimensions Beyond The Known
From Sex to Super-consciousness
The Great Challenge
Hidden Mysteries
I Am The Gate
The Inner Journey
Psychology of the Esoteric
Seeds of Wisdom

Meditation

The Voice of Silence
And Now and Here (Vol 1 & 2)
In Search of the Miraculous (Vol 1 &.2)
Meditation: The Art of Ecstasy
Meditation: The First and Last Freedom
The Path of Meditation
The Perfect Way
Yaa-Hoo! The Mystic Rose

Buddha and Buddhist Masters

The Book of Wisdom
The Dhammapada: The Way of the Buddha (Vol 1-12)

The Diamond Sutra
The Discipline of Transcendence (Vol 1-4)
The Heart Sutra

Indian Mystics

Enlightenment: The Only Revolution (Ashtavakra)
Showering Without Clouds (Sahajo)
The Last Morning Star (Daya)
The Song of Ecstasy (Adi Shankara)

Baul Mystics

The Beloved (Vol 1 & 2)
Kabir
The Divine Melody
Ecstasy: The Forgotten Language
The Fish in the Sea is Not Thirsty
The Great Secret
The Guest
The Path of Love
The Revolution

Jesus and Christian Mystics

Come Follow to You (Vol 1-4)
I Say Unto You (Vol 1 & 2)
The Mustard Seed
Theologia Mystica

Jewish Mystics

The Art of Dying
The True Sage

Western Mystics

Guida Spirituale (Desiderata)
The Hidden Harmony
(Heraclitus)
The Messiah (Vol 1 & 2) (Commentaries on Khalil Gibran's The Prophet)
The New Alchemy: To Turn You On (Commentaries on Mabel Collins' Light on the Path)
Philosophia Perennis (Vol 1 & 2) (The Golden Verses of Pythagoras)
Zarathustra: A God That Can Dance
Zarathustra: The Laughing Prophet (Commentaries on Nietzsche's Thus Spake Zarathustra)

Sufism

Just Like That
Journey to the Heart
The Perfect Master (Vol 1 & 2)
The Secret
Sufis: The People of the Path (Vol 1 & 2)
Unio Mystica (Vol 1 & 2)
The Wisdom of the Sands (Vol 1 & 2)

Tantra

Tantra: The Supreme Understanding
The Tantra Experience
 The Royal Song of Saraha
 (same as Tantra Vision, Vol 1)
The Tantric Transformation
 The Royal Song of Saraha
 (same as Tantra Vision, Vol 2)
The Book of Secrets: Vigyan Bhairav Tantra

The Upanishads

Behind a Thousand Names
(Nirvana Upanishad)
Heartbeat of the Absolute
(Ishavasya Upanishad)
I Am That (Isa Upanishad)
The Message Beyond Words
(Kathopanishad)
Philosophia Ultima (Mandukya Upanishad)
The Supreme Doctrine (Kenopanishad)
Finger Pointing to the Moon
(Adhyatma Upanishad)
That Art Thou (Sarvasar Upanishad, Kaivalya Upanishad, Adhyatma Upanishad)
The Ultimate Alchemy, Vol 1&2
 (Atma Pooja Upanishad Vol 1 & 2)
Vedanta: Seven Steps to Samadhi (Akshaya Upanishad)
Flight of the Alone to the Alone
(Kaivalya Upanishad)

Tao

The Empty Boat
The Secret of Secrets
Tao:The Golden Gate (Vol 1&2)
Tao:The Pathless Path (Vol 1&2)
Tao: The Three Treasures (Vol 1-4)
When the Shoe Fits

Yoga

The Path of Yoga (previously Yoga: The Alpha and the Omega Vol 1)
Yoga: The Alpha and the Omega (Vol 2-10)

Books by Osho in English Language

Zen and Zen Masters

Ah, This!
Ancient Music in the Pines
And the Flowers Showered
A Bird on the Wing
Bodhidharma: The Greatest Zen Master
Communism and Zen Fire, Zen Wind
Dang Dang Doko Dang
The First Principle
God is Dead: Now Zen is the Only Living Truth
The Grass Grows By Itself
The Great Zen Master Ta Hui
Hsin Hsin Ming: The Book of Nothing
I Celebrate Myself: God is No Where, Life is Now Here
Kyozan: A True Man of Zen
Nirvana: The Last Nightmare
No Mind: The Flowers of Eternity
No Water, No Moon
One Seed Makes the Whole Earth Green
Returning to the Source
The Search: Talks on the 10 Bulls of Zen
A Sudden Clash of Thunder
The Sun Rises in the Evening
Take it Easy (Vol 1 & 2)
This Very Body the Buddha
Walking in Zen, Sitting in Zen
The White Lotus
Yakusan: Straight to the Point of Enlightenment
Zen Manifesto : Freedom From Oneself
Zen: The Mystery and the Poetry of the Beyond
Zen: The Path of Paradox (Vol 1, 2 & 3)
Zen: The Special Transmission

Zen Boxed Sets
The World of Zen (5 vol.)
Live Zen
This. This. A Thousand Times This
Zen: The Diamond Thunderbolt
Zen: The Quantum Leap from Mind to No-Mind

Zen: The Solitary Bird, Cuckoo

of the Forest
Zen: All The Colors Of The Rainbow (5 vol.)
The Buddha: The Emptiness of the Heart
The Language of Existence
The Miracle
The Original Man
Turning In

Osho: On the Ancient Masters of Zen (7 volumes)*

Dogen: The Zen Master
Hyakujo: The Everest of Zen–
With Basho's haikus
Isan: No Footprints in the Blue Sky
Joshu: The Lion's Roar
Ma Tzu: The Empty Mirror
Nansen: The Point Of Departure
Rinzai: Master of the Irrational
*Each volume is also available individually.

Responses to Questions

Be Still and Know
Come, Come, Yet Again Come
The Goose is Out
The Great Pilgrimage: From Here to Here

Books by Osho in English Language

The Invitation
My Way: The Way of the White Clouds
Nowhere to Go But In
The Razor's Edge
Walk Without Feet, Fly Without Wings and Think Without Mind
The Wild Geese and the Water
Zen: Zest, Zip, Zap and Zing

Talks in America

From Bondage To Freedom
From Darkness to Light
From Death To Deathlessness
From the False to the Truth
From Unconsciousness to Consciousness
The Rajneesh Bible (Vol 2-4)

The World Tour

Beyond Enlightenment (Talks in Bombay)
Beyond Psychology (Talks in Uruguay)
Light on the Path (Talks in the Himalayas)
The Path of the Mystic (Talks in Uruguay)
Sermons in Stones (Talks in Bombay)
Socrates Poisoned Again After 25 Centuries (Talks in Greece)
The Sword and the Lotus
(Talks in the Himalayas)
The Transmission of the Lamp
(Talks in Uruguay)

Osho's Vision for the World

The Golden Future
The Hidden Splendor

The New Dawn
The Rebel
The Rebellious Spirit

The Mantra Series

Hari Om Tat Sat
Om Mani Padme Hum
Om Shantih Shantih Shantih
Sat-Chit-Anand
Satyam-Shivam-Sundram

Personal Glimpses

Books I Have Loved
Glimpses of a Golden Childhood
Notes of a Madman

Interviews with the World Press

The Last Testament (Vol 1)

Intimate Talks between

Master and Disciple – Darshan Diaries
A Rose is a Rose is a Rose
Be Realistic: Plan for a Miracle
Believing the Impossible Before Breakfast
Beloved of My Heart
Blessed are the Ignorant
Dance Your Way to God
Don't Just Do Something, Sit There
Far Beyond the Stars
For Madmen Only
The Further Shore

Books by Osho in English Language

Get Out of Your Own Way
God's Got A Thing about You
God is Not for Sale
The Great Nothing
Hallelujah!
Let Go!
The 99 Names of Nothingness
No Book, No Buddha, No Teaching, No Disciple
Nothing to Lose but Your Head
Only Losers Can Win in This Game
Open Door
Open Secret
The Shadow of the Whip
The Sound of One Hand Clapping
The Sun Behind the Sun Behind the Sun
The Tongue-Tip Taste of Tao
This Is It
Turn On, Tune In and Drop the Lot
What Is, Is, What Ain't, Ain't
Won't You Join The Dance?

Compilations

After Middle Age: A Limitless Sky
At the Feet of the Master
Bhagwan Shree Rajneesh: On Basic Human Rights
Jesus Crucified Again, This Time in Ronald Reagan's America
Priests and Politicians: The Mafia of the Soul
Take it Really Seriously

Gift Books of Osho Quotations

A Must for Contemplation Before Sleep
A Must for Morning

Contemplation

India My Love

Photobooks

Shree Rajneesh: A Man of Many Climates,
Seasons and Rainbows through the eye of the camera
Impressions... Osho Commune International Photobook

Books about Osho

Bhagwan: The Buddha for the Future by Juliet Forman
Bhagwan Shree Rajneesh: The Most Dangerous Man Since Jesus Christ by Sue Appleton

Bhagwan: The Most Godless Yet the Most Godly Man by Dr. George Meredith
Bhagwan: One Man Against the Whole Ugly Past of Humanity by Juliet Forman
Bhagwan: Twelve Days That Shook the World by Juliet Forman
Was Bhagwan Shree Rajneesh Poisoned by Ronald Reagan's America? by Sue Appleton.
Diamond Days With Osho
by Ma Prem Shunyo

For any information about Osho Books & Audio/Video Tapes please contact:

OSHO Multimedia & Resorts Pvt. Ltd.

17 Koregaon Park, Pune–411001, MS, India
Phone: 020 4019999 Fax: 020 4019990
E-mail: distrib@osho.net Website: www.osho.com